# REALMS OF GOLD
## THE CLASSICS IN CHRISTIAN PERSPECTIVE

## Other Books by Leland Ryken

# REALMS OF GOLD

## THE CLASSICS IN CHRISTIAN PERSPECTIVE

## Leland Ryken

Harold Shaw Publishers
Wheaton, Illinois

The *Wheaton Literary Series*

ISBN 0-87788-717-9

---

**Library of Congress Cataloging-in-Publication Data**

Ryken, Leland.
    Realms of gold : the classics in Christian perspective / Leland Ryken.
        p. cm. — (The Wheaton literary series)
    Includes bibliographical references and index.
    ISBN 0-87788-717-9
    1. Christianity and literature.    2. Literature—Religious aspects. I. Title.
  II. Series
  PN49.R89 1991
  809'.93382—dc20                 91-8686
                                   CIP

---

99  98  97  96  95  94  93  92  91

10  9  8  7  6  5  4  3  2  1

To my colleagues
in the English Department

# Contents

# Preface

Had I really heard what I seemed to have heard, or had my end-of-the-semester paranoia made me imagine things? David, a bright and godly student on the verge of graduation from college, had just said to me, "In my last semester in college I could not justify the time it would take to read *Great Expectations.*"

I said nothing. I was shocked. The chasm between David and me was so great on this subject that it took me a long time to grasp it. How could anyone not justify taking time to read *Great Expectations?* I wondered. Or Homer's *Odyssey* and many other indispensable, life-changing books? What accounts for the difference between David's attitude and mine? Most obviously, I have acquired a taste for literary classics and David has not. To me they are treasures that I cannot live without. This is an acquired taste only in the sense that people must read these books before they are captivated by them. Once we open ourselves to their beauty and power, they can be trusted to win us. David did not reject the classics because he found them lacking but because he left them unread.

In the book that follows, I have written to share my enthusiasm for some of my closest friends. For students who are reading the classics in a literature course, I have envisioned myself as introducing these friends to people who do not yet know them as friends. I have also written for people who have not read these books in a long, long time, in the hope that they will be motivated to renew their acquaintance with books that can delight them anew. For people who already know the classics as intimate friends, I have tried to share some of my own experience of them in the hope of imparting a fresh perspective. My cherished goal is to create a hunger to read and reread the works I discuss.

This book is part of the *Wheaton Literary Series* published by Harold Shaw. As that series abundantly shows, the world of worthy literature is not limited to the classics (a concept I will explain in my introductory chapter). But the classics should play an important role in any Christian's experience of literature. They are works of indisputable cultural importance and inherent value. It would be as deficient to omit a Christian consideration of the classics as it would be to limit one's attention only to them.

The introduction to this book lays out a framework of literary theory that explains what I think literature is and how it should be read. The chapters dealing with individual classics combine general commentary on the works with a Christian critique of them. In addition, as my chapter titles indicate, I have addressed a specific critical issue in each chapter. My goal is to cover the "classic issues" of Christian literary theory and to apply each one to a literary classic that provides an ideal occasion to explore a given issue. The organization of the book is chronological, tracing the course of Western literature from Homer through modern literature, and in some cases this chronological framework influenced the works I selected and omitted.

The title for the book comes from John Keats' sonnet entitled "On First Looking into Chapman's Homer." This poem dealing with the rapture of discovery begins with a geographical metaphor in which reading literature is compared to traveling through a landscape in which poets hold various realms under the rule of Apollo, classical god of poetic inspiration. The lines are these:

> Much have I traveled in the realms of gold,
>   And many goodly states and kingdoms seen;
>   Round many western islands have I been
> Which bards in fealty to Apollo hold. . . .

These lines provide provocative metaphors for what I have attempted in this book. I have looked upon myself as a helpful travel guide—determining the itinerary, pointing out features of the landscape, sharing the delights of the journey through my selected works. I have envisioned my readers as fellow travelers pursuing a journey of discovery, recognition, and sheer enjoyment. For both author and reader, the classics are what Keats implies—treasures to be possessed.

# *Introduction*

*Reading the Classics for All They're Worth*

## Why the Classics Matter

There are some things in life whose value is apparent if we simply define what they are. If we know what love or mercy or fairness is, we already know that we want them in our lives. This is how I propose to address the question of what we mean by a literary classic. I do not want the process to be a purely academic exercise. By the time I define a classic, I trust that it will be evident that the classics are something to be possessed and prized.

*What Is a Classic?* We can profitably begin by examining four thought-provoking descriptions of great literature:

[A masterpiece] modifies our very being and makes us feel . . . that we are not the same men and women we were when we began it.[1]

We speak of a book as a classic when it has gained a place for itself in our culture, and has consequently become a part of our educational experience. But the term conveys further meanings implying precision of style [and] formality of structure.[2]

There are many reasons why certain works of literature are classics, and most of them are purely literary reasons. But there's another reason too: a great work of literature is also a place in which the whole cultural history of the nation that produced it comes into focus.[3]

[A great book] lays its images permanently on the mind [and] is entirely irreplaceable in the sense that no other book whatever comes anywhere near reminding you of it or being even a momentary substitute for it.[4]

*How to Recognize a Classic When You Read One.* With these thoughts as a starting point, we can isolate the ingredients that allow us to call some works of literature classics. One is endurance. A classic has stood the test of time and is still current. It is both timeless and timely. When I am shopping for clothes and my wife comments that a given item is "a classic," she means that it will not be unfashionable a year later. Classics in any field, from cars to novels, have this quality of permanence.

To achieve such permanence, a classic possesses excellence in both content and form. In fact, the word "classic" has become a common honorific term in everyday life. A literary classic rises above most other members of its class. Thus Homer's epics are the best Greek epics and Shakespeare's tragedies are the best of Renaissance drama. Literary scholars keep coming back to the classics because there is so much to do with them. They have a multiplicity of both content and technique that makes them inexhaustible. By comparison, ordinary works seem a little thin, no matter how much we may like them.

The definitions that I cited above also imply a subjective test for a classic. Before we willingly call a work a classic, we have to be deeply affected by it. It has to be in some sense a landmark in our intellectual, spiritual, or literary experience. Classics "do" something for us, as we say. The author of an essay entitled "Why Read the Classics?" has said that "the classics are books that exert a peculiar influence, both when they refuse to be eradicated from the mind and when they conceal themselves in the folds of memory."[5]

Finally, the classics are influential—in cultures, for readers and critics, and (significantly) in the work of other writers. The classics have traditionally been part of the educational program of cultures. They "are the books that come down to us bearing upon them the traces of readings previous to ours, and bringing in their wake the traces they themselves have left on the culture or cultures they have passed through (or, more simply, on language and customs)."[6] We do not personally have to like every classic, but we have to acknowledge the importance of these books as a cultural phemonenon. For this reason, I have limited my focus in this book to Western classics that have been a cohesive cultural force in my own culture. There are classics that I teach, whose cultural importance I defend, but that I myself do not enjoy reading. In this book I have indulged the luxury of discussing classics whose worth I genuinely admire.

*Summary.* A definition of a literary masterpiece that brings together the strands I have been discussing is this one:

> What we tend to require for something called a literary masterwork is a display of great craftsmanship [and] . . . striking originality. . . . Beyond this . . . the text must make a powerful emotional and intellectual impact, provide a rich reading experience, and leave behind a larger understanding of our past experience and perhaps a new way to think about our lives. In the case of the greatest works we return to them time and again in our minds, even if we do not reread them frequently, as touchstones by which we interpret the world around us.[7]

When I speak of "the classics" in this book, I refer to works whose excellence as literature and whose importance to Western culture are indisputable. I am an enthusiast for the works that I have chosen to discuss, and my particular goal is to show why and how Christians should read them. Great literature is not limited to the works that I discuss in this book, but any reader's experience is deficient that does not include them. They will repay all that a reader invests in them.

## Five Fallacies about Literature

The classics are of interest partly because they highlight the basic issues of literature itself. This, in fact, is one reason why literary scholars return to the classics to test and prove their theories. How we view the classics will depend on how we view literature generally. To prize the classics— or even read them at all—we must avoid five common fallacies about literature.

*Fallacy 1: We should read something true rather than something fictional.* An acquaintance of mine recently asked someone what she had been reading lately. In clinching the point that she preferred to spend her time reading informational and religious books, she said, "I want truth when I read." The response reflects a common equation of fiction with untruth.

But the equation of fact with truth and fiction with falsehood is an incorrect equation. Behind the common bias is the premise that facts give us true information about our world. But so does fiction. A fictional story corresponds to life in the world just as thoroughly (though in a different way) as a biography or the daily newspaper does.

In fact, fiction can illuminate human experience better than facts ordinarily do. Facts by themselves are devoid of meaning and insight. But in a good piece of fiction the details are selected, molded, and interpreted in such a way as to embody meaning. Madeleine L'Engle is right to say that the encyclopedia gives us facts but the arts give us truth.[8] Facts give us a very limited kind of truth. By contrast, the truth of fiction is comprehensive, having the potential to be intellectual, moral, emotional, and spiritual at the same time.

The parables of Jesus are an authoritative example of this. They have all the earmarks of being stories that Jesus made up from his observations of life. They are not particularized in the way that a factual account is. Yet these fictional stories convey truth about God and people, about the kingdom of God and life in this world, in a way that no one can question. Fiction is true whenever it illuminates or corresponds to life in the world as we know it. History, biography, and the news are true about specific people; fiction usually strikes us as being true about all people, including ourselves.

*Fallacy 2: Everything in a work of literature is offered for our approval.* This is the root of the criticism that some conservative Christians make against literature. They are so preoccupied with the fact that they disagree with the subject matter or behavior portrayed in literature that this discomfort becomes the reason to reject literature itself.

But this reflects a very basic misunderstanding about how literature achieves its effects. Literature is an interpretive presentation of human experience. Writers first portray human experience and then offer an assessment of that experience. Before they can offer evil for disapproval, therefore, they must portray it. Literature communicates its message in two complementary ways—by offering us positive examples to approve and negative examples to avoid. Both strategies are ways of expressing truth.

The Bible itself follows this dual procedure. Like all literature, it portrays life as we know it in a fallen world. Many of the experiences about which we read in the Bible are sordid, evil, and repulsive. This is no reason to avoid reading the Bible. Some literature does, indeed, offer evil for the reader's approval and should be judged as immoral for doing so. But the portrayal of objectionable behavior or attitudes does not by itself mean that the book as a whole approves of these things.

*Fallacy 3: We should read only literature with whose viewpoint we agree.* This was once a common attitude among uncultured Christians. Today it is common among fashionable literary scholars whose ideology is Marxist, feminist, or liberal. Their narrowmindedness extends not only to the big themes of a work but even to specific details that they find objectionable.

There are, however, good reasons to read literature with which we may disagree in big or small ways. First, it is a rare work of literature with which we cannot find truth at some level. This is especially true of the classics. They overwhelmingly tell us the truth about human fears and longings and about what values are important in human experience. They put us in touch with bedrock humanity. Furthermore, literature is usually truthful in its portrayal of life and human experience. We can call this representational truth. We should value the truthfulness of literature at these levels even when it falls short at the level of perspective and ideas. If we decided to read only books with which we totally agree on every point, we would probably never read a book.

And even in areas where we disagree with a work of literature, it can be worthwhile to take the time to read it. Works of literature clarify the human situation to which the Christian faith speaks, even when their viewpoint is wrong. Literature is a catalyst to our thinking, even when its ideas are wrong. And literature is an invaluable index to the thoughts and feelings of people who live around us.

*Fallacy 4: A literary work written by a non-Christian cannot tell the truth.* On the logic of this fallacy, a non-Christian cannot be a good mathematician or ball player or teacher or mechanic. But we know otherwise. When we go to a restaurant, we do not ask whether the cook is a Christian. We want to know whether he or she can prepare delicious food.

The Bible itself shows us that non-Christian writers can express the truth for our edification. In the New Testament, Paul several times quotes from pagan poets. In his speech in Athens to the Areopagus, for example, he quoted from the Greek Stoic poets Cleanthes, Aratus, and Epimenides, drawing attention to his quotations by saying, "As even some of your poets have said" (Acts 17:28). First Corinthians 15:33 ("Bad company ruins good morals") is a quotation from the play *Thais* by the Greek dramatist Menander. Titus 1:12 is a quotation from Epimenides, a native of Crete, and Paul follows the quotation with the approving comment, "This testimony is true" (Titus 1:13).

Theologians have rightly spoken of the doctrine of common grace. It asserts that God endows all people, believers and unbelievers alike, with some capacity for truth, beauty, goodness, and creativity. John Calvin put it this way: "All truth is from God; and consequently, if wicked men have said anything that is true and just, we ought not to reject it; for it has come from God."[9]

The relevance of this for our reading of the classics is obvious. Christians can and should spend time reading literature written by non-Christians because they can find the truth and beauty of God there, too.

*Fallacy 5: Old literature is irrelevant to us today.* The myth of the superiority of the contemporary is widely held. People who accept it are unlikely to care for the classics, which (after all) come to us from the past. Yet there are at least six good reasons why any lover of literature should take time to read old books.

One line of defense is hedonistic. It is simply interesting and delightful to be transported to the past. It is one of the leading pleasures of the imagination. We need beneficial escapes from our lives in the burdensome present.

Another argument that opens the door to reading literature from the past is an awareness that at the level of subject matter (human experience concretely presented) literature is essentially universal and perpetually up to date. The English poet Percy Shelley called literature "the very image of life in its eternal form."[10] Similarly, T.S. Eliot, in a famous essay "Tradition and the Individual Talent," wrote that "the historical sense involves a perception, not only of the pastness of the past, but of its presence."[11] With literature, the past is present.

The contemporaneity of the past is likewise asserted by the archetypal approach to literature. Archetypes are images (such as light and darkness), character types (e.g., the hero and the villain), or plot motifs (e.g., quest and initiation) that recur throughout literature and life. The presence of the same archetypes throughout the history of literature and the human race shows that the world of literature partly (though not wholly) transcends time. T.S. Eliot rightly speaks of how literature "has a simultaneous existence and composes a simultaneous order."[12] If the same archetypes are present in Homer and Hemingway, then there is a sense in which Homer is as contemporary as Hemingway.

Of course literature from the past is only partly contemporary in this way. If it confirms what is true in the modern world, it also challenges it. This leads to yet another reason for reading old books: we need the literature of the past in order to be introduced to alternate possibilities and to be liberated from bondage to the contemporary. Northrop Frye thus claims that when we study an author "in relation to his own time we are led into a different kind of culture, with unfamiliar assumptions, beliefs, and values. But contact with these is what expands our own view of human possibilities, and it is what is irrelevant, in the narrow sense, about what we study that is the liberalizing element in it."[13] G.K. Chesterton wrote an essay entitled "On Man, Heir of All the Ages," in which he asserted, "An heir is one who inherits, and any one who is cut off from the past . . . is a person most unjustly disinherited."[14]

Reading literature from the past also helps us to understand the present and be protected from it. C.S. Lewis stated the case admirably in his famous sermon "Learning in War-Time":

> We need intimate knowledge of the past. Not that the past has any magic about it, but because we cannot study the future, and yet need something to set against the present, to remind us that the basic assumptions have been quite different in different periods and that much which seems certain to the uneducated is merely temporary fashion. A man who has lived in many places is not likely to be deceived by the local errors of his native village: the scholar has lived in many times and is therefore in some degree immune from the

great cataract of nonsense that pours from the press and the microphone of his own age.[15]

Not that we always have to prefer the old ways to our own age. But one of the uses of the past is to help us understand the present. Thus T.S. Eliot claimed that the historical sense of the past is what makes a person "most acutely conscious of his place in time, of his own contemporaneity."[16]

There is, finally, a line of defense that has nothing to do with time and instead concerns the quest for excellence. The Victorian enthusiast for culture Matthew Arnold defined literary criticism as the "endeavour to learn and propagate the best that is known and thought in the world."[17] Elsewhere he expressed the view that "the best poetry is what we want."[18] If it is the best literature that we want, we will necessarily take lengthy and frequent excursions into the past, because much of the best was written long ago.

*Summary.* Before we will value the classics, we need to think clearly about literature itself. If we doubt that we can profit from fiction, literature written by non-Christians, or literature from the past, we will obviously leave the classics unread. We will also avoid the classics if we think that we should read only literature with whose viewpoint we agree or if we assume that everything portrayed in a work of literature is offered for our approval.

But all of these premises are faulty. Fiction *can* tell the truth. So can literature written by unbelievers. Literature from the past *is* relevant. We are not asked to approve everything that is portrayed in a work of literature. And we can gain profit and delight from works of literature with whose viewpoint we only partly agree.

### How to Misread the Classics

Misconceptions can prevent our reading the classics. But pitfalls remain even after we have decided to read them. Next to not reading the classics, the greatest abuse we can heap on them is to misread them. Here are eight easy ways to misread them.

*Misreading 1: Be sure to read the classics for their ideas.* If you do, you will soon find that you don't need the classics themselves. All you need is a list of ideas. You will also find that these abstracted ideas look very much like a collection of lifeless platitudes. C.S. Lewis rightly debunks the "idea" approach to literature by observing that "many of the comments on life which people get out of Shakespeare could have been reached by very moderate talents without his assistance."[19] To reduce a piece of literature to its ideas, adds Lewis, "is an outrage to the thing the poet has made for us."[20]

This is not to deny that works of literature embody ideas, express a sense of life, and make us think. But the first claim that a work of literature has on us is to get us to relive an experience. The experience that we enact *is* the meaning of the story or poem. That is why fiction writer Flannery O'Connor has said that "the whole story is the meaning, because it is an experience, not an abstraction."[21]

*Misreading 2: Assume without question that the classics tell the truth.* It is easy to see why defenders of literature have made the claim that literature by definition universally tells the truth. Faced with the perennial charge that literature is not useful, enthusiasts for literature have tried to meet the utilitarian challenge on its own ground by arguing that literature by its very nature "teaches truth."

Often this is simply a naive equation of the ideational content of literature with truth. But obviously the ideas of literature can be false as well as true. Furthermore, literature as a whole is contradictory in what it tells us. The classics, we will quickly see, disagree with each other on some very basic issues, with the result that they cannot simply be said to assert the truth.

Viewed from a Christian perspective, the values that the classics offer for our approval are suspect. The case has been argued very ably by C.S. Lewis in one of his best essays. He notes that "the values assumed in literature have seldom been those of Christianity."[22] Instead, the value structure of most literature is "sub-Christian." The list with which Lewis fleshes this out will be a helpful roadmap to the works that I discuss in this book:

> Some of the principal values actually implicit in European literature were . . . (a) honour, (b) sexual love, (c) material prosperity, (d) pantheistic contemplation of nature, (e) *Sehnsucht* [longing] awakened by the past, the remote, or the (imagined) supernatural, (f) liberation of impulses.

Conspicuously absent from the list is the Christian God. And when we start to read the "fine print" of the ideas embodied in the classics, we will find even more with which to disagree.

*Misreading 3: Look upon the classics as "improving literature."* An equally common misconception is that the classics are "serious stuff"— something you *have* to read but would not choose to read. Because most people first encounter the classics in high school or college literature courses, the idea has gotten around that they are something we have to read as a solemn duty. In many people's thinking, reading a classic is more like listening to a sermon or lecture than attending a ballgame.

As a corrective, I suggest that we view the classics as a form of entertainment first of all. Any usefulness they might hold can come as a byproduct. The classics are, to use T.S. Eliot's definition of the purpose of literature, "superior amusement."[23] I prefer them over most other reading material because I think they are more fun. I recommend that they be read in the spirit of Charles Williams' comment that *"Paradise Lost is much more fun written in blank verse than it would be in prose, or is so to anyone capable of enjoying that particular kind of fun. Let us have all the delights of which we are capable."*[24]

*Misreading 4: Regard the classics as beyond criticism.* The classics can be overvalued and wrongly valued as well as undervalued. In a society where cultural literacy is in serious decline, this is not a temptation that is widely indulged. But it is possible among the cultured. The classics are worthy of our admiration and should make us feel humble, but we should not venerate them as something sacred.

A work of literature or art is always subject to criticism. As Christian readers we are *obligated* to disagree with some things that the classics assert. Enthusiasts for literature have too readily given the impression that if a work is great by literary criteria, all we need to do is affirm and celebrate it. But Francis Schaeffer has rightly observed that the fact that a great artist portrays a world view "does not mean that we should automatically accept that world view. Art may heighten the impact of the world view (in fact, we can count on this), but it does not make something true."[25] In a similar vein, T.S. Eliot cautioned that "the 'greatness' of literature cannot be determined solely by literary standards," and that a mark of maturity in a Christian reader is the ability to say of a Dickens or Thackeray, "This is the view of life of a person who was a good observer within his limits. . . ; but he looked at it in a different way from me."[26]

*Misreading 5: Assume that moral considerations are irrelevant to the classics.* A century ago Oscar Wilde, notorious British author and critic, gave this viewpoint its official creed when he wrote, "There is no such thing as a moral or an immoral book. Books are well written, or badly written. That is all."[27]

But this mistakes both the nature of literature and our experience as readers. Because literature deals with human behavior and is itself an influence on a reader's behavior, it always potentially has moral implications. Reading literature is not a neutral activity like riding in a car. It is much more like food that we digest by taking it into ourselves. Once we have assimilated it, it always has some impact on us.

The morality of literature depends on three factors. In the order of increasing importance, they are: the subject matter that the work puts before us, the perspective toward that subject matter embodied in the work itself, and the influence of a work on the behavior of the reader. In all three areas, moral literature can be defined as literature that offers moral behavior for the reader's approval or that influences a reader to behave in a moral way. Immoral literature reverses this.

When we apply these criteria to the classics, they fare rather well. The best confirmation is simply to notice what types of behavior a work regards as virtues and vices. The classics generally espouse a system of virtues and vices with which a Christian can agree. But when we turn from virtues and vices to the *values* espoused by the classics, we suddenly have to scale down the claims that we make for their compatibility with Christianity.

*Misreading 6: Be sure that you do not see anything in the classics that the author and original audience did not see in it.* This premise is known as the intentional fallacy—the fallacy of believing that the author's intention must govern our interpretation of a work of literature. The reasons for believing that this is a fallacy are impeccable.

There are few works of literature for which we know the writer's intention. What we *infer* to be the intention is highly speculative. An author may be unaware of his or her total intention. The achieved product may vary widely from the writer's intention, in which case the intention can only mislead us. Later generations of readers may see something valid in a work that its original audience missed or misread.

Finally, to tie the interpretation of a work to a single moment in history is to deny the very nature of history—that attitudes change. Every generation of readers, including the first, has its blind spots. Homer's original audience relished the battle scenes that figure in his stories. A modern reader is more likely to see the limitations of such violence. From antiquity through the Renaissance, authors and their audiences accepted a strongly hierarchical view of society. Modern readers, with a bias toward egalitarianism, will assess the behavior of characters in the old stories differently from the original viewpoint.

A classic is in one sense an organism. Once it has been created, it takes on a life of its own. In fact, writers cannot control how readers will interpret their works. This is not to say that we should disregard a writer's viewpoint or make a work say something that is the opposite of what the writer meant. We must protect an author's right not to be misunderstood. But having understood a writer, we are not limited to see in a work only what the author saw there.

*Misreading 7: Assume that all that matters is what a work says to you.* This is known as the affective fallacy—the fallacy of basing an interpretation solely on the impressions or feelings of a given reader. The effect of this view is to remove any final court of appeal by which to test interpretations of literature. If a reader's response is the sole basis for interpretation, every reader's interpretation is equally valid. The work itself ought to be the final court of appeal, but the affective fallacy removes its rightful place as arbiter.

Furthermore, a reader's response to a work of literature may tell us a great deal more about the reader than about the work. As we know from real life, responses can be inaccurate and unfair. And finally, a work of literature had a meaning before we read it and will continue to have a meaning after we have read it. We have a responsibility to find what this inherent meaning of the work is.

The proper role of our responses is as a starting point for analysis. We should not try to suppress our responses. They are important. But they are always subject to modification and correction by the work itself.

*Misreading 8: View the classics as relics in the museum of the past.*
Earlier I defended the reading of old books. People who share my viewpoint on this issue frequently believe that the classics exist chiefly to tell us about the past. This is *one* of their uses, but in itself a knowledge of the past offers nothing beyond an academic interest.

Current defenses of the classics tend to assign an arbitrary value to the idea of tradition. But traditions can be either good or bad. Some of them are worthy of our time and study, but others are not. The mere fact that the classics tell us about past eras is of only passing interest.

I myself am interested in the classics for the delight and illumination that they can give me in the present. This does not mean that I doubt their value as admitting me to modes of thought and feeling remote from my own culture and potentially better than it. But even here I am not indiscriminately interested in the past for its own sake. Much more valuable to me is what is universal in the classics. They have an unparalleled ability to capture what is true for all people at all times in all places.

## In Defense of Old Swords

The antidote to misreading the classics is to read them in the right way. In outlining the right way, I will do so under a formula that I borrow from the Old English epic *Beowulf*. The warriors in that story prefer old swords to new ones because they regard them as more useful and reliable. In a similar way, I have taken my principles of reading from older sources that the avant-garde world of contemporary literary criticism would scorn as old-fashioned but whose usefulness readers can prove for themselves. To read the classics with profit and delight we do not need esoteric literary terms that only a handful of scholars can understand. We need time-honored principles that stand out luminous in their clarity and trustworthiness.

*A Keen Eye for the Obvious.* I begin with a comment that C.S. Lewis makes in his book on Renaissance literature. He criticizes the humanists of the sixteenth century for losing the ability "to respond to the central, obvious appeal of a great work."[28] The concept of the simple, obvious appeal of a work yields a lot. It leads a reader to ask, What makes this a good story or poem? Answering that question generates insight into both the subject and form of a work, since both are likely to be part of the work's obvious appeal.

We can profitably theorize about why the selected content struck the writer as promising subject matter for a story or poem. Among other considerations, great writers gravitate toward stories and situations in which (to use an old sword from the French writer Charles Baudelaire) "the deep significance of life reveals itself."[29] But content does not by itself insure a successful piece of literature. Knowing this should propel us to an additional level of concern, accompanied by such questions as, What is skillfully done in this work? What engages my interest at the level of technique? What elements of superior artistry raise this work above lesser works that deal with the same subject matter?

*What Is Literature For?* One of the oldest swords of literary theory can be traced all the way back to the Roman author Horace. It concerns the purpose or effect of literature. The writer aims to do two things, said Horace—to produce a piece of writing that is both useful and delightful.[30] Sixteen centuries later, the English Renaissance poet Sir Philip Sidney echoed Horace when he wrote in his *Apology for Poetry* that the purpose of literature is "to teach and delight."[31] The twentieth-century American poet Robert Frost reformulated the twofold formula in a way that is even better when he said that a poem "begins in delight and ends in wisdom [and] a clarification of life."[32]

If literature truly is (in the words of Shelley) "a fountain for ever overflowing with the waters of wisdom and delight,"[33] we can profitably ask questions like this of the works that we read: What makes this an entertaining story or poem to read? What are the sources of my delight in this work? What wisdom does it impart? What does this story or poem clarify about life?

Literature as a whole is particularly adept at clarifying the values, fears, and longings of the human race. The world of the imagination is dualistic. Northrop Frye is the one who has particularly popularized this view, so we can allow him to supply our key statement of the idea: "There are two halves to literary experience. . . . Imagination gives us both a better and a worse world than the one we usually live with. . . . In literature we always seem to be looking either up or down."[34] Literature does not escape from reality. It names our fears so we can cope with them. It also gives shape to our longings.

Paradoxically, regardless of whether we are looking up or looking down, the effect of literature is to awaken our longings for the good life. In the one case we say, "This is better than life often is." In the other case we say, "Surely there must be something better than this." One of the best ways of reading literature is also one of the simplest: we should simply allow literature to awaken good longings within us. Of course literature cannot by itself satisfy the longings that it arouses, but this is a religious issue that I will note later.

*How the Imagination Expresses Life.* The modern poet T.S. Eliot provides a sword that we can manage with good effect when he writes that "it is a function of all art to give us some perception of an order in life, by imposing an order upon it."[35] Eliot's statement offers a double usefulness to us. On the one hand it alerts us that literature is never a mere recording of the raw flow of life. It is a distillation of life. Writers select and arrange their material. For any work of literature, we can profitably analyze what order the writer's imagination has imposed on the material. In a story, for example, such ordering includes plot conflict, plot structure, dramatic irony, and the principles that governed the writer's selection of details for characterization or setting.

But Eliot's comment also implies that this artistic distillation of life enables us to discern something about life itself with heightened clarity. The conventions of literature that make it different from ordinary life give us a perception of an order in life that we ordinarily miss. This is the consciousness-raising value of literature. We rarely get new information from reading imaginative literature. Instead we find something that we already know raised to a level of awareness. If, as Simon Lesser writes, the function of literary form is "to facilitate perception—to silhouette the material with the desired degree of clarity,"[36] the question that we should ask is, How do the literary features of the work contribute to the clarification of life that I experience as I read this work? In other words, good reading is bifocal: first we look *at* the work and then we look *through* it to real life.

When we look at the work and enter its world, we find much that is unlifelike or even preposterous. In real life, events are not self-contained and complete in themselves as they are in stories. In real life, heroes are not ideally heroic and villains ideally villainous. These are conventions of literature rather than of life. Yet paradoxically the un-lifelike conventions of literature remind us of life.

An old sword that brings this issue into focus is the following statement by the twentieth-century artist Pablo Picasso: "We all know that Art is not [literal] truth. Art is a lie that makes us realize truth."[37] This is similar to the observation of the eighteenth-century writer and critic Samuel Johnson that works of literature are "not . . . mistaken for realities, but . . . they bring realities to mind."[38] On the one hand this reminds us not to make false claims for the realism of literature. Literature is never the same as life. It is life at the remove of the imagination.

Before literature puts us in touch with life, it removes us from it and transports us to a world of the imagination. In this sense literature is like a game. Games temporarily divert us from life. They have their own rules—different from the rules that apply in the real world. But the fact that literature is first of all an escape does not mean that it is necessarily escapist in the sense of making us lose contact with reality. Having removed us from life to a world merely imagined, literature allows us to see out of that imagined world to everyday reality. In real life people do not sit on the shore of the island of a goddess for seven years weeping for their wife and home (as Homer's Odysseus does), but that imagined spectacle reminds us of fidelity as we find it in the world around us.

*Literature as a Picture of Reality.* The reality that we encounter vicariously by means of the literary imagination is universal human experience. Great literature never goes out of date. Northrop Frye brings the issue into focus with his statement that the writer's task "is not to tell you what happened, but what happens: not what did take place, but the kind of thing that always does take place. . . . You wouldn't go to *Macbeth* to learn about the history of Scotland—you go to it to learn what a man feels like after he's gained a kingdom and lost his soul."[39]

It is a convention of literature that the imagined world that we enter as we read a poem or story is offered to us as the writer's picture of reality. What a writer portrays makes implied truth claims and assertions about reality. Novelist Joyce Cary made the point very succinctly when he wrote, "All writers . . . must have, to compose any kind of story, some picture of the world, and of what is right and wrong in that world."[40] The imagined world of literature is thus laden with meaning, though of course a reader is under no obligation to agree with the picture of reality or claims of truth that the writer presents. All we need to do is take the writer's world seriously. Twentieth-century fiction writer Flannery O'Connor thus wrote that "it is from the kind of world the writer creates, from the kind of character and detail he invests it with, that a reader can find the intellectual meaning of a book."[41]

*The Role of the Reader and Author.* Literature is an affective art, by which I mean that it achieves its effects by getting a reader to respond to details in the text. David Lodge brings this subjective element of literary experience into focus with this admirable comment: "The writer expresses what he knows by affecting the reader; the reader knows what is expressed by being receptive to effects."[42] This old sword alerts us to the central importance of the reader in the literary enterprise. Readers collaborate with the author to produce the work of literature. The words on the page are only a potential. The author is dependent on the reader to transform the words into meaning.

The practical result of knowing this is to activate us as readers, chiefly in two ways. First, a good reader enters into the world of a story or poem as completely and vividly as possible. A work of literature asks us to relive an experience. In addition, we must pay attention to our responses to the images, characters, and events in a work of literature. These responses tell us something about ourselves. They are also a chief means by which a work of literature communicates its truth. When we respond favorably to a character in a story, for example, we thereby accept that character's morality and values as good. This affirmation is part of the meaning of the work.

But if David Lodge's comment draws attention to the role of the reader, it also attributes a central role to the author. As readers we are not free to make a story or poem say just anything. The author is the one who laid out the pathway for us to follow. The writer as a presence in the work is our travelling companion—the one who arranges the itinerary and points out things as we go along. "Reading is directed creation," wrote Jean-Paul Sartre, adding that "the author's whole art is bent on obliging me to *create* what he *discloses*."[43] The author is the writer of the script and director of the play. Readers enact the script under the author's direction. The author, writes Sartre, "has preceded [the reader] along the way. . . . A gentle force accompanies us and supports us from the first page to the last."[44]

***On Being Oneself as a Christian Reader.*** Once we acknowledge the role of the reader in the literary enterprise, it becomes apparent that readers do not agree in their interpretation of the details in a work and its overall meaning. Variability of interpretation is a fact of people's experiences with literature. We see in a work of literature what our own experiences of life and our own world view enable us to see. Christian readers therefore view literature through the lens of their Christian beliefs and experiences. If authors reveal a bias, so do readers. Here is an old sword that clarifies the issue:

> It is the whole person who responds to a poem or novel; and if that person is a believing Christian, then it is a believing Christian who judges. . . . Literary criticism is as much a personal matter, as much the product of a personal sense of life and value as literature itself.[45]

Here is an acknowledgement that Christian readers constitute an interpretive community—a group of readers who share an agenda of interests, beliefs, and values. But Christians also belong to the human race.

This dual dimension of reading has been stated in definitive form by T.S. Eliot, who writes,

> Literary criticism should be completed by criticism from a definite ethical and theological standpoint. . . . What I believe to be incumbent upon all Christians is the duty of maintaining consciously certain standards and criteria of criticism over and above those applied by the rest of the world; and that by these criteria and standards everything that we read must be tested.[46]

Eliot insists on two phases to our reading experience. The first is a stage of self-forgetfulness in which we surrender ourselves to the work we are reading. As C.S. Lewis describes it, "The first demand any work of art makes upon us is surrender. Look. Listen. Receive. Get yourself out of the way."[47] The value of literature, writes Lewis, is that "it admits us to experiences other than our own."[48]

But in addition to allowing for this enlarging self-forgetfulness in which we view the world through someone else's eyes, a Christian reader must also become self-conscious about his or her status as a Christian reader. At this point we are interested in assessing the morality and truth claims of the literature that we read. Having listened to a work of literature, we must also talk back to it.

*Summary.* Reading literature is a complex experience that requires a balance among competing interests. A diagram that brings this into focus is the following one, which shows the four ingredients that converge in any reading experience:

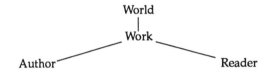

Reading literature begins with a focus on the work itself. That work is always experienced, though, as the response of a particular reader, with his or her own experiences and beliefs. The work, moreover, is the product of a writer, who remains a presiding presence in the story or poem. And because the subject of literature is human experience, we always relate the world of the work to the world in which we live. A complete reading experience maintains always a balance among these ingredients.

## Notes to the Introduction

[1]Sheldon Sacks, *Fiction and the Shape of Belief* (Berkeley: University of California Press, 1964), p. 253.

[2]Harry Levin, "Introduction" to *The Scarlet Letter and Other Tales of the Puritans* (Boston: Houghton Mifflin, 1960), p. vii.

[3]Northrop Frye, *The Educated Imagination* (Bloomington: Indiana UP, 1964), p. 123.

[4]C.S. Lewis, review of *Taliessin through Logres, The Oxford Magazine* 64 (14 March 1946): 248-250.

[5]Italo Calvino, "Why Read the Classics?" *New York Review of Books* 9 October 1986: 19.

[6]Ibid.

[7]Nina Baym, *The Scarlet Letter: A Reading* (Boston: G.K. Hall, 1986), p. xviii.

[8]Madeleine L'Engle, "The Mysterious Appearance of Canon Tallis," in *Spirit and Light: Essays in Historical Theology*, ed. Madeleine L'Engle and William B. Green (New York: Seabury, 1976), p. 26.

[9]John Calvin, commentary on Titus 1:12.

[10]Percy Shelley, *A Defence of Poetry*, in *Criticism: The Major Statements*, ed. Charles Kaplan (New York: St. Martin's, 1975), p. 360.

[11]T.S. Eliot, "Tradition and the Individual Talent," in *Criticism: The Major Statements*, ed. Kaplan, p. 476.

[12]Ibid.

[13]Northrop Frye, *Spiritus Mundi: Essays on Literature, Myth, and Society* (Bloomington: Indiana UP, 1976), p. 43.

[14]G.K. Chesterton, as quoted in C.S. Lewis, *A Preface to Paradise Lost* (New York: Oxford UP, 1942), p. 64.

[15]C.S. Lewis, *The Weight of Glory and Other Addresses* (1949; rpt. Grand Rapids: William B. Eerdmans, 1965), pp. 50-51.

[16]Eliot, p. 476.

[17]Matthew Arnold, "The Function of Criticism at the Present Time," in *Criticism: The Major Texts*, ed. Walter Jackson Bate (New York: Harcourt, 1952), p. 465.

[18]Matthew Arnold, "The Study of Poetry," in *Criticism: The Major Statements*, ed. Kaplan, p. 405.

[19]C.S. Lewis, *An Experiment in Criticism* (Cambridge: Cambridge UP, 1965), pp. 84-85.

[20]Ibid, p. 82.

[21]Flannery O'Connor, *Mystery and Manners*, ed. Sally and Robert Fitzgerald (New York: Farrar, Straus & Giroux, 1961), p. 73.

[22]C.S. Lewis, "Christianity and Culture," as reprinted in *The Christian Imagination: Essays on Literature and the Arts*, ed. Leland Ryken (Grand Rapids: Baker, 1981), p. 33.

[23]T.S. Eliot, "Preface" to *The Sacred Wood* (London: Methuen, 1920) 1960), p. viii.

[24]Charles Williams, *Reason and Beauty in the Poetic Mind* (Oxford: Oxford UP, 1933), p. 5.

[25]Francis Schaeffer, *Art and the Bible* (Downers Grove: InterVarsity, 1973), p. 41.

[26]T.S. Eliot, "Religion and Literature," as reprinted in *The Christian Imagination*, ed. Ryken, pp. 142, 149.

[27]Oscar Wilde, "Preface to *The Picture of Dorian Gray*," printed in 1891; quoted from *The Norton Anthology of English Literature*, 4th ed., ed. M. H. Abrams (New York: W. W. Norton, 1979), 2:1682.

[28]C.S. Lewis, *English Literature in the Sixteenth Century Excluding Drama* (Oxford: Oxford UP, 1944), p. 26.

[29]Charles-Pierre Baudelaire, as quoted by J. Middleton Murry, *The Problem of Style* (London: Oxford UP, 1922), p. 30.

[30]Horace, *The Art of Poetry*, in *Criticism: The Major Statements*, ed. Kaplan, p. 104.

[31]Sir Philip Sidney, *An Apology for Poetry*, in *Criticism: The Major Statements*, ed. Kaplan, p. 114.

[32]Robert Frost, "The Figure a Poem Makes," in *Writers on Writing*, ed. Walter Allen (Boston: The Writer, 1948), p. 22.

[33]Shelley, p. 372.

[34]Frye, *The Educated Imagination*, p. 97.

[35]Eliot, *On Poetry and Poets* (New York: Farrar, Straus and Cudahy, 1957), p. 93.

[36]Simon O. Lesser, *Fiction and the Unconscious* (Chicago: University of Chicago Press, 1957, 1975), p. 125.

[37]Pablo Picasso, *The Arts*, May 1923.

[38]Samuel Johnson, "Preface to Shakespeare," in *Criticism: The Major Statements*, ed. Kaplan, p. 264.

[39]Frye, *The Educated Imagination*, pp. 63-64.

[40]Joyce Cary, *Art and Reality: Ways of the Creative Process* (Garden City, N.Y.: Doubleday, 1961), p. 174.

[41]Flannery O'Connor, p. 73.

[42]David Lodge, *Language of Fiction* (London: Routledge and Kegan Paul, 1966), p. 65.

[43]Jean-Paul Sartre, *What Is Literature?*, trans. Bernard Frechtman (New York: Philosophical Library, 1949), pp. 45, 61.

[44]Ibid., p. 54.

[45]Vincent Buckley, *Poetry and Morality* (London: Chatto and Windus, 1959), pp. 217, 225.

[46]T.S. Eliot, "Religion and Literature," pp. 142, 153.

[47]C.S. Lewis, *An Experiment in Criticism*, p. 19.

[48]Ibid., p. 139.

# Chapter 1

## Homer's Odyssey *and the Value of Myth*

## "A Man Who Was Never at a Loss"

✳

*This is the story of a man, one who was never at a loss. He had travelled far in the world, after the sack of Troy, the virgin fortress; he saw many cities of men, and learnt their mind; he endured many troubles and hardships in the struggle to save his own life and to bring back his men safe to their homes. He did his best, but he could not save his companions. . . .*

*At the time when I begin, all the others who had not been killed in the war were at home, safe from the perils of battle and sea: but he was alone, longing to get home to his wife. He was kept prisoner by a witch, Calypso, a radiant creature, and herself one of the great family of gods.*[1]

✳

This famous opening at once alerts us to the kind of story *The Odyssey* is. It is an epic—a ritualistic form of narrative in which the storyteller begins by announcing the subject of his story. Every formal occasion begins with ritual. The Anglican marriage ceremony, for example, begins thus: "Dearly beloved, we are gathered together here in the sight of God, and in the face of this congregation, to join together this man and this woman in holy matrimony." The preacher, as he utters these words, announces the occasion in stately language, invokes God's presence at the event, and conveys the impression that some great event is now beginning. Homer's epic, like other members of its species, does some of these same things.

The first thing we learn is that the poet plans to tell a story. That story is one of the most famous in the world. The translator of the edition I prefer calls it "the best story ever written and . . . a favourite for three thousand years." *The Odyssey* is one of the foundational stories of Western literature—a veritable model of storytelling technique.

Having announced that he is about to tell a story, Homer hints at the single most important feature of that story—its hero. He is a man, says the epic narrator, who was never at a loss. In other words, his most noteworthy trait is his resourcefulness. This means that we are always left wondering how the hero will get out of his difficulty *this* time. He certainly will not always win by sheer physical strength, as most epic heroes do. He will win by his wit and intelligence. It is no wonder that the story of Odysseus (whom the Romans called Ulysses) has been told and retold through the centuries. Odysseus is, along with some of the characters in the Bible, the dominant character of Western literature.[2]

Homer's hero embodies the Greek spirit. To be never at a loss is to exhibit an ethic of efficiency and effectiveness. It also hints at the prevailing humanism that the story absorbed from the culture that produced it. Odysseus is largely a self-reliant hero. When Calypso offers him the chance to become one of the gods, he chooses his proud humanity instead.

The Greek urge for action is also part of the picture. When Odysseus visits fallen Greek warriors in the underworld and tells Achilles how famous he has become, Achilles silences Odysseus with the curt rejoinder, "Don't bepraise death to me, Odysseus. I would rather be plowman to a yeoman farmer on a small holding than lord Paramount in the kingdom of the dead."

Another thing that the storyteller wants us to know about his hero right at the outset is that "he endured many troubles and hardships in the struggle." Homer's story, like so much great literature, portrays human suffering and endurance. A common way to read *The Odyssey* is to view the individual episodes as all built around the motif of the hero's living up to his name and identity as the one who endures difficulty in order to achieve his goal. The commentator who has popularized this interpretation suggests "trouble" as a good translation of the hero's name.[3]

The story of this colorful hero is a travel story, we are also told in the opening statement of theme. Odysseus is always on the move. In fact, he has been traveling for ten years, a punishment for having angered the sea god Poseidon. The story of his travels, as we could predict, is an adventure story. It is also a quest story in which the hero's goal is to return home after having fought at the ten-year Trojan War that forms the central myth of Greek culture.

When Homer tells us that Odysseus was "longing to get home to his wife," he hints at the central role domestic values will play in his story. Most ancient epics celebrate heroic values. In these stories the chief action occurs on the battlefield and the goal of the hero is to win fame and a kingdom for himself. *The Odyssey* is an anomaly: whenever heroic and domestic values clash in this story, domestic values are elevated above the warrior's code. We might note also that in the world of this story home means a kingdom and possessions as well as a wife and son.

The mention of the goddess Calypso and the family of gods suggests another important feature of the poem—its status as myth. Myth is a story in which some of the characters are gods and bigger-than-life characters and in which marvelous events happen. The gods and goddesses play a key role in Homer's story. In most ways they are like people. They are of both sexes. They have a social structure that approximates that of the human community. The only thing that finally separates them from mortals is that they are immortal.

My analysis of *The Odyssey* will focus on its status as myth. Some Christians object to myth. While respecting their concerns, I will explore the value of myth and what it can contribute to our reading and life.

## Myth as Story

Whatever else myth is, it is first of all story. As such, it invites us to consider the value of narrative as a literary form. The scholarly study of narrative is currently so prolific that it is in danger of collapsing under its own weight. Nearly every month brings a new book on narrative theory.

*Why Stories Matter.* This interest in narratology reflects a universal human longing for stories. In fact, one of the most enduring human impulses can be summed up in the four-word request, "Tell me a story." The appeal of story is partly that stories consist of the same ingredients that make up our daily lives—action, setting, and characters. In other words, life itself has a narrative quality, and we are the protagonists of our own stories.

Another reason we like stories is that we are programmed to want to know the answer to the three questions, What happened? What happened next? How did it turn out? It is no wonder, then, that someone has written that

> humankind is addicted to stories. No matter our mood, in reverie or expectation, panic or peace, we can be found stringing together incidents, and unfolding episodes. We turn our pain into narrative so we can bear it; we turn our ecstasy into narrative so we can prolong it. . . . We tell stories to live.[4]

We tell stories both to ourselves and to others—in our daydreaming about past or upcoming events, at the table, in the office.

We do so partly because stories are entertaining, but also because stories are a means by which we grapple with reality and make sense of life. A story, after all, is not a random flow of events. It is a selection of events arranged into a meaningful pattern. A story is life given meaning, framed as a picture is framed. It is an ordering of human experience. When we are asked at the supper table how our day went, we do not give objective facts. Even our selection of material for the story we tell is an interpretation of the day's events. When we speak of having had a good day or a bad day and then tell the story that supports our claim, we are imposing an order on life's untidy flow.

Neil Postman has expressed the significance of stories in our lives very well:

> Human beings require stories to give meaning to the facts of their existence. . . . Ever since we can remember, all of us have been tell-ing . . . stories about ourselves, composing life-giving autobiog-raphies of which we are the heroes and heroines. . . . A story provides a structure for our perceptions; only through stories do facts assume any meaning whatsoever. This is why children everywhere ask . . . ,

"Where did I come from?" and, shortly after, "What will happen when I die?" They require a story to give meaning to their existence.[5]

A study of successful American companies concluded that "we are more influenced by stories . . . than by data. . . . A story [has] . . . connectedness which we call relevance. . . . This is indeed how people think."[6]

Not only do individuals organize their lives and values around stories—so do communities and nations. It is therefore easy to see why narrative is so important to the Christian faith. Christians live their faith not only in terms of doctrines, but also in terms of stories. If we listen to the words of such a basic summary of the Christian faith as the Apostles' Creed, we find that it tells a story about what God has done. The Christian sacraments tell a story about redemption in Christ.

The Bible likewise highlights stories. Henry R. Luce, founder of *Time* magazine, once commented on his magazine's interest in personalities with the quip, "*Time* didn't start this emphasis on stories about people; the Bible did." The Bible as a whole is organized on a narrative plan, telling the story of human history from its beginning to its end and framed on both ends by timeless eternity. The Bible has a central plot conflict between good and evil. The protagonist in this story is God. His emerging characterization and his actions with his creatures are the main concerns of the entire book. Amos Wilder has rightly said that "the narrative mode is uniquely important in Christianity. . . . A Christian can confess his faith wherever he is . . . just by telling a story or a series of stories."[7]

Everyone lives by a world picture (comprised of images, stories, and characters) as well as a world view (comprised of ideas). That world picture includes the stories of the literature we have absorbed. Through the centuries, the stories that the classics tell have loomed large in the world picture of the societies where they circulate. They can speak with the same power to us.

*The Delight of Homer's Story.* A story begins in delight and ends in wisdom. Before we even know what a story is going to be about at the level of theme, the storyteller has to interest us in the story itself. Novelist E. M. Forster acknowledged this when he wrote that a story "can only have one merit: that of making the audience want to know what happens next."[8] Great storytellers know how to make us want to know what happens next, and paying attention to the specific means by which they do so is often a good first step toward literary analysis.

Our delight in a long story such as Homer's epic depends partly on the storyteller's ability to impose a satisfactory unity on the story as a whole. The big pattern in Homer's story is the quest in which the hero journeys for ten years from Troy to his home in Ithaca. This quest has a happy ending and follows the U-shaped structure that literary critics call a comic plot. It descends into potential tragedy but rises to a happy ending as a series of obstacles are overcome.

This quest story falls into three well-defined sections. The first four books of the epic, known as *The Telemachia*, tell the story of the initiatory journey of Telemachos, son of Odysseus, to find his father. Books 5-12 narrate the ten-year wanderings of Odysseus in the Mediterranean region. Books 13-24 are the homecoming or return phase of the action. They tell how Odysseus regained his kingdom from the plundering suitors and was reunited with his family.

Readers sometimes wonder how the first four books, in which the hero does not even play an active role, fit into the story. But Homer knew what he was doing. These books picture the goal of the quest—a faithful wife, a son reaching maturity, and a rich kingdom being plundered by villainous suitors. With all this fixed vividly in our imaginations, we follow the progress of the hero toward that goal with anticipation, suspense, and occasional heartbreak.

*Conflict, Progression, and Adventure in Homer's Story.* The soul of a plot is conflict, and here, too, Homer's story is a model. Telemachos and Penelope are engaged in a life-and-death struggle with the suitors. Odysseus struggles against the environment (with death by drowning a constant threat on his sea voyage), the hatred of the god Poseidon, and the threats posed by such characters as the Cyclops, Calypso, and Circe. The most subtle and engaging conflict occurs within Odysseus himself. Odysseus is often his own worst enemy. He is overly curious and sometimes greedy. Throughout his wanderings he is torn within himself between his fixed purpose to return home and his curiosity to explore the unknown.

Stories require a sense of progressive movement, and most of them give us some version of a problem-solution format. The problem that needs solving in *The Odyssey* is the absence of Odysseus from Ithaca. Virtually everything in the story adds to our understanding of this problem or to the progress that the hero makes in solving it. The story that Homer builds around this problem-solution format is notable for its suspense. At first the problem seems insurmountable. Then as Odysseus nears home we begin to wonder *how* he will regain his kingdom and restore order to his household.

The best known part of Homer's story is the middle section, dealing with Odysseus' twelve adventures. Each of the adventures is an obstacle that must be overcome. Each episode is also a temptation for the hero to do something forbidden, and an occasion on which the hero passes the test by displaying a virtue (sometimes after having gotten himself into trouble by imprudent behavior). Homer thus began a strategy that later storytellers often imitated: he made his hero pass through a series of landscapes that are both physical and moral.

Within the framework of constant elements, Homer avoids monotony with an amazing variety in the series of adventures. There is variety in the length or brevity of the episodes, for example. Episodes such as those involving the lotus eaters and Sirens are narrated briefly. The stories involving Calypso and Circe are told with leisurely fullness. Some of the events are violent (such as those involving Polyphemos the Cyclops and the sea monsters Scylla and Charybdis), while others are mild (the lotus eaters and the visit to the utopian Phaiacia).

Some of the adventures involve supernatural agents such as Calypso and Circe, others involve human opponents such as the Ciconians, and still others involve nature (the winds of Aeolus and the parching winds on the island of Helios). While the idea of temptation underlies all of these adventures, the specific sin to which Odysseus is tempted varies, from the temptation to consume the food and drink of the gods on the island of Calypso to curiosity to explore the unknown in the cave of the Cyclops to fear in the journey to the underworld. In each episode Odysseus displays the general virtue of faithfulness to home, but the specific virtue varies (abstinence, courage, self-control, wit).

***Dramatic Irony and Climax.*** Storytellers can scarcely tell a story without employing the device of dramatic irony, a situation that arises when readers know something that characters in the story do not. The homecoming phase of *The Odyssey* is perhaps the most sustained performance in the art of dramatic irony among the classics. When Odysseus returns home disguised as an old beggar, the people in Ithaca (including his own wife and son) do not recognize him. Virtually every encounter that Odysseus has with people around his home is filled with dramatic irony, which accounts for much of the reader's delight in reading this part of the story. The effect is reminiscent of the dramatic irony in the story of Joseph and his brothers in Egypt.

And of course a good plot needs a suitable climax. Homer's story has it, a feat all the more remarkable when we stop to consider that Homer builds his entire long story around the single climax of the defeat of the suitors and reunion between Odysseus and Penelope. One thing that makes the homecoming of Odysseus so climactic is Homer's use of foreshadowing. From the opening lines of the story we are never allowed to forget the eventual outcome of the action. In fact, Homer takes the first four books of the epic to establish with great clarity the goal of the hero's quest. The story is filled with references to Odysseus' need to return home and to what will happen, especially to the villainous suitors, if he ever does return. Because the climax is artfully foreshadowed and delayed, it comes with great impact when it finally occurs, an impact heightened by the pervasive "just in time" motif that governs the return story.

*Setting and Characters.* Stories require vivid settings, and here, too, Homer delights us. Odysseus' home, for example, becomes an evocative picture of the archetypal "good place" early in the epic:

> *Telemachos went down to his father's storehouse, a room lofty and wide where heaps of gold and bronze were kept, with clothes in coffers and plenty of fragrant oil; jars of delicious old wine stood . . . in rows along the wall, ready for Odysseus when he should come home again after all his troubles.*

In the opposite vein we find the terror that we relive as Odysseus' ship approaches Scylla and Charydis: "suddenly I saw smoke, and a great rolling wave, and heard a loud noise. The men were terrified, the oars flew out of their hands and fell in the sea with a splash, dragging down at the ship's sides by their loops."

C.S. Lewis, in his classic little essay "On Stories," stresses the importance of atmosphere in a story and claims that "it is here that Homer shows his supreme excellence."[9] The description of Calypso's earthly paradise illustrates this feature of Homer's imagination at its best:

> A great fire blazed in the hearth, and the burning logs of cedar and juniper wafted their fragrant scent far over the island. . . . There the birds would sail to rest on their outspread wings. . . . Over the gaping mouth of the cave trailed a luxuriant grape-vine, with clusters of ripe fruit; and four rills of clear water ran in a row close together, winding over the ground. Beyond were soft meadows thick with violets and wild celery. That was a sight to gladden the very gods.

It is no wonder that Homer's story is praised for its realism. We find it not only in his descriptions, but also in his celebrated epic similes that compare an event in the story to something in real life. Here is how he makes the capture of Odysseus' men by the monster Scylla come alive:

> As a fisherman stands on a projecting rock with a long rod, and throws in ground-bait to attract the little fishes, then drops in hook and line with its horn-bait, and at last gets a bite and whips him out gasping, so Scylla swung them gasping up to the rock; there in the cave she devoured them, shrieking and stretching out their hands to me in the death-struggle.

Despite the seeming remoteness of myth from everyday life (a remoteness reinforced by the grand scope of epic), *The Odyssey* is never far from actual life.

Finally, a good story requires vivid and striking characters. *The Odyssey* gives us a gallery of memorable characters. One is many-sided Odysseus. The density or "thickness" of his character can be attributed partly to the complex qualities that he exhibits—physical prowess and courage, intelligence and wit, faithfulness in personal relations, and piety to the gods. He is a paradoxical character, capable of both strong emotions and remarkable self-control, of both fixed purpose to get home and self-defeating curiosity to explore everything along the way. He displays both warmth and hardness toward his friends and family. We also see Odysseus in a range of roles: leader, father, husband, son, king, worshiper of the gods, victim, victor.

Next to Odysseus in importance are his son and wife. Penelope is an idealized heroine—a fit companion to the epic hero. She is faithful, beautiful, courageous, clever—a figure to inspire admiration. Telemachos is the maturing son who begins the story incapable of filling the void of his father's absence and ends as a worthy son to perpetuate the family line (an important value in ancient cultures).

Beyond these family members is a cast of characters whom we never forget: the beautiful and seductive Calypso, the unhappily reunited celebrity couple Menalaos and Helen, the youthful Nausicaa (whose father tried to interest Odysseus in her), the one-eyed Cyclops (a curious blend of the pastoral and cannibal), the irresistible Sirens who eat gullible men for breakfast, the faithful swineherd and nurse, Antinoos (the ringleader of the villainous suitors who flings a cowsfoot at Odysseus in the dining hall), and Laertes, the pathetic and aged father of Odysseus.

*Summary.* Homer's *Odyssey* is the very touchstone of storytelling. It fulfills the first demand of myth, that of creating an irresistibly compelling narrative. Before we interpret myth, we must simply experience it as story and not ask too many deeper questions of it. Myth first entertains us, partly by its sheer strangeness. C.S. Lewis goes so far as to define myth as a "story which has a value in itself—a value independent of its embodiment in any literary work."[10]

The story of Odysseus is such a story, but in Homer's handling it is beautified by all the best resources of the storyteller. Someone has rightly said that "all of Homer is a study in story magic."[11] Odysseus himself, while being entertained by an epic poet at a banquet in Phaiacia, expresses the delight I am claiming for Homer's story: "What a pleasure it is, my lord, to hear a singer like this. . . . I declare it is just the perfection of gracious life: good cheer and good temper everywhere, rows of guests enjoying themselves heartily. . . . I think that is the best thing men can have."

## Myth as Fantasy

Myth is not only a story. It is also fantasy. The realm of fiction falls into two types, or two degrees. Fictional realism is "made up" rather than factual, but it does not violate what happens in the world in which we live. Fantasy, by contrast, does not reproduce the empirical world but creates an alternate world that part of the time violates the limits or rules of the real world. Neither type of fiction is better than the other, but it is important that we understand the dynamics of both. In a later chapter I will take a look at realistic fiction. The older literature was more inclined to be fantasy.

*The Pleasures of Fantasy.* Readers either have a taste for fantasy or they don't. About half of my students prefer fantasy to realism. They do so partly because of the distinctive pleasures that fantasy affords.

One of these is remoteness from everyday life. To read fantasy is to take a holiday from ordinary life. Fantasy transports us from a world of asphalt parking lots and boredom at stoplights to a world merely imagined. It is simply a more interesting and exciting world than the world of the local grocery store, just as a dragon is more interesting and exciting than a check-out clerk. The appeal of fantasy is akin to poring over an issue of *National Geographic.*

Once we enter the imagined world of fantasy, we find ordinary experience defamiliarized. Fantasy has what J.R.R. Tolkien, in his famous essay "On Fairy-Stories," calls "arresting strangeness."[12] A writer of high school mathematics books took the educational world by storm several years ago when he replaced conventional math problems with ones involving fantasy. Instead of having to read problems built around apples in a box and three men rowing upstream in four hours, students found themselves confronted by such flights of fantasy as fairies and wood nymphs. Someone else who did a doctoral dissertation on algebra textbooks found that students pay more attention to problems with a touch of fantasy.[13]

The concept of wonder or mystery is also a common theme in recent defenses of fantasy. By putting us in touch with other-worldly events and places, fantasy awakens both our longing for transcendence and our awareness that it is real. The more completely technology dominates our society, the stronger will be the appeal of fantasy.

Homer's story capitalizes on the pleasures of fantasy. Homer makes no attempt to stay within the bounds of observable reality. Instead he flaunts the fantastic element in his story. He whisks us away to a world where a goddess entertains a traveler for seven years on an earthly paradise island, where a one-eyed giant eats men for supper when they invade his cave, and where the king of the winds lives in a domestic utopia on a floating island. The pleasures of such fantasy are the pleasures of enchantment, mystery, and "otherness."

This sense of wonder is something that we can carry over to real life. C.S. Lewis said that a person "does not despise real woods because he has read of enchanted woods: the reading makes all real woods a little enchanted."[14]

*Fantasy and Reality.* The case for fantasy extends beyond its value as entertainment to its usefulness in clarifying life. We can begin by noting that for all its apparent remoteness from everyday life, fantasy is actually filled with elemental human experience. Tolkien makes much of this in his essay. Fairy stories, he notes, deal "with simple or fundamental things . . . made all the more luminous by their setting. . . . It was in fairy-stories that I first divined the potency of the words, and the wonder of the things, such as stone, and wood, and iron; tree and grass; house and fire; bread and wine."[15] For all its far-flung fantasies, Homer's story keeps us rooted in the world of water and sunlight, eating and drinking, and the geography of the Mediterranean region (in fact, retracing the supposed trip of Odysseus has become a hallowed ritual in our century, as documentary books and commercial cruises attest).

Fantasy and myth are particularly adept at expressing universal human experience, emancipated from changing social conditions and historical particularities. Stripped of the surface clutter of transient social conditions, elemental human experience stands out fully illumined. The enduring quality of myth is evident from the fact that Homer's story is still up-to-date twenty-nine centuries later.

During his wanderings, Odysseus encounters approximately what anyone taking a journey away from home would encounter today: violence, sexual temptation, drugs (the island of the lotus eaters), the occult, physical danger, death, lost luggage, homesickness, getting lost, culture shock (for example, the overnight in the Cyclops' cave and the spectacle of Odysseus' seeing his fellow sailors transformed into animals as he arrives at Circe's house), hospitality, the impulse to give up, inadequate transportation, a lost passport (Odysseus arrives stark naked and without identity at Phaiacia), and personal conflict with fellow travelers.

Homer's fantastic story presents images of life as we know it—images of courage, heroism, mystery, deity, beauty, and a dozen others. Odysseus is tempted by the things that tempt us—fear, forbidden food and drink, self-pity, greed, harmful self-indulgence, people of the other sex.

*The Misconception about Fantasy.* In view of what I have said, it should be obvious that the common charge of escapism is fallacious. Because fantasy transports us to an alternate world with its own rules, say the debunkers, it is unrelated to life in *this* world. Writers of fantasy are thus criticized for making the problems of life too easy—for deciding to "dress moral problems in fancy clothes and magic, and evade the problems of being merely human," in the words of one critic.[16]

But wait a minute. What are these "fancy clothes" in which fantasy dresses up moral problems? A beautiful goddess who tries to steal a faithful husband by offering him eternal life and sexual fulfillment if only he will eat the ambrosia and drink the nectar of the gods? A palace filled with plundering suitors who are undermining the very basis of civilization? A bloody battle in the great hall of a palace in which over a hundred men are slaughtered and after which the hall has to be cleaned with shovels and sulfur? If the images of the good are magnified in myth, so are the images of evil. Myth does not conceal the terrors of life. In fact, the contrary charge that myth is too fearful is also brought against it by mothers who want fairy stories removed from schools.

Homer's *Odyssey* does, indeed, defamiliarize human experience, but it does not run away from the problems of being human. Ursula LeGuin, a writer of science fiction, expresses the basic principle involved here very well:

A scientist who creates a monster . . . a wizard unable to cast a spell . . . may be precise and profound metaphors of the human condition. The fantasist, whether he uses the ancient archetypes of myth and legend or the younger ones of science and technology, may be talking as seriously as any sociologist—and a good deal more directly—about human life as it is lived, and as it might be lived, and as it ought to be lived.[17]

*Metaphors of the human condition:* this is the key concept. We do not mistake the details of fantasy for everyday life, but those details bring real life to mind.

Sometimes the charge is phrased in terms of the alleged untruth of fantasy. But fantasy *does* have the ability to tell the truth. Homer's story is true to life as we find it in our own world. The story of the suitors and their behavior in Ithaca during the absence of Odysseus is literally preposterous. The scale of thievery is unrealistic. No prince's property would have been sufficient to support the lavish lifestyle of 108 suitors and their hangers-on year after year. The nearly unrelieved evil of these princes does not do justice to the complexity of human psychology as we know it.

But this heightened picture of evil and barbarity is as contemporary as the daily newspaper or a drive through any major city. Homer's story is truthful to the perversion of sexual morality, disrespect for others' property, laziness, callousness, greed, obsession with being entertained, assault on marriage, and decay of manners that we find everywhere around us. What could be more truthful than Homer's mythical picture of a society whose values have been turned upside down? Bruno Bettelheim, who has written so well on the benefits of fairy stories for children, rightly comments that "the child intuitively comprehends that although these stories are *unreal*, they are not *untrue*."[18] We should not forget that the visionary writings of the Bible are filled with fantastic details that picture realities—a red horse, a flying scroll that devours the wood and stones of houses, a great red dragon whose tail sweeps down a third of the stars of heaven.

The test of whether or not fantasy is escapist is an easy one: does reading such literature unfit a reader for dealing with everyday reality, or does it send a reader back to life with renewed understanding and zest? In principle, fantasy is no more subject to being escapist than a computer manual or a biography is. Paradoxically, it is often less escapist than the television news, which bombards us with information about which we are expected to do nothing.

Let me reiterate that fantasy is simply a particular type of fiction. It is subject to the same potential advantages and liabilities as realistic fiction, with two exceptions. On the negative side, it requires the ability to translate the details of the story into recognizable human experience or issues. Not everyone can do such translating, and those who cannot often fail to see the point of fantasy. The goddess Calypso is a picture of sexual seduction and Polyphemos the Cyclops of violence only for people who have developed the knack of building bridges between the mythical world and the ordinary world. Fantasy and myth are a means of evaluating the real world, but not all readers have the antennae that enable them to see this.

On the positive side, fantasy and myth seem to be more adept at portraying some types of experience than realistic fiction is. I do not wish to overstate the case. I remain unconvinced by some of the claims made for myth. It is commonly implied by apologists for fantasy that myth has a virtual corner on the portrayal of such experiences as the conflict between good and evil, heroism, the triumph of the good, and a whole and complete world. But realistic fiction can portray these, too. Still, I think a case can be made for the superior ability of fantasy to portray mystery, beauty, images of greatness, and above all supernatural reality. It also presents experiences on such a heightened scale that some experiences, while open to treatment in realistic fiction, seem more powerfully drawn in fantasy.

## Myth and the Supernatural

By definition, myth includes supernatural reality in its portrayal of life. And therein lies its controversial status in some circles. Myth has, in fact, been caught in crossfire on the subject. People unsympathetic to religion scoff at myth for its inclusion of the supernatural. A reviewer complained that the only people who like the fantasy written by C.S. Lewis are either children or Christians, adding that they "share one quality of imagination—a common willingness to extend reality beyond the visible."[19]

More often the case against the supernaturalism of myth is made by theologically conservative Christians. I receive a steady stream of correspondence from former students now teaching in Christian schools asking how to handle parents' objections to myth. It is not easy to get at the heart of the complaints, but here is a typical statement, from a piece entitled "Christian Fantasy—A Contradiction":

The contradiction comes with the focus on magic, sorcery, witches and mythological creatures born out of civilizations that believed in the gods they created and used the stories that surround them to explain man's existence. . . . It seems a contradiction to use the very things God has spoken so strongly against—witches, casting a spell, etc.—to communicate truth. . . . When held to the light of God's Word, the books become confusing and are seen to be unreliable. Such contributions to literature, inconsistent with God's Word, contribute nothing to our understanding of truth.[20]

Much of the Christian objection to myth has centered on its inclusion of pagan or extrabiblical supernaturalism, and this is the question I will attempt to disentangle. Doing so takes us into the religious dimension of myth.

Let me begin with a fact of literary history. The oldest literature of the world is myth—stories about the gods, about heroes, about marvelous events. The history of literature has been in the direction of displacement toward greater and greater realism, with romance serving as a midway step in this development.

The mythical literature that arose from primitive societies reflects their religious outlook. Many of the old myths were originally believed to express religious truth, though the exact degree to which this was true is hard to determine at this late date. We know from Plato's *Republic* that he was appalled at Homer's portrayal of the gods, whose behavior struck him as unbecoming to the very idea of deity.

But no matter how frivolous the behavior of the gods in Homer might strike us, let us note an important way in which this mythical literature stands as a corrective to our own secular age. C.S. Lewis makes the commonsense observation that "the big division of humanity is into the majority, who believe in some kind of God or gods, and the minority who do not. On this point, Christianity lines up with the majority—lines up with ancient Greeks and Romans, modern savages, . . . etc., against the modern Western European materialist."[21]

The supernaturalism of mythical literature, far from being a mark against it, is part of its truthfulness. In its acceptance of the premise that there is a level of supernatural reality, it is more truthful than contemporary television programs, for example, which presumably raise no objections from Christians who dislike myth because its supernaturalism is not the Christian supernatural.

Some Christians act as if pagan gods do not exist, but this is not how the Bible views the matter. Psalm 82 tells us, "God has taken his place in the divine council; in the midst of the gods he holds judgment" (v. 1). "Who is like thee, O LORD, among the gods?" the Israelites asked following the Red Sea deliverance (Exodus 15:11). God "is to be feared above all gods," the Psalmist declares (96:4). These statements will make a great deal more sense to us if we know something about the other gods as we find them depicted in myth. The superiority of the God of the Bible to the gods of pagan myth is open for any reader to experience, and it is not a waste of time to experience it.

This brings us to the issue of mythical parallels or analogues to stories in the Bible. Genesis 2 is the Bible's version of life in paradise; Homer gives us *his* version of an earthly paradise. He also gives us his picture of a heavenly abode of the gods and of the afterlife. In pagan mythology more generally, we find stories of creation, a fall from innocence, a flood, a dying and reborn god, and so forth. What should be our attitude toward these stories?

Christians through the centuries have disagreed in their answer to that question. The balanced middle position is well summed up by the Renaissance historian Walter Ralegh, who claimed that the old myths are "crooked images of some one true history."[22] In other words, the correct version of the stories is found in the Bible. How, then, should we regard the crooked images of the truth—humankind's memories of a universal story, unaided by supernatural revelation?

Some Christians have asserted strongly that "mythology is not only false, it is evil."[23] Calvin Linton writes, "Satan has . . . from the dawn of history prepared, in anticipation of God's unfolding plan, a great fraud, an intricate imitation, of the kingdom of Christ."[24]

C.S. Lewis takes a more positive view. He speaks of how God "sent the human race . . . good dreams," that is, anticipations or echoes of the truth.[25] Elsewhere Lewis comments that "the resemblance between these myths and the Christian truth is no more accidental than the resemblance between the sun and the sun's reflection in a pond, or that between a historical fact and the somewhat garbled version of it which lives in popular report."[26]

This strikes me as a defensible view of the old myths, and I would relate it to the theory of G.K. Chesterton that mythology is an attempt to arrive at religious truth through the imagination alone.[27] The old myths expressed the right human longings (which we share), but the answers they gave to the great issues lacked certainty. Mythical literature satisfies some of the *needs* that are satisfied by religion, but it does not provide a creed that people believe with the same certainty that Christians believe the Apostles' Creed. The pagan "feels the presence of powers about which he guesses and invents." In a word, writes Chesterton, "mythology is a *search*." It *expresses* a need but does not satisfy it. The pagans "had dreams about realities."

In agreeing with Chesterton, I am taking issue with a longstanding Christian tradition that believes that the gods that pagans worshipped were really demons. I think that Zeus and Athena and Poseidon were figments of the pagans' imagination.

It is always possible, of course, that a person might be satisfied with the dream (though no one today is in danger of converting to Greek paganism as a result of reading *The Odyssey*). It is more likely that a person will find the dream directing him or her to the reality. Someone has claimed that "it is frequently out of a pagan soul that the best Christian soul is made."[28] Missionary Rachel Saint, when asked how she felt about the charge that missionaries deprive natives of their culture, responded,

> I have come to the conclusion that we are actually giving the Indians back that which they lost, maybe hundreds of years ago. In the stories of the Indians, they recognize one God. They do not know his Son, nor his name. . . . We are simply taking them back to their old, old stories and filling in the facts of the Gospel. . . . The more I study their legends, the more I find of their longing to know God.[29]

I have raised the question of the religious dimension of myth because it is an issue raised in some Christian circles. But I myself read myth simply as a branch of fantasy, without regarding it as primarily a religious statement. After all, as Northrop Frye observes, "When a system of myths loses all connexion with belief, it becomes purely literary."[30]

## The Wisdom of Homer's Odyssey

A story begins in delight and ends in wisdom. The wisdom that Homer's story offers us is the kind that I associate with myth—a knowledge of elemental human experience and the common moral wisdom of the human race. Dorothy Sayers notes that myth has an uncanny ability to "disclose the universal pattern of things."[31] G.K. Chesterton also puts us on the right track when he observes (in an essay entitled "The Ethics of Elfland") that "fairyland is nothing but the sunny country of common sense."[32]

First, then, myth puts us in touch with the primeval images of our existence. Carl Jung said that these master images "make up the groundwork of the human psyche" and that "wisdom is a return to them."[33] For example, Homer's *Odyssey* and *Iliad* together give us two of the main paradigms for literature: life is either a journey or a battle. Without consciously thinking about life in these terms, we nevertheless organize much of our life according to them. The following comment catches the flavor of one type of wisdom I am claiming for Homer's mythic imagination:

> In telling the tale of an exiled king striving to return home, Homer is telling the tale of all of us. All of us know what it is like to be desperately lost and to wonder if we shall ever get "home" again. And the *Odyssey* gives us hope, because its central message is simply this: that no matter how long, . . . no matter how desperate we become, we shall eventually return home, and to happiness. It is little wonder, then, that the *Odyssey* has become a key word in Western civilization: all of our individual lives consist of "odysseys" of one kind or another. . . .[34]

*The Odyssey* calls us back to bedrock humanity—to elemental relationships (to nature, the divine, family, friends, enemies, the state) and to elemental activities (eating, sleeping, sex, worship, work, leisure).

The wisdom of the story also consists of its ability to put us in touch with human fears and longings. The fears include death, physical danger, violence, isolation from home and family, social instability, rootlessness, the hostility of nature, and (in the story of Telemachos) underachievement. The longings that the story awakens within us include the longings for security, a stable social order, faithful wedded love, worthy children, home, a sense of belonging, a fixed place of rest, justice, and achieving success in our ventures.

The story's scheme of vices and virtues is part of its wisdom. The vices include greed, thievery, violence, self-destructive curiosity, abandonment of duty, self-indulgence, disregard of property and marriage, and impiety toward the gods. The virtues include hospitality, self-control (which in the wanderings of Odysseus often takes the form of abstinence), intelligence, cleverness, courage, justice, obedience to the gods, and—overshadowing all the others—fidelity to home.

The sense of life that emerges from this mythical story also corresponds in its general outlines to a Christian view. Life emerges as a continuous test. Good and evil are real and absolute. We get repeated and accurate anatomies of how temptation works in a person's life and how it can be overcome. The dangerousness of life, both physically and morally, comes through clearly. Human nature is double—capable of both good and evil. The limitations of violence as a way of life are seen in the fate of the suitors.

One of the things that makes the story seem modern is the central importance allotted to women and domestic values. We notice first the large number of female characters in the story, both humans and goddesses. Women are often the ones in power, and they are frequently threatening to men. Domestic values are elevated to the highest position in the world view of the story. The epic similes and beatitudes scattered throughout the story often draw upon domestic life. All of this led the Victorian writer Samuel Butler to write a book entitled *The Authoress of the Odyssey*, whose thesis was that a woman wrote the poem.

In affirming the truth of *The Odyssey* as I have, I must guard against leaving the impression that the story is above criticism. Since Homer had never read a page of the Bible and lived nine centuries before the incarnation of Christ, the religious details are of course less than Christian. The view of the afterlife is notably deficient. The vision is too humanistic and too lacking in such concepts as acknowledgement of sin, forgiveness, and God-reliance to be fully agreeable to a Christian reader. And the human race has generally decided to settle its disputes in a more civilized manner than through the physical combat described in Homer's story (though this stricture applies equally to the Old Testament).

*Summary.* Homer's story is neither more nor less truthful for being myth. It has exactly the same potential for truth and error that any other work of literature possesses. But the predominant truth and beauty of *The Odyssey* should lay to rest any doubt about the ability of myth to be both delightful and edifying. Perhaps this explains why Paul in the New Testament quotes pagan writers with approval, and why in addressing the Areopagus on the subject of humankind's "feeling after God" (Acts 17:27) he alludes to Homer's *Odyssey* by using the word Homer used to describe the groping of the blinded Cyclops Polyphemus as he sought the entrance of his cave.

## Notes to Chapter 1

[1] Homer, *The Odyssey*, trans. W.H.D. Rouse (New York: New American Library, 1937).

[2] See William B. Stanford, *The Ulysses Theme: A Study in the Adaptability of a Traditional Hero* (New York: Barnes and Noble, 1964).

[3] George E. Dimock, Jr., "The Name of Odysseus," *Hudson Review* 9 (Spring 1956): 52-70. The essay has been reprinted in several anthologies of essays on *The Odyssey*.

[4] John Shea, *Stories of God* (Chicago: Thomas More Press, 1978), pp. 7-8.

[5] Neil Postman, "Learning by Story," *The Atlantic* December 1989: 122.

[6] Thomas J. Peters and Robert H. Waterman, Jr., *In Search of Excellence: Lessons from America's Best-Run Companies* (New York: Harper and Row, 1982), pp. 61-62.

[7] Amos Wilder, *Early Christian Rhetoric: The Language of the Gospel* (Cambridge, MA: Harvard UP, 1972), p. 56.

[8] E.M. Forster, *Aspects of the Novel* (Harmondsworth: Penguin, 1962), p. 35.

[9] C.S. Lewis, "On Stories," in *Of Other Worlds: Essays and Stories*, ed. Walter Hooper (New York: Harcourt, 1966), p. 11.

[10] C.S. Lewis, *An Experiment in Criticism* (Cambridge: Cambridge UP, 1961), p. 41.

[11] Victor Nell, *Lost in a Book: The Psychology of Reading for Pleasure* (New Haven: Yale UP, 1988), p. 48.

[12] J.R.R. Tolkien, "On Fairy-Stories," in *Essays Presented to Charles Williams*, ed. C.S. Lewis (Grand Rapids: William B. Eerdmans, 1966), p. 67.

[13] Janet Cawley, "Fantasy Adds up in Algebra," *Chicago Tribune* 12 September 1982, Section 3: 1-2.

[14]C.S. Lewis, *Of Other Worlds*, pp. 29-30.

[15]Tolkien, p. 75.

[16]Samuel Hynes, as quoted in "Did Christianity Corrupt Lewis?" Editorial, *Christianity Today* 23 (1979): 1663.

[17]Ursula LeGuin, National Book Award acceptance speech, as quoted by Martin LeBar, "Slipping the Truth in Edgewise," *Christianity Today* 27 March 1981: 38.

[18]Bruno Bettelheim, *The Uses of Enchantment: The Meaning and Importance of Fairy Tales* (New York: Vintage, 1975), p. 73.

[19]Hynes, 1663.

[20]*The Capsule* May/June 1981: 11.

[21]C.S. Lewis, *Mere Christianity* (New York: Macmillan, 1960), p. 43.

[22]Walter Ralegh, as quoted by Isabel MacCaffrey, *Paradise Lost as "Myth"* (Cambridge, MA: Harvard UP, 1959), p. 12.

[23]J. Barton Payne, *The Theology of the Older Testament* (Grand Rapids: Zondervan, 1962), p. 140.

[24]Calvin Linton, "And Pilate Said, 'Make It As Sure As Ye Can,'" *Christianity Today* 13 April 1973: 5.

[25]C.S. Lewis, *Mere Christianity*, p. 54.

[26]C.S. Lewis, *Reflections on the Psalms* (New York: Macmillan, 1958), p. 107.

[27]All my citations and quotations from Chesterton here are from *The Everlasting Man* (Garden City, NY: Image Books, 1955).

[28]Charles Peguy, *Clio, Dialogue of History and of the Pagan Soul*, as quoted by Henri Peyre, "Camus the Pagan," in *Camus: A Collection of Critical Essays*, ed. Germaine Bree (Englewood Cliffs, NJ: Prentice-Hall, 1962), p. 65.

[29]Interview with Rachel Saint, *Christianity Today* 12 January 1976: 15-16. Don Richardson's book *Eternity in Their Hearts* (Ventura, CA: Regal Books, 1984) provides numerous examples of how pagan myths and rituals frequently correspond to the Bible and the Christian faith.

[30]Northrop Frye, *Fables of Identity: Studies in Poetic Mythology* (New York: Harcourt, 1963), p. 32.

[31]Dorothy Sayers, "Oedipus Simplex: Freedom and Fate in Folk-Lore and Fiction," in *Christian Letters to a Post-Christian World*, ed. Roderick Jellema (Grand Rapids: William B. Eerdmans, 1969), p. 254.

[32]G.K. Chesterton, *Orthodoxy* (Garden City, NY: Image Books, 1959), p. 49.

[33]Carl Jung, *Psychological Reflections*, ed. Jolande Jacobi (Princeton: Princeton UP, 1953), p. 47.

[34]Hugh McDermott, *Novel and Romance* (Totowa, NJ: Barnes and Noble, 1989), p. 15.

# Chapter 2

## Chaucer's Canterbury Tales
### and the Comic Spirit in Literature

## "Then People Long to Go on Pilgrimages"

✳

*When April with his showers sweet*
*Has pierced the drought of March to the root,*
*And bathed every vein in such moisture*
*That has the power to engender the flower. . . .*
*Then people long to go on pilgrimages,*
*And palmers to seek strange shores*
*And distant shrines known in various lands;*
*And especially from every shire's end*
*Of England they travel to Canterbury,*
*To seek the holy blissful martyr*
*Who helped them when they were sick.*
*It befell that in that season one day*
*In Southwark at the Tabard Inn as I lay*
*Ready to go on my pilgrimage*
*To Canterbury with heart devout,*
*At night there came into that hotel*
*A company of twenty nine*
*Of sundry folk.*[1]

✳

In these lines Geoffrey Chaucer (1343-1400) sets the stage for his major poem—an unfinished collection of stories set within the narrative framework of a pilgrimage from Southwark, a suburb of London, to

Canterbury. The narrative premise is that the pilgrims tell the stories on the pilgrimage to make the time pass more pleasantly.

When Chaucer decided to bring together a group of separate stories into a single work, he faced the task of imposing unity on a mass of heterogeneous material. One element of unity that he imposed was thematic. In the portraits that make up "The General Prologue" and in the stories that the pilgrims tell, we find a tension between the secular and the sacred, the worldly and the spiritual.

A second unifying framework is the journey or pilgrimage, with its ongoing dynamics. The institution of the pilgrimage was the only thing that would have enabled Chaucer to bring together a representative cross-section of medieval society. In Chaucer's handling, moreover, the pilgrimage gives the overall story a sense of progression toward a goal and allows for interaction among the pilgrims, so that the pilgrimage itself becomes a continuous and lively drama as pilgrims get angry at each other and tell stories at each other's expense.

Chaucer is commonly regarded as the third greatest English writer (behind Shakespeare and Milton). Three sources of his greatness are his storytelling ability, his affectionate understanding of human nature, and his comic spirit.

Chaucer's understanding of human nature reveals itself partly in his portrayal of character. Particularly noteworthy are his ability to visualize the appearance of characters, his range of characters (both socially and morally), and his adeptness at portraying universal character types (so that we have the impression of having met the person before in our own experience).

Chaucer's comedy is also one of the reasons why he stays so vividly with people who have read *The Canterbury Tales*, and this will provide the framework within which I will discuss Chaucer's work. Much of Chaucer's comedy is satiric. It laughs at the social and religious abuses of the day. Chaucer seems to have believed that laughter, not loathing, is the best way to expose the vices and foibles of the human race.

In addition to putting us in touch with human nature and making us laugh, Chaucer imparts two particular bits of wisdom to us. He is adept at capturing the hypocrisy that infiltrates the life of every religious person and institution. He has a knack of uncovering the hidden and not-so-hidden attempts that religious people make to be worldly and spiritual at the same time. Chaucer's pilgrims are headed for a religious encounter and are supposedly engaged in a pious activity. Yet what we mainly observe enroute to Canterbury is an abundance of fallen humanity, much of it far from any kind of spiritual holiness. We can profitably compare what occupies the thoughts and conversation of these pilgrims with the sentiments expressed in the "Songs of Ascent" (Psalms 120–135) that Old Testament worshipers sang as they "went up" to worship God at the temple in Jerusalem.

Another of Chaucer's most important themes is the power of sex in people's lives and its capacity for perversion. As Chaucer looks at the pilgrims, he sees sex everywhere. In doing so, he is only being true to life. It is not necessarily evidence of a perverse imagination or diseased moral sensibility that leads a writer to choose this for a subject. The Bible also has its share of the portrayal of eros defiled.

## Comedy of Plot

Comedy means two things in literary scholarship. It refers on the one hand to a U-shaped plot structure in which events begin in prosperity, descend into potential tragedy, and rise to a happy ending. Homer's *Odyssey* is a prototypical example of such a plot. The second meaning, which will be the focus of my discussion here, is the humorous or laughable. Understanding the comic spirit in literature is as necessary as it is elusive. One writer on the subject claims that "the theory of the comic . . . remains one of the permanently unsolved problems of literary study."[2]

It is customary to arrange literary comedy on a continuum or "ladder," ranging from the less subtle or intellectually sophisticated to the more subtle and refined. I have followed that scheme in my discussion of comedy in *The Canterbury Tales*.

At one end of the comic spectrum is humor rooted in the external events of a story's plot. The literary term for this is "situation comedy." It consists of embarrassing or inopportune occurrences, physical mishaps that strike us as funny ("slapstick comedy"), mistaken identity, misunderstanding, and (at the lower end of the comic scale) comedy arising from sex (which can shade off into pornography but does not necessarily do so) or other bodily functions (scatology and obscenity).

*Comedy and the Physical Side of Life.* Chaucer has more than his share of pornography and scatology. In the Middle Ages these stories of sex or obscenity were called fabliaux. Chaucer transformed them into high art with his usual narrative skill, but the potentially offensive nature of the subject matter remains an issue of taste.

Why has the human race decided that references to sex and bodily functions are funny? The more one ponders the question, the more arbitrary the list of comic subjects seems to be. But there is a logic to comedy. A comic handling of a sensitive subject is one way to distance it so it can be viewed from a safe distance. This is why the human race laughs at subjects that bother it or that it finds difficult to discuss because of their private nature. We also know that comedy thrives in a spirit of freedom from ordinary restraints, with the result that we normally find it funny when someone displays a flagrant disregard of normal inhibitions (as the wife of Bath does when she talks about her marriages in the prologue to her story).

*Slapstick Comedy.* Among the lower rungs of the ladder of comedy we also find physical mishap, often in the form of "slapstick comedy." The conventional stage trick of slipping on a banana peel and the pie-in-the-face routine are standard examples.

There is a touch of slapstick comedy in *The Canterbury Tales*. If we leave out of consideration the scatalogical stories, the most delicious example is the brief portrait of the cook in "The General Prologue." The portrait is famous for what *seems* to be a *non sequitur*—something "that does not follow." Chaucer tells us that it was a pity the cook had a mormal on his leg, because he could make blackmanger with the best of cooks. On the surface, the humor seems to lie in the incongruity, as if we were to say, "What a pity he has freckles on his arm, because he can play tennis with the best."

But upon further scrutiny, there is a logic to the pity that Chaucer claims for the cook's ailment. A mormal was either a species of scabbed ulcer or a running sore. In either case, it was the type of thing a person would be tempted to scratch now and then. Blackmanger was an elaborate stew over which a cook would spend a great deal of time. Everything considered, we have a rather gross version of chef's delight.

Why do we find physical mishaps like this funny when we read about them, whereas in real life life we would find them distressing?

Apparently it all has to do with the safe distance from which we view such events in comic literature. An important part of the dynamics of comedy is that the audience feels superior to the comic victim. Secure from the threat of what is happening to the victim, we are in a position to laugh at something that we would find painful if it happened to us in real life. We can laugh at the imagined spectacle of the cook's scabs falling into the stew because we do not have to eat it.

*The Humor of Personality Clashes.* Another of the comic situations that Chaucer exploited was the altercations or grudges that arise among characters on the pilgrimage. Some of these clashes were bound to happen because of the prejudices that pilgrims had toward each other's profession or gender. Personality clashes also occur. Chaucer capitalized on these funny situations both in his narrative links between stories and by having some of the pilgrims tell stories at the expense of other pilgrims.

One of the funniest of these altercations occurs at the end of the pardoner's story. The pardoner, who is the most depraved person on the pilgrimage, has just made a complete revelation of the greed that he has practiced in his career as a traveling preacher supposedly collecting money for a hospital in Spain. His story is an impressive exposure of the self-destructive nature of greed—a story of three young rioters who go on a quest to slay Death and end up killing each other after they find a pile of gold.

As the pardoner finishes this story, capped off with a conventional religious benediction, the pilgrims are momentarily silent and impressed. Tempted beyond measure, the pardoner goes on to make an appeal to his fellow travelers to step forward and buy his fraudulent relics and pardons. He either thinks he can actually get money out of the pilgrims, or he consciously exaggerates his appeal as a way of ridiculing them for having been impressed by him even after he has revealed himself as a scoundrel. Having made the host, Harry Bailey, the butt of his appeal, the pardoner finds himself attacked in a coarse jest from Harry involving his status as a eunuch.

Through the centuries, relations between men and women have been the most common subject of comic literature. It is therefore not surprising that this perenniel "battle of the sexes" makes an appearance in *The Canterbury Tales*. In addition to the overtly sexual stories, Chaucer composed the so-called "marriage group" of stories. They come to focus on the question of authority in marriage. The wife of Bath predictably thinks that the wife should rule in any marriage, but several of the men tell approving stories of submissive wives. The franklin's tale attempts a reconciliation between the opposed viewpoints.

Domestic situations are one of the favorite subjects of literary comedy, and the best of all *The Canterbury Tales* takes its cue from this convention. It is "The Nun's Priest's Tale"—the story of the rooster Chauntecleer and his wife Pertelote. What does a story about a pair of chickens have to do with real life? we might ask. The answer is, Everything—because Chaucer treats them as archetypal husband and wife. He humanizes them and makes both of them domineering personalities with opposite temperaments. Pertelote is the archetypal shrewish wife and Chauntecleer a combination of the henpecked husband and pompous fool.

The main action begins with an utterly realistic domestic situation. Chauntecleer wakes up terrified by a nightmare in which he dreamt that a fox had seized him. Having in turn awakened his "chick" Pertelote to share the dream, Chauntecleer finds himself embroiled in a debate about the meaning of the dream. *He* thinks he has received a prophetic revelation of impending catastrophe. His wife, a frustrated pre-med dropout who loves to prescribe home remedies, thinks her husband has been overeating and needs to take some laxatives. The humor of the debate is not simply that chickens have been endowed with human personalities. We also laugh at the recognizable domestic experience of husband and wife sparring for supremacy.

*Summary.* Literary comedy at its least subtle stems from plot situations that are amusing. In *The Canterbury Tales* these include stories that revolve around the physical side of human experience, slapstick comedy, and rivalry among characters.

## "Of Sundry Folk": The Comedy of Human Nature

Comedy also stems from human character and personality. Virtually every author whom we credit as being good at comedy gains that reputation partly on the strength of characterization. Chaucer is no exception. When the seventeenth-century English poet John Dryden saw the sheer plenitude of human character in *The Canterbury Tales*, he was led to exclaim, "Here is God's plenty." Chaucer himself gave us the magical phrase "of sundry [various] folk" near the beginning of his "General Prologue" to the story. As that phrase suggests, the vision of comedy is social, in contrast to the focus of tragedy on the individual.

Chaucer's "General Prologue," the best known part of *The Canterbury Tales*, is mainly a series of portraits or character sketches of the pilgrims on the trip to Canterbury. To look for action in these portraits is to invite frustration. They exist for the sake of description. The narrator himself tells us that he will mingle three ingredients in his portraits—external appearance, social standing, and inner character. The portraits are notable for their blending of individualizing and typical traits, their combination of idealization and satiric exposure of flaws, hyperbole (as the unreliable narrator naively overpraises virtually every pilgrim), economy of expression (in just a few lines we get to know a character), and a planned randomness in the structuring of each portrait. Already in these portraits we see Chaucer's comic genius.

*Humorous Obsessions.* The portrait of the prioress is perhaps the richest of all the portraits. Obsession is one of the things that makes us smile at her. The prioress, who may have been coerced into that vocation by her aristocratic family, is obsessed with courtly manners.[3] She is misplaced in her calling and would be much happier at court. Chaucer the pilgrim tells us that her chief delight lay in good manners. Indeed, three-fourths of her portrait is devoted to appearance and manners, reflecting an imbalance for someone who was supposed to have renounced worldly preoccupations. The extended catalog of felicities in her table manners assumes a comic effect: she never let a morsel fall from her lips, she did not wet her fingers too deeply in the sauce, she wiped her lips so cleanly that no grease spots appeared in her cup after she had taken a drink, etc., etc.

The comic effect is heightened by the way in which the prioress emerges in our imaginations as "the eternal feminine." Her self-chosen name is Madame Eglantine, a name appropriate for a heroine in a medieval romance. In fact, the portrait itself is based on a passage in a popular medieval romance—a passage, moreover, that described the wiles by which a woman could snare a man.

The narrator (who is overly impressed by external signs of affluence and success) is greatly charmed by this attractive and delightful woman. He tells us that "all was conscience and tender heart," chiefly because the prioress is full of feeling for her dogs (which she fed luxuriously while the poor in medieval society went hungry).

The comic effect in such a passage as the portrait of the prioress depends on a combination of things. We are amused by the obsession of the character with manners and appearance, by the imperfect submergence of the woman in the nun, and by the way in which this feminine charm impresses the men on the trip. The literary source behind the portrait also enters the mirth we see in the portrait, but none of the things I have mentioned would have their impact if we did not see the real-life quality of the person Chaucer describes.

Of course the materials of life become transmuted into literary conventions by the time we encounter them in literature. In real life we find people who are humorously and predictably obsessed by one thing or another, but the comic imagination heightens this into "humor characters." The word "humor" here is based on the old physiological theory that various personality types exist because of a controlling fluid or "humor" in the body.

Most of the portraits in Chaucer's "General Prologue" fit this convention of the root trait, allowing Chaucer to perform one of his favorite feats— giving us a quick glimpse into the inner person. The monk's life, for example, is governed by his passion for hunting (a worldly pursuit that the monastic rules forbade). The Oxford student is stone broke and poorly dressed because he cannot control his impulse to buy books. Money is number one in the scheme of Harry Bailey, the innkeeper in Southwark who ends up serving as host on the trip. The young squire, the eligible bachelor on the pilgrimage (the narrator calls him a "lusty bachelor"), is the archetypal lady's man and dandy. All of these characters make us smile because we see beyond the literary distillation to real-life experiences.

This interplay between literary artifice and real life is well illustrated in the portrait of the Wife of Bath. As a "type" character, she is a combination of the domineering woman, the shrewish wife, and the oversexed female. She dresses conspicuously in red hose, a hat as large as a shield, and such an overabundance of kerchiefs that the narrator judges them (in conscious exaggeration) to weigh ten pounds when Alison is dressed in her Sunday clothes. This incurably competitive woman insists on going to the offering box first in church, and if she does not she pouts.

To fill out the humorous portrait, Chaucer draws the picture of a sexually obsessed woman. She has been married five times, "not counting other company in youth." She goes on pilgrimages frequently, a sure sign in the Middle Ages that she was given to sexual promiscuity. Furthermore, she is "gap-toothed," which according to the medieval physiognomy books was a sign that a person was inclined to lechery. When she tells her story to the other pilgrims, the wife of Bath makes a big hit with her laugh-provoking confession in which she tells about her marriages (including their sexual side) with total lack of inhibition. It is no wonder that the narrator tells us with crowning ambiguity that "she knew a lot about wandering by the way."

*The Humane Vision of Comedy.* The comic vision in literature is rooted in the richness of human personality as we find it in life. When we read comic literature or see comic drama, the foremost response that we carry away from the experience is that we have celebrated human nature. In the very act of laughing at literary characters, we acknowledge that life is this way. We do not wholly approve of human nature as we look at it, but neither do we for the moment sit in harsh judgment of it. The comic spirit, writes someone, "is humane, calling forth a sense of the richness of life, willing participation in it, an acceptance of the full responsibility of being human."[4] Or as Ernst Cassirer put it, "Comic art possesses in the highest degree that faculty shared by all art, sympathetic vision."[5]

## Satiric Comedy

Along with this acceptance of the human condition in comedy, there is an element of discernment. In the very act of laughing at something, we often recognize an inconsistency between the ideal and the actual. When our sense of discernment is fully awakened, we know that we are dealing with literary satire.

Satire is the exposure of human vice or folly. It can be either comic or serious, either laughing or bitter. Satiric humor is often related to human character or personality, and this is the form that it customarily takes in Chaucer. Its effect usually depends on the reader's ability to see inconsistency or incongruity.

Again the portraits in "The General Prologue" furnish the best examples. Repeatedly we smile knowingly at a gap between a character's

profession and actual behavior. The prioress, for example, has supposedly renounced worldliness, yet she is preoccupied with being
fashionable in appearance and manners. The narrator claims that she
is all conscience and tender heart, yet she caters to the dainty appetites
of her dogs in a day of poverty, and she furthermore tells a blatantly
anti-Semitic story.

The most consistent form of satire in *The Canterbury Tales* is ecclesias-
tical satire, as Chaucer exposes the vices of the clergy. The monk, for
example, breaks nearly every rule in the book. His vows committed
him to staying cloistered within the walls of a monastery, except when
looking after the business of the monastery. Monks were supposed to
be engaged in work at specified times. They were forbidden to have
hunting horses. Medieval monks took vows of poverty, chastity, and
obedience (to monastic rules).

With this as the prescribed behavior, virtually every detail that
Chaucer gives us about the monk is satiric. Far from remaining
cloistered, this monk is on a pilgrimage and makes a habit of riding
through the countryside hunting for game. Instead of working, he builds
his life around recreation. In fact, he is a veritable "huntaholic." He
owns a whole stable of valuable hunting horses, as well as "greyhounds
as swift as birds in flight." In a quick glimpse into the inner person, the
narrator tells us that "riding and hunting for the hare were all his
pleasure." And he dresses luxuriously and indulges his gourmet appetite.

Are we angry at this monk? No. We accept his human failings with
a degree of detached tolerance. Our sense of discernment is awakened,
but not a strong sense of judgment. When it is, as in the case of Chaucer's
friar and pardoner, we pass the line from comic satire to biting satire.

*The Function of Comedy.* Aristotle made a provocative comment
about the common subject matter of tragedy and comedy when he said
that they both deal with "some defect or ugliness."[6] The Greek word
that Aristotle uses is *hamartia*—literally a missing of the mark in archery
and the famous "character flaw" of tragedy. In comedy this defect "is
not painful or destructive," while in tragedy it is. Both tragedy and
comedy reconcile us to common human failing. But tragedy makes us
fear it, while comedy makes us comfortable with it. Paradoxically, notes

Bernard Schilling, "in tragedy man seems great after all, in comedy he seems small after all."[7]

It is not easy to say why the spectacle of human defect strikes us as funny in comedy. The same experiences in real life are painful. It is obvious that the angle of vision is part of the explanation. In comedy we ourselves must feel superior to the comic victim before we laugh at his or her misfortune.

Comedy reduces people to the common lot of the human race and declares it good. A book on the comic entitled *The Divine Average* argues that comedy not only endorses the average but idealizes it.[8] Comedy levels us all into a community of ordinary people. In comedy we judge the human condition as limited and flawed, but we are reconciled to it and accept our place in it.

A book entitled *Why Literature Is Bad for You* observes that "the most renowned stories of the Western World are frequently built around a central bungler whose incompetence has the effect of injuring a good many around him" and then draws the conclusion that literature makes us tolerant of incompetence.[9] I would suggest an alternative conclusion: reading stories about human failing can serve the beneficial purpose of helping us cope with a "given" of our own experiences in a fallen world, namely, human failure.

### Verbal Wit

At its most subtle and intellectual, comedy consists not in *what* the author portrays but in *how* he or she portrays it. Here the humor arises from the cleverness with which the writer expresses things. Key ingredients are irony or incongruity, understatement, pun or word play, euphemism (a roundabout way of naming something), and parody (imitating a literary genre or work but with comic effect). It is exactly in these subtle ways that Chaucer's comic genius shows itself most clearly.

The satire that we have noted, for example, depends on the reader's alertness. Chaucer the narrator simply records the facts. Any incongruity we find between a character's ideals and behavior is something we have to discover on our own.

In fact, Chaucer himself repeatedly engages in verbal irony—saying one thing while meaning another. He makes Chaucer the pilgrim (the fictitious persona who narrates the story) praise characters whom we and Chaucer the author know to be blameworthy. Chaucer the narrator is taken in by the success of the pilgrims, not realizing that their very success often condemns them. The narrator, for example, approves of the monk's defense of building his life around recreation. His portrait of the friar shows him to be an utterly depraved person, yet the narrator calls him "a pillar of his [monastic] order." The pardoner is even worse, yet the narrator calls him "a noble ecclesiastic in church."

The effect is to activate the reader to protest against these naively misguided superlatives. The strategy works wonders as it makes us participants in the moral action of the story. Comic effect itself depends on such participation. Before we recognize comedy and respond with laughter, we have to catch the joke.

The narrator's obtuse statements do not account for all of the inconsistency of character in *The Canterbury Tales.* Sometimes the inconsistency is embodied in the portrayal of the character itself. The pardoner, for example, himself tells us that he always preaches against the vice (greed) of which he himself is guilty. The nun's priest, who lives in the nunnery under the governance of the prioress, draws an anti-feminist moral from the story of Chauntecleer and Pertelote. The story, he says, shows what happens when a man takes the advice of a woman. Yet Chauntecleer did *not* take his wife's advice. The anti-feminist moral is *self*-revealing, as the priest projects his own bias onto the story (and then backtracks like mad when he catches the prioress' disapproving look).

Chaucer's subtle humor is also seen in his ability to parody earlier works or genres of literature. He wrote the first and greatest mock epic in the English language in his story of Chauntecleer and Pertelote. He took a realistic farmyard event—the capture of a rooster by a fox—and treated it in the style of ancient epic. Chauntecleer, for example, is described in the high style replete with epic similes: his comb was redder than coral and indented like a castle wall, his bill shone like jet, his legs and toes were like azure, and his color like burnished gold. The capture of this rooster by a flattering fox is handled like an epic battle. The incongruity is funny in itself and becomes more so when a reader is able to recognize ironic parallels in ancient epic literature.

## Christianity and the Comic Vision

We can relate comedy to the Christian faith at two levels. One is simply the refreshment value of comedy. C.S. Lewis has said that "the Christian . . . has no objection to comedies that merely amuse and tales that merely refresh. . . . We can play, as we can eat, to the glory of God."[10] Comedy can be therapeutic for Christians, too, and this is something the world at large benefits from seeing.

The Bible encourages a spirit of playfulness. Elton Trueblood has written a classic little book on *The Humor of Christ*.[11] In it he shows something of the playfulness that characterized the conversations of Jesus (and I might note in passing that the categories that Trueblood finds in Christ's words are ones that are prevalent in Chaucer's writings). God wants his creatures to be refreshed on the journey of their life. He "furnishes us with everything to enjoy" (1 Timothy 6:17). Using ancient images of festivity and refreshment, the writer of Ecclesiastes commends, "Let your garments be always white; let not oil be lacking on your head" (9:8).

In addition to the refreshment that comedy provides, it offers a vision of the world that must also be placed within a Christian context. Some literary critics have made much of the affinities between the comic vision and the Christian faith. Northrop Frye sounds the keynote when he claims that the "romantic and comic myths are those that inform Christianity."[12] Most literary critics would agree with that statement, so it will repay our analysis.

I should note in advance that the claims are often excessive. As we will see, the relation between Christianity and comedy is based on parallels or analogies between the two. Too many writers on the subject act as though the presence of these parallels makes comedy automatically Christian. But obviously not every manifestation of these principles is Christian.

*The Comic Strand in a Christian World View.* The first common bond between Christianity and comedy is the spirit of celebration and joy. When Paul commands us, "Rejoice in the Lord always; again I will say, Rejoice" (Philippians 4:4), he exudes the spirit of zest that is a hallmark of comedy. The comic vision affirms life and festivity. When we attend a comic play or read a comic story, we come away from the experience feeling that we have attended a festival. The Christian faith encourages a similar exuberance.

Comedy and Christianity also share a preoccupation with the earthly, the human, the commonplace. Whereas tragedy requires the grand and sublime, comedy requires the everyday. It immerses itself in the world of flawed humanity and accepts the human condition. So does the Bible, where the sublime influence of God (to quote Erich Auerbach) "reaches so deeply into the everyday" that it produces a style "which does not scorn everyday life and which is ready to absorb the sensorily realistic, even the ugly, the undignified, the physically base."[13] The incarnation of Christ is likewise based on a full immersion in the drama of human life.

It is an easy step from such immersion in the human condition to a celebration of God's creation. In a Christian world view, what God created is good in principle. This includes people, who, after all, were created in God's image. Again, therefore, we can see a kinship between comedy and Christianity. As the author of *The Comic Vision and the Christian Faith* states, "There is in comedy a kind of rock-bottom faith in the essential goodness of what is *natural* to humankind."[14]

Literary critics also stress the similarity in the comic structure and the shape of salvation history. The essential pattern is a U-shaped story in which events descend into tragedy but rise to a happy ending. As Wylie Sypher notes,

> the range of comedy is wider than the tragic range. . . . The comic cycle is the only fulfilled and redemptive action. . . . Should we say that the drama of the struggle, death, and rising—Gethsemane, Calvary, and Easter—actually belongs in the comic rather than the tragic domain?[15]

There is, in other words, a comic structure to the gospel—to the life of Jesus and to the way of salvation that every believer experiences, beginning in an awareness of a lost state and ending in the certainty of heaven. The gospel, writes someone, "is comic . . . in the singularity of the hope and joy it announces to the world."[16]

Comedy and Christianity also share the impulse to look at the temporary misfortunes of life from a superior perspective. To laugh at

human error as we do in comedy is to know that we have surmounted
it. This is similar to the Christian view of history—a perspective that
earlier centuries called life *sub specie aeternitas* ("under the aspect of
eternity"). The Christian has an eternal vantage point from which to
rise above any final earthly defeat. In both comedy and Christianity,
we view earthly mishap with a sense of detached amusement. Ralph
Wood comments that "Christian faith is nowhere more comic than in
this eschatological confidence. No matter how grim the immediate
prospect, . . . the Gospel announces that history's final destiny has been
graciously fixed."[17]

It is not surprising, then, that theorists on comedy have seen comedy
as permeated with a spirit of grace that is akin to the Christian gospel.
Comic characters are a case study in resilience. They beat the odds.
They even escape the reader's condemnation. A spirit of forgiveness
hovers over comedy. There is also something outlandish about comedy
as ordinary rules are suspended.

There is a similar strand in the Christian faith. Paul wrote that "God
made foolish the wisdom of the world" (1 Corinthians 1:20). Whereas
the world of tragedy is a world of inevitability, comedy thrives on the
unexpected or unlikely. In his essay "The Gospel as Comedy," Frederick
Buechner writes about the comic strand in Christianity thus:

> The good news breaks into a world where the news has been so bad
> for so long that when it is good nobody hears it much except for a
> few. And who are the few that hear it? . . . . They are the last people
> you might expect to hear it, themselves the bad jokes and stooges
> and scarecrows of the world, the tax collectors and whores and
> misfits.[18]

The very language that Buechner uses here suddenly reminds us of the
common ground between literary comedy and the Christian gospel.

*The Moral Vision of Comedy.* I noted earlier that comedy tends
toward a humanizing effect. In Chaucer's hands, for example, the comic
vision encompasses an affectionate understanding of human nature and
a compassionate reproof of human weakness. As we participate in
comedy, we celebrate the richness, the diversity, and the failings of
common humanity, recognizing our own place in that community. In

comedy we are reconciled to what it means to be human, even though we might not like all that we see. Perhaps compassion is the dominant tone of comic literature.

But this very acceptance of human failing also raises a moral problem. The customary strategy of comedy is to make us laugh at human failure and immorality. Is this good or bad for our moral sense?

Harry Blamires, in his book *The Christian Mind*, believes that the effect of comedy is essentially moral:

> A comic treatment of adultery or sodomy in a funny story or a bawdy piece of literature is most likely to be thoroughly moral; for the force of humour is frequently dependent upon stirring our sense of the incongruity between what people do and what they ought to do. Humour can rarely afford to dispense with the yardstick of traditional morality.[19]

But *is* laughing at immorality a form of moral judgment?

The skeptics of this position have included some literary giants. John Milton, for all his championing of freedom of the press, reveals an uneasiness about comedy when, in describing his ideal system of education, he claims that students can be introduced to Greek and Roman comedy "with wariness and good antidote."[20] Sir Philip Sidney, in his *Apology for Poetry*, admits that "naughty play-makers and stage-keepers have justly made [comedy] odious."[21] The reason for this uneasiness with comedy is well founded. In the act of laughing tolerantly at human misconduct, we withhold our moral judgment, no matter how temporarily. The strategy of comedy is generally to make us relax our sense of moral judgment against the moral failings that we observe. The Bible, by contrast, does not treat sin as a laughing matter. According to one theorist, "Comedy thrives in an atmosphere of moral holiday."[22] But Christian morality does not take a holiday.

The qualification I would want to make is that morality must be distinguished from standards of good taste. There are many points at which literary comedy will offend what a sensitive person considers decent, and these may be sufficient to make us close a book or turn off the television, but this in itself is not necessarily a comment about the morality of a work. It is instead of matter of taste, refinement, and respect for privacy.

*Summary.* There are important connections between comedy and the Christian faith. While this does not make every comic work automatically Christian in viewpoint, a Christian reader has a framework within which to understand comedy. There is a comic strand in Christianity, including a spirit of celebration of life, affirmation of common experience as part of God's creation, and acceptance of God's grace as something that announces unexpected good news. The moral vision of comedy, meanwhile, requires Christian discernment.

## Notes to Chapter 2

[1] Chaucer wrote *The Canterbury Tales* in Middle English (not Old English, incidentally). "The General Prologue" is written in poetic couplets. I have provided my own translation and have made no attempt to retain the word order and rhyme scheme of the original.

[2] Bernard N. Schilling, *The Comic Spirit* (Detroit: Wayne State UP, 1965), p. 12.

[3] That Chaucer's nun had many real-life prototypes has been documented by Graciela S. Daichman, *Wayward Nuns in Medieval Literature* (Syracuse: Syracuse UP, 1986).

[4] Schilling, p. 17.

[5] Ernst Cassirer, An Essay on May (New Haven: Yale UP, 1944), p. 150.

[6] Aristotle, *The Poetics,* in *Criticism: The Major Statements,* ed. Charles Kaplan (New York: St. Martin's, 1975), p. 26.

[7] Schilling, p. 16.

[8] William G. McCollom, *The Divine Average: A View of Comedy* (Cleveland: Case Western Reserve, 1971).

[9] Peter Thorpe, *Why Literature Is Bad for You* (Chicago: Nelson-Hall, 1980), p. 67.

[10] C.S. Lewis, *Christian Reflections,* ed. Walter Hooper (Grand Rapids: William B. Eerdmans, 1967), p. 10.

[11] Elton Trueblood, *The Humor of Christ* (New York: Harper and Row, 1964).

[12] Northrop Frye, *The Stubborn Structure* (Ithaca: Cornell UP, 1970), p. 53.

[13] Erich Auerbach, *Mimesis: The Representation of Reality in Western Literature,* trans. Willard R. Trask (Princeton: Princeton UP, 1953, 1968), pp. 22, 72.

[14] Conrad Hyers, *The Comic Vision and the Christian Faith: A Celebration of Life and Laughter* (New York: Pilgrim Press, 1981), p. 90.

[15] Wylie Sypher, "The Meanings of Comedy," in *Comedy: Meaning and Form,* ed. Robert W. Corrigan (San Francisco: Chandler, 1965), p. 36.

[16] Ralph C. Wood, *The Comedy of Redemption: Christian Faith and Comic Vision in Four American Novelists* (Notre Dame: Notre Dame UP, 1988), p. 31.

[17]Ibid., pp. 32-33.

[18]Frederich Buechner, *Telling the Truth: The Gospel as Tragedy, Comedy, and Fairy Tale* (San Francisco: Harper and Row, 1977), pp. 70-71.

[19]Harry Blamires, *The Christian Mind* (London: S.P.C.K., 1963), p. 99.

[20]John Milton, *Of Education*.

[21]Sir Philip Sidney, *Apology for Poetry*, in *Criticism: The Major Statements*, ed. Charles Kaplan, p. 127.

[22]McCollom, p. 19.

# Chapter 3

## Shakespeare's Macbeth and the Tragic Spirit in Literature

## "The Way to Dusty Death"

✳

*Come, you spirits*
*That tend on mortal thoughts, unsex me here,*
*And fill me from the crown to the toe top-full*
*Of direst cruelty. Make thick my blood;*
*Stop up th' access and passage to remorse. . . .*
*Come to my woman's breasts*
*And take my milk for gall, you murd'ring ministers,*
*Wherever in your sightless substances*
*You wait on nature's mischief. Come, thick night,*
*And pall thee in the dunnest smoke of hell,*
*That my keen knife see not the wound it makes,*
*Nor heaven peep through the blanket of the dark*
*To cry "Hold, hold!"*

✳

*To-morrow, and to-morrow, and to-morrow*
*Creeps in this petty pace from day to day*
*To the last syllable of recorded time,*
*And all our yesterdays have lighted fools*
*The way to dusty death. Out, out, brief candle!*
*Life's but a walking shadow, a poor player*
*That struts and frets his hour upon the stage*

*And then is heard no more. It is a tale*
*Told by an idiot, full of sound and fury,*
*Signifying nothing.*[1]

✳

These two speeches are spoken by Lady Macbeth and Macbeth, respectively, early and late in the play. They represent a great experiment in evil in its planning stages and in its final phase of disillusionment. They frame what one critic has called "Shakespeare's most profound and mature vision of evil."[2] The world of the play is heavy with the atmosphere of darkness, demonic influence, and blood, as Lady Macbeth's words in the quoted excerpt foreshadow.

The two protagonists in this universe of evil are among Shakespeare's great character creations. Macbeth is a case study in ambition. His sheer energy in pursuing that ambition compels our attention. He speaks a poetry unsurpassed among Shakespeare's characters. As he is torn apart by inner struggles of conscience, we see the dynamics of guilt as clearly as anywhere in literature.

Lady Macbeth is scarcely less impressive. Early in the play the initiative in evil rests with her. She acts as an overpowering agent of temptation—a latter-day Jezebel pushing her husband to kill the king and usurp what he wants. Following her domineering calmness in the murder scene, she begins a long slide into a psychological collapse that culminates in her famous sleepwalking scene and subsequent death (which forms the context for Macbeth's "To-morrow" soliloquy). Like her husband, Lady Macbeth is a thoroughly developing character, though halfway through the play the initiative in evil passes from one to the other.

The plot of the story also makes the play memorable. It is a crime and punishment story that follows the usual three-part pattern of antecedents, occurrence, and consequences of the crime. The opening act, moreover, is one of the most impressive temptation stories in literature. Four agents of temptation gradually overpower the hero's resisting conscience—the prophecies of the witches that predict kingship for Macbeth, Macbeth's rising political fortunes, his own "vaulting ambition," and Lady Macbeth's browbeating.

The story also follows the scheme of what literary critics call the well-made plot. The exposition introduces us to the hero and idealizes him as a brave soldier and loyal subject to the king. The inciting moment is the ladder-like prophecies of the witches. The rising action centers on the conflict between Macbeth's ambition and its foes, both internal (his conscience) and external. The turning point (the point from which we can see how the plot will be resolved) occurs midway through the play when we hear for the first time of an organized resistance to Macbeth. Further complication takes the form of Macbeth's struggles against the consequences of his crime, especially in the form of external agents of justice. The climax is Macbeth's defeat on the battlefield, and the denouement (tying up of loose ends) consists of a brief re-establishment of order at the end of the play. Thus is reenacted the pyramid structure of Shakespeare's plays.

Like Shakespeare's other plays, *Macbeth* is written mainly in poetic form. The verse form is unrhymed and is known as blank verse. The language, too, is poetic—filled with metaphors, images, and periphrasis (a roundabout way of expressing a thought). Shakespeare is so poetic as to be difficult for a modern reader. A reader's best allies are reading aloud, reading an edition that has footnotes or marginal notes to explain difficult phrases, and not worrying about lines that remain elusive.

For all its high artistry, *Macbeth* also has affinities with folk literature and as such is an example of "popular" literature that appeals to the whole cross section of society. It has the ingredients of television drama that we can view any night of the week—violence, villains and villainy, portrayal of the criminal mind, suspense, heightened conflict between good and evil, and the triumph of justice at the end. The classics do not bypass popular taste. They do, however, use the ingredients of popular storytelling to present significance of content, intellectual stimulation, and superior artistry.

A classic like *Macbeth* thus confirms the theory of T.S. Eliot that great literature meets readers at whatever level they are equipped to receive it. Here is Eliot's framework:

In a play of Shakespeare you get several levels of significance. For the simplest auditor there is the plot, for the more thoughtful the character and the conflict of character, for the more literary the words and phrasing, for the more musically sensitive the rhythm, and for auditors of greater sensitiveness and understanding a meaning which reveals itself gradually. . . . At none of these levels is the auditor bothered by the presence of that which he does not understand, or . . . in which he is not interested.[3]

For those able to grasp it, Shakespeare gives stylistic excellence and subtlety of insight in addition to the foundational elements of plot and character.

Part of the artistry of *Macbeth* is the unifying image patterns. The imagery of darkness creates an atmosphere of evil and secrecy. References to blood first picture the physical horror of the murder and then quickly come to represent the principle of guilt and retribution for sin. Hand imagery, equally pervasive, shows the same evolving meaning from crime to punishment. The imagery of ill-fitting garments reminds us continuously that Macbeth is attempting to fill a position that is not his by right, while disease imagery and sleeplessness are pictures of moral and psychological decay.

## The Tragic Spirit in Macbeth

Through the centuries tragedy has held a hallowed place among serious students of literature. Tragedy at its best brings forth great art, and that for an explainable reason. When the subject matter of literature is threatening, a writer must find ways to enclose it in a reassuring framework so we can contemplate it from a safe distance. Stylization is one of these distancing devices. Most great tragedies have been written in poetry, for example, as a way of conveying an impression that "this is art, not life." Tragedians also tend to reach back into history, myth, or legend for their story material, further distancing the action.

*The Elements of Tragedy.* Aristotle's *Poetics* remains the starting point for understanding literary tragedy, and I have drawn upon it heavily in the discussion that follows. To begin, tragedy requires an exalted hero on whom the action focuses. This is in contrast to the more social vision of comedy. The tragic hero is essentially a good person who is socially elevated (usually he is a ruler) and who possesses greatness of spirit. The tragic hero is greater than common humanity but is subject to the natural order and moral criticism.

For all his or her greatness, a tragic hero possesses a tragic flaw of character. Aristotle called it "hamartia"—literally a missing of the mark in archery and implying sinfulness when applied on a moral plane. This tragic flaw becomes fully evident in the tragic hero's moment of choice, which in turn leads inevitably to the hero's catastrophe.

From the scenario I have described it is possible to see the underlying elements of tragedy. Tragedy is the spectacle of exceptional calamity and irremedial loss. It makes us confront what we most fear and wish to avoid facing—the destructive potential of evil in human life. Literary tragedy depicts a painful misfortune brought about by human error.

Tragedy thus deals with *caused* suffering. This is one of the things that allows us to contemplate the pain with pleasure or at least calmness. The hero is always responsible for his or her downfall and is usually deserving of it, even though the punishment seems disproportionate to the crime. We are also reconciled to the hero's fate because he or she ordinarily shows grandeur in the suffering and because tragedy demonstrates a redemptive potential in suffering.

*Tragic Form.* A large part of the impact of any great tragedy is the six-part tragic form that virtually all tragedies follow. This is the order that the literary imagination imposes on life as a way of disclosing an order *in* life. It produces a literary experience and vision of life that are virtually the opposite from what we find in comedy.

The opening movement in tragedy focuses on a *dilemma* that the hero faces. Within the given tragic world, the hero is drawn in two directions. Macbeth, for example, is on the one hand attracted to the idea of usurping the throne, an act that would require him to commit a murder. But he vacillates between that longing and his healthy conscience that sets up an equally strong resistance to the act of murder that he imagines so vividly. Ambition and conscience form the two magnetic poles between which Macbeth hangs suspended early in the play. Part of the genius of this play is the way in which Shakespeare elaborated the tragic hero's dilemma into a full-fledged temptation story.

The tragic dilemma is always resolved by the hero's *tragic choice.* In *Macbeth* it occurs at the end of Act I. Having waged a losing battle with his conscience, Macbeth utters the fateful words, "I am settled, and bend up / Each corporal agent to this terrible feat." It would be wrong to say that Macbeth here kills his conscience, since it continues to plague him until relatively late in the play. But his conscience ceases to control his actions and curb his bent toward evil. In a tragic hero's moment of choice we always see the tragic flaw of character, which in Macbeth's case is uncontrolled ambition.

The tragic choice leads inevitably to a *catastrophe*. Tragedy is by definition a fall from prosperity to calamity. In *Macbeth* the catastrophe is initially internal and moral instead of external. It consists first of the self-destructive effects of guilt. For Macbeth this journey into psychological collapse begins already in the murder scene, where his mind breaks. In his hallucinations he hears accusing voices. In stunned repetitions he utters statements having no relevance to the moment, such as his memorable poetic description of sleep.

Eventually the catastrophe takes the form of an organized political resistance to Macbeth. Like other tragic heroes, Macbeth moves to a state of increasing bondage. His political fortunes, once on the ascent, collapse around him. Lady Macbeth, who shared her husband's crime, also shares his catastrophe.

The fourth phase of a tragedy is the hero's tragic *suffering*. Oscar Mandel, whose book *A Definition of Tragedy* remains the best overview of literary tragedy, speaks of the hero's "grave physical or spiritual suffering."[4] In *Macbeth* the suffering is mainly spiritual and psychological. Long before the world at large knows of the Macbeths' crime, we are given a scene (III. ii) in which husband and wife share their misery. They both express a death wish. As subsequent scenes unfold, Macbeth becomes the most completely isolated of all Shakespeare's tragic heroes (an important aspect of tragedy is that the hero gradually becomes isolated from society, in contrast to comedy, where the hero becomes integrated into society). Lady Macbeth's suffering is comparable, consisting of an emotional breakdown culminating in premature death.

The suffering of Macbeth is so intense that it permeates the next phase of the tragic pattern, the tragic *perception*. In most tragedies this moment of recognition is the tragic hero's insight into what he or she did wrong, accompanied by an element of confession of wrongdoing. In the case of Macbeth, two speeches are in the running as potential moments of tragic perception, but both stop short of the conventional expectations we have for this feature of tragedy.

Here is one of the candidates for the moment of tragic recognition (V. iii. 22-28):

> My way of life
> Is fall'n into the sear, the yellow leaf,
> And that which should accompany old age,
> As honor, love, obedience, troops of friends,
> I must not look to have; but, in their stead,
> Curses not loud but deep, mouth-honor, breath,
> Which the poor heart would fain deny, and dare not.

In this speech we observe Macbeth's sensitivity to the precious human values that he has violated and that he must forego as an outcast. "This is truly the poetry of the soul in anguish," writes Alfred Harbage.[5] But Macbeth expresses no sense of personal responsibility for his sorry plight. Someone has said that Macbeth suffers from "a terrible anxiety that is a sense of guilt without becoming . . . a sense of sin. It is not a sense of sin because he refuses to recognize such a category."[6] This is a moment of tragic perception only if we redefine it to mean an insight into what the tragic hero has lost by his tragic choice.

The second potential moment of tragic epiphany or insight is the most famous speech in the play—the "tomorrow, and tomorrow, and tomorrow" speech quoted at the beginning of this chapter. It is one of the most memorable expressions in literature of the futility and meaninglessness of life. Macbeth here denies a basic premise of existence— that life has meaning. But here, too, Macbeth stops short of an awareness of personal wrongdoing or sinfulness. He does not link the meaninglessness of his life to his own tragic error. In fact, if we compare the moral sensitivity that Macbeth shows early in the play to his responses late in the play, we can see that one of the unifying strands in his characterization is his progressive moral dereliction.

The final phase of a tragedy is the hero's *death*. Shakespeare's play runs true to form. Macbeth, who had wrongly interpreted the witches' second series of prophecies as conferring immunity from death upon him, is killed in battle by Macduff. But the horror of his death is delayed until the last minute of the play, when a group of soldiers runs across the stage with Macbeth's head displayed on a pole as a traitor's head.

*The Artifice of Tragedy.* Like other literary forms, tragedy is based on unlifelike conventions. No one's life falls naturally into the six-phase pattern of literary tragedy. In order to fit a person's life into this pattern, we have to omit most of a person's biography and select only a few relevant aspects. Tragedy does not cover the whole of life. It is a distillation from available materials.

C.S. Lewis has emphasized this point. He objects to people's mistaking the conventions of tragedy for real life. He writes,

> The tragedian dare not present the totality of suffering as it usually is in its uncouth mixture of agony with littleness, all the indignities . . . of grief. It would ruin his play. It would be merely dull and depressing. He selects from the reality just what his art needs; and what it needs is the exceptional. . . . Next to a world in which there were no sorrows we should like one where sorrows were always significant and sublime. But if we allow the 'tragic view of life' to make us believe that we live in such a world, we shall be deceived. Our very eyes teach us better.[7]

We should note that Lewis is not objecting to the unlifelike conventions of tragedy but only to a common failure of people to recognize them as unlifelike. The function of art, said T.S. Eliot, consists of "imposing a credible order upon ordinary reality, . . . thereby eliciting some perception of an order *in* reality."[8] The conventions of tragedy highlight selected features of life as we know it, and to these features I now turn.

## The Meaning of Tragedy

There can be no doubt that the tragic pattern I have noted reveals something significant about life. Tragedy is based on presuppositions that are laden with philosophic and moral implications, which perhaps explains why philosophers and theologians through the centuries have been unable to keep their hands off literary tragedy.

*The View of the Person.* Tragedy is based on a high view of people. The tragic hero is a person of exalted stature, and this exaltation is more than a matter of social hierarchy. Tragic heroes possess an intangible quality that I call greatness of spirit. They exert themselves strenuously and test their human limits. They are bigger-than-life figures with an overflowing vitality.

Tragedy's high view of the individual is also evident in the power of moral choice with which tragedy endows the tragic hero. By definition, tragedy focuses on the person at the crossroads. Contrary to the prevailing modern view of the person as an amoral set of conditioned reflexes, tragedy presupposes that people have a power of choice, with accompanying moral responsibility.

One reason why tragedy did not survive intact into the twentieth century is that its high view of the person could not be accommodated to the naturalistic view that regards people as the helpless victims of psychological, environmental, and cosmic determinism. The vision of tragedy is such that (to quote from the esteemed Victorian scholar A.C. Bradley) "no one ever closes a tragedy with the feeling that man is a poor mean creature. He may be wretched and he may be awful, but he is not small."[9]

*The Power of Evil.* Tragedy bases itself on the bedrock of what Christianity calls sin. It asserts human fallenness and the reality of evil in the world. It pictures the flaw in human nature, and in this regard it is worth noting that Aristotle's word for the tragic flaw—*hamartia*—is the word that is translated as "sin" in English translations of the New Testament. Part of the power of tragedy is its ability to express the dangerousness of life—the ease with which people make the wrong choice.

*Macbeth* illustrates tragedy's vision of radical evil in the world and in the individual. It is a classic picture of people's failing to live up to what their conscience tells them they should do. Shakespeare here tells a story of more-than-human evil. Throughout the early scenes of the play, Macbeth and Lady Macbeth entertain the thought of doing something monstrously wicked to which they are strongly attracted.

In fact, their attraction to evil is stronger than their ability to do it. Macbeth is beside himself—a psychological wreck—during the scenes surrounding the murder. Lady Macbeth prays for evil forces to unsex her and fill her, "from the crown to the toe, top-full / Of direst cruelty" (I. v. 40-41). The impact of the knocking at the gate at the end of the murder scene and the drunken porter speech immediately following stems from the way in which these scenes draw a boundary around the demonic evil that has prevailed in the preceding scenes. The Victorian essayist Thomas De Quincey, in his famous essay "On the Knocking at the Gate in *Macbeth*," explored why he had always found the knocking at the door at the end of the murder scene so awesome. His conclusion was this:

> [During the murder scene] the entrance of the fiendish heart was to be expressed and made sensible. Another world has stept in; and the murderers are taken out of the region of human things, human purposes, human desires. They are transfigured. . . . The world of devils is suddenly revealed. . . . The knocking at the gate is heard; and . . . the human has made its reflux upon the fiendish.[10]

In a similar vein, Alfred Harbage comments that the drunken porter's speech produces the effect of "isolating the Macbeths in their monstrous universe and returning us to a seamy but sane normality. He opens the gate not into but out of inferno, and we are able to breathe again."[11]

*Human Responsibility for Evil.* Tragedy is also based on the premise of human responsibility for evil. Evil does not simply happen in tragedy. It is chosen through human agency. Shakespeare's *Macbeth* is a particularly clear example of this. In the opening act of the play, Macbeth momentarily resists all of the agents of temptation, including even the valor of his wife's tongue (her own designation). The very fact that Macbeth is repeatedly able to establish momentary control over these voices of temptation shows that he has a power of choice and also helps to answer a perennial question about this play, namely, why we sympathize with such a flawed and eventually depraved person as Macbeth.

Macbeth does not fall unknowingly into the crime he commits. He knows what he is doing. We observe his titanic struggles with his own conscience. The thought of murdering Duncan is to Macbeth a "horrid image" that unfixes his hair and makes his heart knock at his ribs (I. ii. 135-136). Before, during, and after the murder Macbeth wishes he were not committing it. A critic observes that "Macbeth is never in doubt of the difference between good and evil,"[12] while another says that *"Macbeth* is the tragedy of a man who, in full knowledge of what he was doing, destroyed his own soul."[13] As in the Bible, external forces of temptation provide the occasion for the tragic choice but do not cause it.

Shakespeare's anatomy of guilt in this play reinforces our awareness of human responsibility for evil. Few works of literature depict with such clarity the experience of guilt stemming from evil actions. Shakespeare has given us the classic story of human guilt in English literature. Five scenes in particular trace the crescendo of guilt: the dagger scene in which Macbeth's hallucination pictures a blood-smeared dagger that leads him to Duncan's chamber just before the murder (II. i), Macbeth's mental collapse immediately after the murder (II. ii), the scene in which Macbeth and Lady Macbeth share their mutual fears and misery (III. ii), the appearance of Banquo's ghost (which only the guilt-haunted Macbeth sees) at the banquet (III. iv), and Lady Macbeth's sleepwalking (V. i).

*Human Suffering.* Another principle that underlies tragedy is suffering. Tragedy's ability to portray human suffering is part of its power. All people know what it is like to suffer. We would prefer to avoid the subject, but life will not allow us to do so, hence the appeal of tragedy for thinking people who do not run away from life as it is, even at its worst.

Aristotle in his definition of tragedy claims that tragedy deals with a human "defect that is painful or destructive." So close is this link between tragedy and the spectacle of human suffering that some works of literature get smuggled into the category of tragedies because they portray human suffering, even though overall they do not fit the form of tragedy.

Literary tragedy does more than simply portray suffering. It also offers an explanation of it by assigning a human cause to it. Tragic heroes bring suffering on themselves through their tragic mistake—a fatal missing of the mark. Literary tragedy thus removes the arbitrary element from human suffering.

Of course this is only part of the truth about human suffering. Again we can profitably heed the caution of C.S. Lewis:

> Flaws in character do cause suffering; but bombs and bayonets, cancer and polio, dictators and roadhogs, fluctuations in the value of money or in employment, and mere meaningless coincidence, cause a great

deal more. Tribulation falls on the integrated and well adjusted and prudent as readily as on anyone else.[14]

This caution reminds us only that tragedy does not tell the whole truth. The same stricture applies to other literary forms.

*The Triumph of Justice.* Yet another principle that tragedy asserts is the triumph of justice in the world. So does some comedy, but with contrasting effect. In a comic plot like Homer's *Odyssey,* we welcome the retribution that befalls the guilty. In lighthearted comedy, we laugh goodnaturedly as ridiculous characters get their comeuppance.

The effect of justice in tragedy is more complex. On the one hand we recognize the justness of the downfall of Macbeth and Lady Macbeth. We resign ourselves to the inevitability of a tragic hero's downfall because it is in some sense deserved. But we also find ourselves drawn toward pity. We feel uncomfortable with the pessimistic doom and helplessness that settle upon us in the later phases of a tragedy. Often the tragic hero's punishment seems disproportionate to the offense that set it in motion.

Shakespeare's *Macbeth* at first strikes us as an exception to this pattern because the tragic hero is such a deeply flawed character who becomes utterly villainous in the late stages of the play. But even here we find a certain ambivalence. Macbeth is a pitiable figure in his final isolation. He experiences only suffering and no enjoyment from his evil actions. Furthermore, even in his moments of depravity he utters sentiments that represent the common moral wisdom of the human race. His famous aphorism, "It will have blood, they say: blood will have blood" (III. iv. 122), echoes the biblical principle, "Whoever sheds the blood of man, by man shall his blood be shed" (Genesis 9:6). Nor should we overlook the degree to which we can see our own experiences in Macbeth's. We have all done something wrong and then hoped that we could conceal it and avoid punishment for it.

*Wisdom through Suffering.* The presence of perception as part of the tragic pattern suggests yet another underlying principle—the redemptive potential in human suffering and failure. Tragedy does not depress us the way modern naturalism does. It is pessimistic but not ultimately depressing. It holds out the possibility that suffering can lead to insight and even renewal.

We should not overstate the point. Tragedy is the bearer of bad news. I cannot agree with critics who call tragedy optimistic. But tragedy typically shows the possibility of learning from error and achieving wisdom through suffering. Of course that wisdom comes too late to help the tragic hero. But the reader or viewer, distanced from the hero's defeat, leaves a tragedy feeling that he or she has learned from the hero's failure and can avoid a similar fate.

*Summary.* It is no wonder that tragedy has held an honored place in the annals of literature. It embodies so many significant aspects of human experience: human assertiveness, the reality of evil, human choice, the dangerousness of life, justice, human suffering, wisdom through suffering, human significance, and the momentousness of life.

Overall, tragedy is an anatomy of human failure. But this is itself an ambivalent subject. If failure brings great suffering and exposes human weakness, it can also be the occasion for perception and even grandeur.

## Can Tragedy Be Christian?

It remains to discuss whether the literary form of tragedy as I have described it can be accommodated to Christian doctrine and experience. As a preliminary answer to this perennial question, I would simply ask if any of the traits and underlying principles I have noted seem incompatible with the Christian faith.

*The Scholarly Consensus.* Most scholars who have written on the subject have concluded that literary tragedy is incompatible with Christianity. "No genuinely Christian tragedy can exist," writes a critic.[15] "It is a frank contradiction in terms to equate religious with tragic experience," writes someone else.[16] Other representative views are that "the religion of the Bible is inimical to Tragedy,"[17] that "Christianity reverses the tragic view and makes tragedy impossible,"[18] and that "Christianity is intransigent to tragedy."[19] A book-length study has restated the case that "Christian (religious) vision and tragic vision offer different views and versions of reality" and that they "contain irreconcilable differences."[20]

When critics such as these begin to defend their case, they typically argue that Christianity and tragedy present opposed viewpoints on certain key issues. A Christian believes in an eternal destiny, while tragedy limits its focus to the hero's earthly life. Tragedy is pessimistic, while the Christian gospel of redemption is optimistic. Christianity asserts human freedom, but tragedy mingles a note of determinism alongside the hero's choice. The suffering of tragedy is punitive (the sufferer as sinner), while Christianity exalts innocent suffering (the sufferer as saint or suffering servant). The Christian message has a happy ending, while tragedy ends in defeat and irremedial loss.

These contrasts, while important, also point up the unwarranted assumptions of those who deny that tragedy can be a Christian form. Critics in this camp assume that the tragic hero will be a Christian believer whose destination is heaven. But why would we make such an assumption? More importantly, these critics assume that tragedy is sub-Christian because it does not embody the whole truth about the Christian gospel. By the same criterion, every other literary form also falls short of Christianity.

*Tragedy in the Bible.* We know that tragedy is not incompatible with Christianity because there are tragedies in the Bible.[21] The Old Testament story of King Saul is a full-fledged tragedy based on the same principles as Greek and Shakespearean tragedy, and Saul himself is "a tragic figure of the same stature as Oedipus or Othello."[22] The story of Samson is a tragedy on a briefer scale.

Several other biblical stories are nearly as complete in their adherence to the tragic pattern. Genesis 3, the story of the fall, is the prototype of all biblical tragedies. It possesses all of the usual ingredients of tragedy. The story of David as told in Second Samuel is likewise tragic: the hero's life is prosperous until the sordid episode involving Bathsheba and Uriah sends it tumbling in the direction of exceptional calamity. The life of Solomon is equally tragic.

Beyond these complete tragedies in the Bible, we find a host of partial tragedies—stories where the essential tragic ingredients are present, but where the story is too brief to be a full tragedy or where the tragic elements are mingled with other historical material. The Old Testament historical chronicles and the New Testament gospels and book of Acts provide numerous examples. Jesus' parables are an equally rich source of brief tragedies. We think at once of the slothful servant cast into outer darkness, a rich man condemned to torment after death for his indifference to a beggar at his gate, wedding guests who missed the messianic banquet because of their worldlymindedness, and many more.

*The Common Ground of Christian Doctrine and Tragedy.* A similar concord between Christianity and tragedy emerges if we compare the common premises of both. Tragedy presupposes that people have the power to choose between good and evil, and that their destiny depends on the choice they make. A major premise of Christianity is likewise that people must choose between life and death, God and evil, and that the pattern of their lives is a result of the choices that they themselves make. Jesus' image of the broad way that leads to death and the narrow way that leads to life (Matthew 7:13-14) opens the possibility for either a tragic or comic pattern in a person's life, and Jesus made it clear that the life story of most people is a tragedy.

The view of the person is similar in Christianity and tragedy. In both schemes the individual is significant for either good or evil. In neither system are people helpless pawns. Instead, they have the power of choice. Both outlooks agree that people are flawed and have a fatal tendency to choose the wrong thing. But people also have the potential to learn from their mistakes and snatch something redemptive from their suffering. Of course the redemptive potential of tragedy stops far short of Christian regeneration and eternal life, but even here there are the common ingredients of moral perception, conviction of wrongoing, and inner transformation. Furthermore, although Christianity offers an ultimate escape from the consequences of sin, it never denies that temporal consequences take their toll, even in a believer's life.

The principle of justice is also common to Christianity and tragedy. Both operate on the premise that people reap what they have sown and that doing evil brings inevitable retribution in the sphere of earthly life. The world of tragedy is closed: once the tragic choice has been made, doom is inevitable. Christianity postulates an open world in which God's forgiveness is always possible. But no work of literature is obliged to cover every aspect of life. Tragedy tells *part* of the Christian truth.

*Shakespeare's* Macbeth *as a Christian Tragedy.* I have implicitly made a case for *Macbeth* as a Christian tragedy. Although biblical allusions do not by themselves make a work Christian, they represent the initial point at which *Macbeth* intersects with Christianity.

The plot of Shakespeare's play came from Holinshed's *Chronicles of English History*, but Shakespeare's treatment of the inherited story follows biblical models. The world of the play, so heavy with atmosphere, is less Scottish than biblical. We move in a world of Old Testament histories of kings whose evil can taint a whole nation. The evil that people do in the world of the play is given a supernatural dimension, in keeping with biblical precedent. There are thirty-seven images of hell and demons in the play.[23] Eschatalogical overtones of God's judgment against evil brood over the play in the form of such images as blood, darkness, and disruptions in nature, a strategy probably influenced by the visions of moral and natural collapse in the book of Revelation.[24]

Specific scenes are also modelled on the Bible. The spectacle of a king's wife urging, planning, and helping to execute a crime to gain something for her husband is the story of Ahab, Jezebel, and Naboth in a new setting. The false welcome of King Duncan into the castle of Macbeth reenacts the treason of Judas. When Lady Macbeth attempts to pass off the effect of the murder of the king with the nonchalant comment that "a little water clears us of this deed," and even more when she washes her hands in the sleepwalking scene, she becomes another Pilate, futilely trying to wash the hands in a false innocence. Macbeth's murder of Macduff's children takes shape as the motif of the murder of the innocents by Herod. And at the end of his career, Macbeth becomes another King Saul—a doomed king on the verge of death consulting a witch.

Smaller poetic effects in the play are also influenced by the Bible. Macbeth's "tomorrow and tomorrow and tomorrow" soliloquy that appears at the beginning of this chapter furnishes some examples. The image of "the way to dusty death," for example, echoes the psalmist's statement about being brought into "the dust of death" (Psalm 22:15) and the creation principle that "dust thou art, and unto dust shalt thou return" (Genesis 3:19, KJV). Macbeth's image of life as a candle quickly extinguished alludes to the statement in Job 18:6 that the wicked person's "candle shall be put out" (KJV). Equally biblical are the images of life as a shadow (Ecclesiastes 8:13; Job 8:9, 14:2; Psalm 102:11, 144:4) and as a tale that is told (Psalm 90:9, KJV).

Primarily, though, the Christian allegiance of *Macbeth* consists of the ideas that it embodies—its implicit moral patterns and world view. These, in turn, are inseparable from its tragic pattern. They revolve around ideas of evil, moral responsibility, guilt, temptation, the sanctity of human life, and order as a moral good. The fact that these are not exclusively Christian ideas and that the play presents a rather rudimentary version of them does not make them any less Christian.[25]

*Summary.* Shakespeare's *Macbeth* shows us what a Christian tragedy looks like. As it reenacts the usual tragic pattern and displays the ordinary ingredients of tragedy, it also embodies such Christian ideas as human choice, the reality of evil and the human propensity toward it, the inevitability of justice, and a redemptive potential even in human failure. Shakespeare highlights these affinities between tragedy and the Christian faith by implicitly placing his story into a biblical framework.

## Notes to Chapter 3

[1]I have used the Pelican edition of Shakespeare's *Macbeth,* ed. Alfred Harbage (New York: Penguin, 1956, 1971).

[2]G. Wilson Knight, *The Wheel of Fire* (1930; reprint edition Cleveland: World, 1957), p. 140.

[3]T.S. Eliot, *The Use of Poetry and the Use of Criticism* (Cambridge, MA: Harvard UP, 1933), p. 146.

[4]Oscar Mandel, *A Definition of Tragedy* (New York: New York UP, 1961), p. 20.

[5]Alfred Harbage, *William Shakespeare: A Reader's Guide* (New York: Noonday, 1963), p. 394.

[6]Harold S. Wilson, *On the Design of Shakespearian Tragedy* (Toronto: Toronto UP, 1957), p. 74.

[7]C.S. Lewis, *An Experiment in Criticism* (Cambridge: Cambridge UP, 1965), pp. 78-79.

[8]T.S. Eliot, *On Poetry and Poets* (New York: Farrar, Straus and Cudahy, 1957), p. 94.

[9]A.C. Bradley, *Shakespearean Tragedy* (Cleveland: World, 1955), p. 28.

[10]Thomas De Quincey, "On the Knocking at the Gate in *Macbeth,*" as excerpted in *Shakespeare and His Critics,* ed. F. E. Halliday (New York: Schocken, 1963), pp. 94-95.

[11]Harbage, p. 384.

[12]Kenneth Muir, "Introduction" to the Arden Edition of *Macbeth,* 9th ed. (New York: Ramdom House, 1962), p. lii.

[13]Virgil K. Whitaker, *The Mirror up to Nature* (San Marino: Huntington Library, 1965), p. 265.

[14]Lewis, pp. 77-78.

[15]Karl Jaspers, *Tragedy is Not Enough* (Boston: Beacon, 1952), p. 38.

[16]Una Ellis-Fermor, *The Frontiers of Drama* (London: Methuen, 1945), pp. 17-18.

[17]D.D. Rapheal, *The Paradox of Tragedy* (Bloomington: Indiana UP, 1961), p. 51.

[18]Richard B. Sewell, *The Vision of Tragedy* (New Haven: Yale UP, 1962), p. 50.

[19]Laurence Michel, "The Possibility of a Christian Tragedy," *Thought* 31 (1956): 427.

[20]Barbara J. Hunt, *The Paradox of Christian Tragedy* (Troy, N.Y.: Whitston, 1985), pp. 92, 94.

[21]For more commentary on biblical tragedy than I can provide here, see chapter 6 of my book *Words of Delight: A Literary Introduction to the Bible* (Grand Rapids: Baker, 1987).

[22]Edwin M. Good, *Irony in the Old Testament* (Philadelphia: Westminster, 1965), p. 80. Good's full-scale explication of the story of Saul is the best treatment of a biblical tragedy that I have seen.

[23]S.L. Bethell, "Shakespeare's Imagery: The Diabolic Images in Othello," *Shakespeare Survey* 5 (1952): 68.

[24]Jane Jack, "Macbeth, King James, and the Bible," *English Literary History* 22 (1955): 173-193.

[25]For more on the incompleteness of the Christian patterns in *Macbeth*, see my book *The Liberated Imagination: Thinking Christianly about the Arts* (Wheaton: Harold Shaw, 1989), pp. 190-192.

# Chapter 4

## Milton's Paradise Lost
### and the Bible as Literary Influence

### "This Delightful Land"

✳

*With thee conversing I forget all time,*
*All seasons and their change, all please alike.*
*Sweet is the breath of morn, her rising sweet,*
*With charm of earliest birds; pleasant the sun*
*When first on this delightful land he spreads*
*His orient beams, on herb, tree, fruit, and flow'r,*
*Glist'ring with dew; fragrant the fertile earth*
*After soft showers; and sweet the coming on*
*Of grateful ev'ning mild, then silent night*
*With this her solemn bird and this fair moon,*
*And these the gems of heav'n, her starry train:*
*But neither breath of morn when she ascends*
*With charm of earliest birds, nor rising sun*
*On this delightful land, nor herb, fruit, flow'r,*
*Glist'ring with dew, nor fragrance after showers,*
*Nor grateful ev'ning mild, nor silent night*
*With this her solemn bird, nor walk by moon*
*Or glittering starlight without thee is sweet.*[1]

✳

This is Eve's love song addressed to her husband in the part of *Paradise Lost* (Book 4) where Milton portrays life in Paradise. I have chosen it for my entry into the poem not only because it is my favorite passage in

*Paradise Lost* but also because it epitomizes the poem and challenges some misconceptions that people have about Milton's masterpiece. The misconceptions arise partly because many readers cannot get beyond Book 1 in their minds and imaginations, and Book 1, as students enrolled in literature courses know, is Milton's murky vision of Hell, written in the most difficult style of the whole poem.

Instead of beginning there, I propose that we listen to Eve's love song. The first thing we notice about it is that it is the poetry of longing. It awakens our longing for nature, for example, and alerts us that *Paradise Lost* is a great nature poem. It also awakens our longing for human love and companionship, reminding us that *Paradise Lost* is also the greatest love poem in the English language. As a nature poem and love poem, Eve's speech underscores the abundance of recognizable human experience that *Paradise Lost* contains, something obscured from many readers by the high style in which the poem is written. Milton's adeptness at the poetry of longing means that one of the best strategies for reading the poem is simply to allow it to elicit good longings from us—longings for perfection, for beauty, for God, for freedom from evil, for reconciliation, and much more. One of the chief triumphs of *Paradise Lost* is Milton's ability to make the good attractive.

The passage also typifies the style in which Milton's poem is written. It is a high style that flaunts its eloquence and the beauty of its language. It is a golden or ostentatious style. Its words invite emotion and sensuous ("sensory") imagining. Even though Milton is a poet of ideas, the style of his poetry is not abstract. It is as dense with poetic texture as the poetry of any English Renaissance poet other than Shakespeare.

The verse form in which *Paradise Lost* is written is blank verse (unrhymed lines with ten syllables per line), but it is not predominantly end-stopped like Shakespeare's dramatic blank verse. It is epic blank verse, with long, flowing sentences that run right past the ends of the lines. The verse paragraph is the basic structural unit in the poem. In its sheer grandeur, *Paradise Lost* is to English literature what Handel's *Messiah* is to music: it gives us the grand themes in the grand style. The poetry is there for our enjoyment. In the words of Charles Williams, "*Paradise Lost* is much more fun written in blank verse than it would be in prose."[2] C.S. Lewis, in what is still the best book on *Paradise Lost*, speaks of our need to "be receptive of the true epic exhiliration" that Milton's grand style can create.[3]

The style is also an affective style, by which I mean several things. Milton's poetry gains its effects by getting the reader to feel a certain way toward the subject matter. How much we visualize is an irrelevance. How we feel toward a character or scene is what counts. It is also a commonplace that Milton requires the reader to supply the content for his images. He does not paint a picture of Paradise for us in the quoted excerpt. He gives us the outline; we fill in the details.

The impact of such poetry depends on the poet's ability to arouse our own experiences of the things about which he writes. C.S. Lewis has this to say about Milton's description of Paradise (and it applies equally to Milton's portrayal of Hell and Heaven): "While seeming to describe his own imagination [Milton] must actually arouse ours. . . . We are his organ: when he appears to be describing Paradise he is in fact drawing out the Paradisal Stop in us."[4]

The style of *Paradise Lost* is also an oral style. It will produce its best effects if we read it aloud or hear it read. Not only will this allow us to enjoy the music of the poetry and the eloquence of the language, it will also make the meaning much easier to grasp. Eve's love song is filled with the rhetoric of oral poetry. It is replete with repetition and echo, as nearly every image in the first half of the poem is repeated in the second half.

This careful structuring is another of Milton's characteristic gifts. Despite its wealth of images, Eve's speech turns on a simple design. It begins with the phrase "with thee." In the middle comes the pivot, as signalized by the word "but." The last line completes the pattern with the phrase "without thee." Eve's strategy is first to catalog the sensations in the garden that she finds pleasant when Adam is with her, and then to catalog the same features but declare them indifferent to her when Adam is absent.

This structural clarity shows on a small scale what the poem as a whole presents on a grand scale. If we stand at the greatest distance from the poem, the organizing principle is a prolonged conflict between good and evil, both in the universe and in the individual human soul. The shape of the plot exhibits this same classical simplicity of design.

The plot is a single action in three phases—the antecedents, the occurrence, and the consequences of the central event in the story, Adam and Eve's eating of the forbidden fruit.

The poem has four great scenes of action, and these, too, organize the poem in our imagination. They are Hell, Heaven, Paradise, and the ordinary earthly sphere. These places are both literal, physical places and spiritual states. In reading the poem we thus live simultaneously in a physical and spiritual cosmos. We begin the poem in Hell, then reside in Heaven and Paradise, and eventually descend, not as low as we started, but still considerably below the heights to which we soar in the middle books. Heaven is high and light, Hell is low and dark, and earth with its human citizens is poised midway between the two. The human potential for good or evil and the need for moral choice are thus built into the very setting of the story.

Milton also organized his long poem by books. *Paradise Lost* is reminiscent of the structure of other epics by being divided into twelve books, thereby conveying a sense of shapeliness and completeness. There are several subordinate patterns discernible in this arrangement. *Paradise Lost* progresses by pairs of books devoted, in sequence, to Satan and the fallen angels in Hell, the perfection of Heaven and Paradise, the war in Heaven, God's creation of the world, the Fall into sin, and the consequences of the Fall in human history.

At the same time, we can see the customary "ring composition" in which the second half of the poem recalls the first half in reverse order. Thus the first three books describe Satan's sinful actions and the last three narrate humankind's sinful actions. Book 4 is our entry into Paradise, while Book 9 describes the loss of Paradise. The destructiveness of the war in Heaven in Books 5-6 is balanced by God's creativity in Books 7-8.

Eve's love song shows another Miltonic trait by belonging to a conventional genre. This love poem follows the standard motif of praising the beloved as the source of one's joy. Equally common is the idea of couching a love poem in rural or pastoral imagery, based on the premises that our sentiment for nature will be transmuted into romantic sentiment and that an idealized setting is appropriate for a story of happy love.

Milton always wrote in well defined genres like this. *Paradise Lost* is an epic, written in conscious imitation of classical and biblical epics.

Epic is an encyclopedic form that sums up what a whole age wanted to say. It has a cosmic setting that includes both earthly and supernatural realms. It is constructed around a hero of national or racial importance who performs an epic feat (usually military in nature) and is told in the high style of poetry. Within the overriding framework of epic, Milton incorporates a host of individual genres, making *Paradise Lost* a compendium of virtually every genre that had appeared on the scene when the blind Milton wrote the poem in a five-year span around 1660.[5]

A final feature of Eve's love song that will concern us here is its indebtedness to the Bible. The affective style that Milton gives us is also the prevailing style of the Bible, which tends to give us only the outline of events and activates us to fill in the specific details. Eve's speech to Adam is filled with elemental images, as is the Bible. And it was partly the Song of Solomon that taught Renaissance love poets how to write pastoral love poetry like this.

The influence of the Bible on *Paradise Lost* is the framework within which I will explore the great English and Christian epic. The Bible gave Milton his story and subject matter. The epic genre came from the classical tradition, but what Milton did with the inherited epic forms was based on biblical models.

## The Bible as Literary Source and Influence

The Bible is *the* book, not only of Christendom, but also of the literary writers of the Western world. While this is preeminently true of a Christian writer like Milton, writers continue to draw upon the Bible right up to the present day, even when they do not believe its religious message.

The Bible is therefore an essential context for readers of literature as well. Northrop Frye has said that the Bible is "the major informing influence on literary symbolism. . . . Once our view of the Bible comes into proper focus, a great mass of literary symbols from *The Dream of the Rood* to *Little Gidding* begins to take on meaning."[6] Someone else writes that the Bible "becomes one with the Western tradition, because it is its greatest source."[7]

The starting point for any discussion of the Bible as a presence in imaginative literature remains C.S. Lewis' famous monograph *The Literary Impact of the Authorized Version*. It was here that Lewis bequeathed the distinction between the Bible as a literary source and a literary influence: "A source gives us things to write about; an influence prompts us to write in a certain way."[8]

We can thus view the indebtedness of literature to the Bible as existing on a continuum. At one end of the spectrum we find a direct borrowing of material from the Bible. As we move across the continuum, literary works move by stages away from direct ties to the Bible.

Writers most directly use the Bible as a source for titles of works, names of fictional characters, and subject matter (including plots and characters). At a further remove, the Bible supplies literary genres, such as the lament psalm, the praise psalm, or epic. Even when literary subject matter does not come from the Bible, writers can derive a "mythology" and ideas from the Bible—the world view within which they locate their own subject matter. Of course writers allude to the Bible as they elaborate their stories and poems. At the most remote end of the continuum, writers allow the Bible to influence their characterization, plots, and genres (even when these are not derived from the Bible), as well as their style.

Why would writers from Caedmon (who wrote the oldest extant piece of literature in the English language) to Hemingway and Faulkner draw upon the Bible in these ways? For several reasons, chief of which is that the Bible is itself largely a work of literature. The characteristic way of presenting truth in the Bible is not the treatise or sermon but the story, the poem, the vision, and the letter. If we apply a rigorous definition of literature (such as that literature is an interpretive presentation of human experience in an artistic form), at least three-fourths of the Bible fits the definition. It is, moreover, literature of a very high order. Throughout the history of Western literature, writers have repeatedly claimed that the Bible has shown them how to write.

Writers have also been impressed by the Bible's truthfulness. Writers are always on the lookout for authentic human experience and insight—for stories and situations in which the deep significance of life reveals itself. The Bible consistently meets this criterion. Furthermore, because the Bible has through the centuries been accepted as an authority for life and belief, it has supplied writers a "language" of stories and images that they know their readers will understand.

For Christians writers, an additional factor enters the picture. The Bible is for them an authoritative source of belief. They accept it as the true account of God, reality, and morality. Since every writer portrays a world view, and since Christian writers derive their world view ultimately from the Bible, it is inevitable that the Bible will enter their work at many points.

Milton's poetry is a case study in how a Christian poet's imagination can be influenced by the Bible. Without the Bible, Milton's poetry would not exist.

## Milton's Biblical World View

Even an initial reading of *Paradise Lost* shows that Milton's world view is informed by the Bible. Ideas are part of that world view, but a world view consists of more than ideas. It also includes a world picture or a "mythology." We do not live by ideas alone but also by master images and stories that we accept as true and in terms of which we live our lives. It would be arbitrary to assign primacy to the ideas rather than the images. Because Milton read the Bible with a poet's heart (as someone has put it), I begin with the rootedness of his poetry in the Bible's world picture rather than its doctrinal system.

*The Mythological Universe of* **Paradise Lost.** Literary critics use the term "mythology" to refer to the framework of stories and symbols by which a culture expresses its experiences and values, especially in its art forms. A sociologist provides as good a definition as we can hope for: "The mythology of a culture is the framework of beliefs, values, expressive symbols, and artistic motifs in terms of which individuals define their world, express their feelings, and make their judgments."[9] The Bible has provided the dominant storehouse of such images throughout the history of Western culture (so much so that the Romantic poet William Blake called the Bible "the great code of art"), but never with more authority and pervasiveness than it did for Milton's Puritan milieu.

Of particular importance in this regard is the overall shape and coherence of the Bible. The Bible starts with the story of creation and the beginning of human history. It concludes with the events that bring history to its conclusion. Between these points stretches human history with its ups and downs. The overall pattern is a U-shaped story beginning with perfection, followed by the Fall and its consequences, until these are reversed in a vision of perfection restored and consummated.

No work of English literature draws upon this pattern so directly and fully as does *Paradise Lost*. The plot begins in eternity before earthly history has begun. This phase of action pictures the perfection of Heaven and the violation of that perfection by Satan and his rebellious angels, who are cast into the eternal realm of Hell. To compensate for this blemish on heavenly perfection, God creates the world and places Adam and Eve in Paradise. In Book 9 they disobey God and are subsequently expelled from the garden. Before that expulsion, though, God sends the angel Michael to give Adam a preview of fallen history, including its final consummation.

Northrop Frye speaks of the Bible as "a vast mythological universe, stretching in time from creation to apocalypse, and in . . . space from heaven to hell."[10] The same description applies to *Paradise Lost*. We can see at once, moreover, that Milton accentuated the supernatural aspect of this mythological world. Most of his story is set in timeless eternity (including Paradise before the Fall). Through thousands of lines supernatural agents are the only characters. No ordinary human characters enter the story until Book 10.

Milton's story material thus posed an unusual but not insurmountable difficulty—the need to portray in human terms an action and setting that are not directly accessible to human experience. It is no wonder that Milton claims in one of his invocations that he will tell "of things invisible to mortal sight" (III. 55). The skill with which he succeeded in the venture is one of the chief triumphs of the poem.[11] He could never have achieved that success without the Bible to serve as a model and source. The Bible gave him the materials for creating what one critic calls "authoritative reality." In other words, the Bible was a source of details that enabled Milton to make "his action, characters, and setting believable, probable, and real, even in the invented parts" of the poem.[12]

The overall story that the Bible tells is structured as a prolonged conflict between good and evil. Reality is pictured as being claimed by God and counter-claimed by Satan. This character conflict is reinforced by the scenic conflict of Heaven against Hell. Individual actions by people participate in this conflict, as every choice that people make shows a motion toward God or away from him.

Milton imported this overall situation straight from the Bible into his epic. It, too, is a carefully invented system of contrasts between good and evil, God and Satan, Heaven and Hell. A council in Hell is balanced by a council in Heaven. The demons in Hell bow in adoration toward Satan, and the angels in Heaven bow in worship toward God. Satan journeys through space to destroy the world after the Son had journeyed through space to create it.

From what I have said, it is apparent what Milton owed to the Bible's world picture and imaginative universe. The Bible supplied the big framework within which to fit his entire story. In fact, it provided both the subject matter and the structure of his poem.

**Biblical Ideas in Paradise Lost.** The Bible also supplied the big ideas for *Paradise Lost*, and these ideas are part of the greatness of the poem. We can begin where Milton begins—with the idea of the goodness of God. In his opening invocation, Milton first announces that his plot is the story of humankind's fall from innocence. At the end of the invocation he states that his theme (what he intends to do *with* that story) will "assert Eternal Providence / And justify the ways of God to men" (I. 25-26).

Milton's portrayal of God has proved controversial, but for Christian readers it should not be. It is rooted at every point in the portrayal of God in the Bible. C.S. Lewis correctly observes that "many of those who say they dislike Milton's God only mean that they dislike God: infinite sovereignty. . . , combined with infinite power . . . , and love which, by its very nature, includes wrath also—it is not only in poetry that these things offend."[13] Not only the attributes that Milton ascribes to God but usually the images in which he embodies those attributes as well come from the Bible.

Another of the big ideas in the story is the reality of evil in the universe. Milton calls our attention to this aspect of his story in the statement of theme with which he opens his poem:

*Of man's first disobedience, and the fruit*
*Of that forbidden tree, whose mortal taste*

*Brought death into the world, and all our woe,*
*With loss of Eden, till one greater Man*
*Restore us, and regain the blissful seat,*
*Sing, Heav'nly Muse.*

*Paradise Lost* is a poem about loss. It gives us the most powerful delineation of evil in English literature. Yet as the opening statement of theme shows, it is also a story about redemption through Christ.

In portraying evil at such length, the poem naturally exhibits a theological understanding of evil. For Milton the essential identity of evil is disobedience against the will and commands of God. It is, moreover, the perversion of goodness, which partly accounts for why Milton portrays an impressive Satan in Book 1. To be the greatest of all evil forces, Satan had to have originally possessed qualities and virtues that in themselves are superlative. But Satan's progressive degeneration throughout the story shows a related idea that is important in the poem—the self-destructive effects of evil on the doer.

If we combine these first two ideas—the goodness of an all-powerful God and the fact of evil and suffering in the world—we can see at once that Milton's poem is a theodicy. Theodicy is the attempt to solve the so-called "problem of evil"—to reconcile God's goodness and power with the existence of suffering and evil in human experience. Milton invites us to read his story partly in terms of the logic of his theodicy. The usual tendency of theodicies is to impair either God's power or his goodness, but to reduce either of these is to violate attributes that the Bible ascribes to God.

We know that Milton's theodicy was important to his poem not only because he elevated it to the status of the formal statement of epic theme, but also because he invented a scene in which he lays out the four main principles of his theodicy. It is the so-called "dialogue in Heaven" that comes at the beginning of Book 3, the first scene set in Heaven. In this exalted drama of the glory, authority, justice, and mercy of God, the Father and the Son discuss the ramifications of the fact that Adam and Eve will fall from innocence.

As the dialogue unfolds, four main principles emerge: evil will eventually be destroyed (III. 84-86); Adam and Eve were endowed with original perfection, combined with freedom of will that would allow them to persist in that perfection (98-102); God permits evil but is not the cause of it (112-118); God's mercy is available to save fallen people (130-134). Each of these can be related to a specific biblical text that especially teaches the same principle—the book of Revelation for the final defeat of evil, Genesis 2–3 for Adam and Eve's original perfection and free choice, the book of Job for the permissive theory of evil, and the Gospels and Epistles for the availability of God's redemption.

The great battle between good and evil makes choice necessary on the part of people, and this is another of Milton's big ideas in the poem. "The ideological center of the whole poem," writes Kester Svendsen, "is the fact of choosing; the center of the narrative is the act of choosing. Everything in it relates to . . . the antecedents of that act, its occurrence, and its consequences."[14]

The human-divine relationship also figures prominently in the story. A major premise of the action is that God and people are inescapably related to each other. The story itself explores variations on that theme— God's unremitting care over his creation, how God intended for people to relate to him, the ways in which the human race disrupts the relationship, the effects when it does, and the way in which the relationship can be restored after its disruption.

*Paradise Lost* exhibits a moral system as well. C. M. Bowra has written that for Milton "the question of right and wrong was more important than any other question," adding that "*Paradise Lost* sets forth the noblest virtues and the darkest sins."[15] Someone else says that "more than any other English poet Milton may be said to express the moral energy of his race."[16] Milton's ethical viewoint is a combination of biblical and classical emphases. Central to the scheme is the importance of reason as the pathway to virtue, with a corresponding distrust of emotion and appetite as moral guides. This is combined with a belief that God has built a hierarchical principle into the very fabric of reality at every level—cosmic (the great chain of being idea, with God at the top), familial (where the husband/father is the head), and individual (where reason is meant to rule).[17]

An important part of the moral system in Milton's poem is also the idea that goodness consists of obedience to God and that evil is disobedience to what God has prescribed. "The one great moral . . . which reigns in Milton," wrote Joseph Addison in the first rigorous literary analysis of *Paradise Lost*, "is the most universal and most useful that can be imagined: . . . that Obedience to the will of God makes men happy, and that Disobedience makes them miserable."[18]

Modern aesthetic theory generally downplays the role of ideas in literature. After all, one cannot create a work of literature out of ideas. But it is good to be reminded that ideas are part of the greatness of a great work. Douglas Bush has written,

> The quality of Milton's poetry is inseparable from his vision of life, and his vision of life, in its essentials, remains significant, whatever the changes in our ways of thought—and indeed to a large measure because these have changed so much. . . . [In Milton's poetry we hear a] voice of heroic magnitude proclaiming that good is good and evil evil, that man is a religious and moral being in a religious and moral universe, and that the destiny of the race depends upon the individual soul. To be moved by the poetic presentation of such elementary convictions is to enjoy the experience which [Milton's] poetry gives.[19]

***Form and Meaning in* Paradise Lost.** The foregoing discussion of Milton's world view has treated Milton's mythological world and ideas separately, but this is somewhat misleading. The amazing thing about *Paradise Lost* is the degree to which form and meaning are fused and inseparable. Milton invented scenes and episodes that embody his ideas, so that the moment we name an idea we are reminded of scenes in the story.

Take, for example, the idea of original perfection. It is an important idea in Christian theology. But in Milton's poem it is hardly an idea at all. It is instead a host of images, descriptive passages, and narrative episodes in which Milton portrays Adam and Eve in Paradise. It is Eve's love song. It is the gradual approach to Paradise (IV. 131-153) and the narrator's first description of Adam and Eve (IV. 288-299). It is Adam's first speech in the poem in which he praises God's wonderful provision (IV. 411-439). It is Adam and Eve's evening hymn (IV. 720-735) and morning hymn (V. 153-208).

Milton even manages to make style bear a moral and spiritual meaning. It is a commonplace that Milton writes in two distinct styles in *Paradise Lost*. His demonic or internal style, used in scenes depicting

Satan and evil, is filled with epic similes and allusions to classical mythology. The sentence structure is elaborate. In Book 1 Milton deliberately creates a suffocating effect that gives shape to Lady Macbeth's comment that "Hell is murky." Milton's celestial style, by contrast, is relatively plain and easy to follow. It is devoid of epic similes and mythological allusions. What it *does* possess is an abundance of biblical language as Milton creates the effect of the plain truth of Scripture for his scenes depicting God and Heaven.

*Summary.* The Bible is the source of Milton's imaginative universe and the big ideas that make up an important part of his poetry. Because Milton was both a poet and a theologian (he wrote his own theological treatise), image and idea are inseparable in his poetry.

## Plot and Characters

The Bible supplied Milton with his story material as well as his world view. He relied on the Bible for details regarding his plot, characters, and settings. It is important to note at the outset, though, that no single biblical text supplied this material. Poets who use the Bible as a source ordinarily synthesize a vast array of biblical passages as they create their works. This is especially true of an epic poet who must elaborate his story far beyond what the Bible supplies on a given subject. Milton's characters and settings are a mosaic of biblical allusions.

*The Biblical Plot of* **Paradise Lost.** The core of Milton's plot comes from Genesis 1–3. From this foundational biblical text Milton took his story of an eternal God stepping forward from the stage of eternity to create a world. At the beginning of the history thus initiated stand two perfect human creatures in a perfect garden. Creation and Paradise are followed by a third phase of action—the Fall from innocence and expulsion from the garden. This is Milton's Ur-text, but it is so brief that it supplied only a bare outline for Milton's plot.

We should pause to ask why Milton was attracted to this story for his epic. Milton in effect spent the first fifty years of life preparing to write his major life's work, and during that time he changed his mind several times regarding what the subject would be. We can assume that Milton was attracted to the story of Paradise and its loss because this story enabled him to say what he wanted to say about reality. It was a story in which the deep significance of life revealed itself.

This means that we should not read the story about life in Paradise primarily as Milton's version of how Adam and Eve lived before the Fall. How does Milton know what happened day by day in Paradise? He can only imagine. The relevance of his paradisal vision is that it is his imagined picture of how God intended (and still intends) all people to live. In filling out this picture of the good life, Milton drew upon the whole tenor of biblical teaching. For Milton, Paradise is "the model for human happiness" and "a moral center against which traditional assumptions about heroism and the proper end of human activities are tested."[20]

According to Milton's imagined picture of Paradise, then, how *does* God intend human life to be lived? He intends it to be lived in communion with him, first of all. Adam and Eve's pastoral day begins and ends with prayer addressed to God. According to Milton's paradisal vision, God intends every human need to be satisfied, including the need for beauty, food, harmony with nature, human companionship, and sex. The issue of sex is especially important to Milton. Writing in the Puritan tradition that exalted married sexuality, Milton goes out of his way to insist that Adam and Eve enjoyed sexual love before the Fall (see especially IV. 736-765).

Equally Puritan is Milton's insistence that God intended people to work and that work gives purpose to life. In fact, if we compare Milton's earthly Paradise with its precedessors, we find that its most original feature is that Milton made work not only pleasurable but also necessary.[21] The work consists of Adam and Eve's keeping the garden's profuse growth from getting out of control, thereby contributing to the sense Milton wanted us to have that the garden has the potential to be lost.

Milton's Paradise is, in fact, a master image of equilibrium. It is an intricate balance between order and abundance, art and nature, realism and a more-than-earthly quality, the physical beauty of the garden and our awareness that it is also a spiritual state, continuing innocence and the way in which Adam and Eve increasingly reveal their vulnerability. "The overall feeling we have," writes someone, "is of stability on the brink of change: it can, will fall, but it could be no more blessed than it is."[22]

The keynote of Milton's imagined picture of how God wants people to live is the God-centeredness of life in Paradise. Nothing in Adam and Eve's life in *Paradise Lost* is self-contained. Everything points beyond itself to God. Just listen to Adam and Eve's evening hymn (IV. 724-735):

> *Thou also mad'st the night,*
> *Maker Omnipotent, and thou the day,*
> *Which we in our appointed work employed*
> *Have finished happy in our mutual help*
> *And mutual love, the crown of all our bliss*
> *Ordained by thee, and this delicious place*
> *For us too large, where thy abundance wants*
> *Partakers, and uncropped falls to the ground.*
> *But thou hast promised from us two a race*
> *To fill the earth, who shall with us extol*
> *Thy goodness infinite, both when we wake,*
> *And when we seek, as now, thy gift of sleep.*

Everything in their lives reminds Adam and Eve of God—their work, their mutual love, the beauty of Paradise, day and night, and even their sleep. This is the sacramental vision of Puritanism in which all of life is God's—a much more genuine sacramentalism than the multiplying of ritual within the church. Puritan spirituality is rooted in the Bible, as evidenced by the way in which Adam and Eve's evening hymn begins by paraphrasing Psalm 74:16 ("Thine is the day, thine also the night") and ends by alluding to Psalm 127:2 ("He gives to his beloved sleep"). While Genesis 2 supplied the skeleton for Milton's story of life in Paradise, in telling that story at full epic length his imagination ranged over the whole Bible.

The same thing is true of his story of the fall in Book 9. Genesis 3 supplies the core action of the temptation of Eve by Satan in the form of a crafty serpent, Eve's eating the forbidden fruit and then becoming the agent of her husband's also eating, and the cosmic effects of this representative action. But to fill this out, Milton invents a wealth of narrative material.

In doing so, he makes use of whatever further hints the Bible supplies. He bases the falls of Eve and Adam on two key New Testament verses, for example. One is the comment that Eve was deceived by the serpent's cunning (2 Corinthians 11:3). The other is Paul's differentiation between the falls of the man and the woman: "Adam was not deceived, but the woman was deceived and became a transgressor" (1 Timothy 2:14). Milton fleshes this out in *Paradise Lost*. Eve falls only after a long process of temptation, and she falls completely deceived by the false claims that Satan has made. Adam, by contrast, falls instantaneously and "against his better knowledge" (IX. 997).

Here, too, we can infer that Milton's purpose is not simply to show what happened in the garden on that fatal day but also to show us how the Fall into sin *happens* in our own lives. According to Milton's story, it happens when we unnecessarily open ourselves to temptation and prolong the occasion of temptation (as Eve does), when we think ourselves invulnerable, when we allow ourselves to be deceived, when we disobey what God has commanded, when we choose a lesser good over obedience to God (Adam's situation), when we indulge our selfish feelings, amd when we mistakenly think that sin has no price tag attached.

In other parts of *Paradise Lost* Milton similarly invents episodes based on biblical details. In portraying life in Heaven, he draws upon scenes of heavenly ritual in such apocalyptic passages as Ezekiel 1 and Revelation 4. For a dialogue in which God's mercy and justice progess toward a resolution regarding what to do about human sinfulness (the dialogue in Heaven in Book 3), Milton draws upon the story of Abraham's intercession on behalf of Lot and the cities of Sodom and Gomorrah (Genesis 18:16-33). To fulfill the epic expectation of a battle involving supernatural agents, Milton's imagination gravitates toward hints in the Bible of a war in Heaven (for example, Revelation 12:7-10).

*Biblical Characters in* **Paradise Lost.** Epic poets take their characters from existing myth or legend. Milton took his from the Bible. I have already noted that the characterization of God is based on biblical pictures of God. Since readers are often offended by speeches in which God asserts the need for judgment against human sinfulness, let me focus for a moment on the way in which Milton's characterization at this point is thoroughly biblical.

Here is the speech that readers have found particularly offensive (it occurs early in the dialogue in Heaven, at III. 95-99):

> *so will fall*
> *[Adam] and his faithless progeny. Whose fault?*
> *Whose but his own? Ingrate, he had of me*
> *All he could have; I made him just and right,*
> *Sufficient to have stood, though free to fall.*

There is nothing here with which the Bible would disagree. The writer of Ecclesiastes states, "God made man upright, but they have sought out many devices" (7:29). In Psalm 14, God "looks down from heaven upon the children of men," and what he sees is as unflattering as what he is said to see in Milton's dialogue in Heaven: "They have all gone astray, they are all alike corrupt; there is none that does good, no, not one" (14:2-3). Elsewhere the psalmist asserts to God, "No man living is righteous before thee" (Psalm 143:2). No part of *Paradise Lost* is as saturated with biblical allusions as the dialogue in Heaven, as Milton lends biblical authority to his portrayal.

Nor is God defensive in the speech quoted above. He is simply stating the facts of the matter. Stanley Fish writes,

> The emotional content of a word like "ingrate" (if it is felt) is provided by the reader who receives it defensively, his pride resisting the just accusation. . . ; the recalcitrance of the sinner, not the vindictiveness of his God, is the source of the difficulty. . . . Equally illusory is God's vaunted defensiveness. He does not argue, he asserts. . . . The tendency to argue with God, like the sense of injury we feel at hearing his words, is *self*-revealing.[23]

Milton also insures a positive response to God's speech because it represents the voice of authority after the prior actions of Satan have presented the reader with a disquieting authority vacuum.

If the characterization of God is thus modelled on the Bible, so are the portraits of Adam and Eve. The original parents of the human race have three primary roles in the Bible: they are the original prototypes of humanity (people as God intended them to be), the representatives of the human race, and the original sinners. They fill these same roles in *Paradise Lost*. We do not meet them for the first time when we encounter them in Milton's poem. They already have an identity in our imagination.

As prototypes of the human race, Adam and Eve are idealized beyond ordinary humanity. T. S. Eliot captured this quality well:

> These are not a man and woman such as any we know; if they were, they would not be Adam and Eve. They are the original Man and Woman, not types, but prototypes. . . . They have ordinary humanity to the right degree, and yet are not, and should not be, ordinary mortals.[24]

Adam and Eve are given a grandeur that elevates them beyond ordinary humanity. This grandness is evident in their exalted manner of speaking before the Fall in *Paradise Lost* (they lose it after the Fall in Milton's story) and in their intellectual and moral superiority. They utter poetry extemporaneously in whatever style they choose (V. 146-50).

Milton also draws upon a tradition of Adam and Eve as the first Christians. This is largely an extrabiblical tradition,[25] though it is hinted at in Genesis 3:15, where God the judge predicts that from the seed of Adam and Eve the redeemer will come who will defeat Satan. But again Milton's chief strategy is to flesh out his characters with a wealth of relevant biblical material. In Milton's story, Adam and Eve after the Fall enact the process of salvation, including conviction of sin, contrition, prayer for forgiveness, and faith in God's grace. They leave the garden redeemed people.

Milton's Satan is likewise modelled on the Bible. Milton's imagination begins with the few descriptions that the Bible affords. In the Bible he is above all "the adversary" (the literal meaning of his name), the antagonist of God and good on every possible front. He appears in such varied roles as tempter, leader of demonic forces (including those who fought against Michael in the war in Heaven), and the one who is judged by God and ultimately defeated by Christ.

But this supplies only the foundation on which Milton builds his extended portrait of Satan. Milton's Satan is an angelic figure with impressive qualities. In fact, the first picture we have of Satan in Book 1 is so impressive that many readers have thought him a heroic or even sympathetic character. There are several reasons why Milton gave us an initially impressive Satan. Milton's view of evil as the perversion of goodness means that the leader of the evil angels possessed qualities that are good in themselves. The problem is that with Satan these good qualities are perverted to a bad end. As one critic comments, "Satan's impressiveness is only half the picture. Against it we must set his evil motives and his evil actions. There is an apparent contradiction between his heroic spirit and his corrupt motives, between his courageous acts and the end to which they are directed."[26]

A powerful and attractive Satan also accorded with what Milton knew about the power of evil in a fallen world, where it is at least as powerful as goodness. There are also literary reasons for Milton's portrait of an impressive Satan. His design with Satan was to show the degrading effects of sin, and this required him to show Satan first at his height and then trace his decline. A good plot conflict, moreover, requires an adequate antagonist to do battle with the protagonist. Milton gives us the greatest plot conflict ever imagined.

Equally importantly, Milton's initially impressive Satan is part of his technique of the guilty reader.[27] By means of this technique, Milton gets his readers to reenact the Fall in their own reading experience. For example, he conducts the opening description of Satan in such a way that any reader would find it easy to be swayed emotionally and imaginatively by Satan's eloquence, no matter what the reader knows rationally about this figure of evil. From time to time the narrator alerts his readers to the error of their fallen responses, informing them, for example, that despite Satan's boasting, he is "in pain" and "racked with deep despair" (I. 125-126).

Satan is not ultimately heroic in *Paradise Lost*. As his story unfolds, Milton links him by way of language and allusion with a host of biblical villains, including the rich man of Jesus' parable who was punished in Hell for his indifference to the beggar Lazarus, Nebuchadnezzar, Herod, Esau, Belshazzar, Pharaoh, and Judas Iscariot.[28]

One effect of this eclectic approach is to make Satan and his demons universal images of evil. In Milton's story we first look *at* the supernatural world of Hell, but we then look *out of it* to life as we, too, know it. The demonic world that Milton creates in the first two books of his poem is a window through which we see a wealth of recognizable human experience, much of it psychological. We witness images of defeat, loss, pain, suffering, aspiration, revenge, hatred, egomania, confusion, ineptitude, poor judgment (Satan is forced to admit that he miscalculated his attack on the Almighty), defiance, punishment, denial, and disappointment. Satan emerges as "the quintessential loser,"[29] a picture of "the aspiring mind . . . forcibly concerned with its own crushing failure."[30]

Even as we observe all of this, we realize that these are experiences to which we also fall prey. To choose what Satan stands for, writes Lewis, "is possible. Hardly a day passes without some slight movement towards it in each one of us. That is what makes *Paradise Lost* so serious a poem. The thing is possible, and the exposure of it is resented. Where *Paradise Lost* is not loved, it is deeply hated."[31] It is, indeed. More books have been written against Milton and his poem than is true of any other author's work.

But this confrontational quality that makes readers take sides is also characteristic of the Bible. An unsympathetic critic of Milton once grumbled, "With the best will in the world, we cannot avoid Milton's God or refuse to react to him."[32] The Bible elicits similar reactions. In the words of Erich Auerbach, "The Bible's claim to truth is not only far more urgent than Homer's, it is tyrannical—it excludes all other claims. . . . The Scripture stories . . . seek to subject us, and if we refuse to be subjected we are rebels."[33]

*Summary.* Milton took his story material from the Bible, but not only in the obvious sense that his plot and characters have a pre-existence in the Bible. In filling out his story and characters to full epic scope, Milton's imagination operates on a principle of association that brings a wide range of biblical details to bear upon his own story.

## The Bible as Influence

I have thus far considered ways in which the Bible was a source that gave Milton something about which to write. But equally interesting is how the Bible influenced his handling of material that he took from the classical tradition.

We should note in the first place that while classical epic prescribed the motifs that Milton needed for his epic, Milton was careful to give us the biblical version of each one. For a Christian reader one of the pleasures of reading his epic is to note the biblical version of familiar epic motifs.

A standard feature of epic is the inclusion of a supernatural realm with characters who participate in events on earth. Milton replaces the classical paraphernalia of Mt. Olympos and Hades with the Christian supernatural—God and Satan, Heaven and Hell, angels and demons. Epic is built around an epic hero of national importance. Milton wrote about Adam and Eve, representatives of the whole human race. In classical epic, gods assist human warriors. Milton shifts the battle entirely to Heaven, where God and his angels battle Satan and his followers in a three-day conflict finally won by the Son of God.

In all these cases, classical epic was the source of the motif, but the Bible influenced the precise form that the motif took in *Paradise Lost.* The same thing is true of one of the most striking of all of Milton's effects—his writing a poem that is an anti-epic as well as an epic.[34] *Paradise Lost* incorporates the forms of classical epic but inverts the meaning of those forms. The Bible was the key influence in Milton's management of the feat.

*Pastoral and Domestic Epic.* When Milton decided to write his epic about Adam and Eve, he at once revolutionized the epic tradition by writing a domestic epic. The distinctiveness of what one critic calls "Milton's household epic"[35] becomes obvious if we compare it to its classical predecessors. Classical epics are about public heroes—warriors and rulers of nations. The premise of all these stories is that the crucial events of history occur on the battlefield. Their focus is on public glory won through prowess in war.

Milton rejected this basic premise of classical epic and medieval romance. To show that he set no store in public honor won by military strength, Milton modelled Satan and the fallen angels on the old epic warriors and their standards of value. He even reserved his classical epic style, replete with long epic similes and allusions to classical mythology, for the scenes devoted to Satan and his followers.

Milton replaced military action with domestic action. His human heroes are husband and wife living their private life in a garden. The memorable scenes assigned to this married couple are domestic in nature: expressions of love, discussions about daily work at supper or breakfast, a conversation recalling their first meeting, entertaining an angelic guest with ideal hospitality, praying together, enjoying sexual love, discussing a troubling dream of the preceding night. In this domestic climate, Eve gets more space and prominence than does any heroine of classical epic.

Milton elevates these domestic scenes to the status of epic norm. This is Milton's version of epic heroism and moral virtue. Milton locates virtue "not in military glory . . . but in the everyday, the domestic."[36] As Milton wrote his domestic epic, pastoral became a natural ally to him. Pastoral literature, which pictures humble characters in a rural setting, praises such ideals as contentment, humility, and simple virtue. It is at the same time a rejection of courtly civilization, public glory, and the aspiring mind. It is obvious that Milton substituted pastoral values for heroic values in his epic.[37]

What model helped Milton in his venture of writing a domestic and pastoral epic? Primarily the Old Testament book of Genesis. It, too, tells stories of family life in a pastoral setting, within an epic framework of national destiny. The heroes of Genesis are family leaders, not deliverers of nations on the battlefield. Abraham's epic quest, for example, is thoroughly private and domestic. It consists of having a baby and raising a son. Milton likewise wrote about an epic feat (eating an apple) that is in itself so commonplace and even trivial that the focus is naturally diverted from the physical act to the primacy of the spiritual meaning represented by the act. The book of Genesis and *Paradise Lost* share a blend of domestic activity and pastoral simplicity, both invested with a quality of ultimate spiritual significance.

*The Satiric Epic.* A second part of Milton's anti-epic strategy was to discard the theme of human greatness in favor of the twin themes of divine greatness and human weakness. The epic tradition that Milton inherited praised a human hero or patron. Milton reserved his praise for God. In contrast to classical epics, Milton's story attributes ultimate glory to God, not to a human hero.

Balancing this elevation of the divine is Milton's exposure of human sinfulness. His opening announcement of theme, "Of Man's first disobedience," announces a revolution. John M. Steadman comments thus:

The uniqueness of *Paradise Lost* is implicit in the first enunciation of its theme. . . . Unlike the usual heroic poem, it does not propose a victory, but a defeat. Its action is not some illustrious "act of benefit," but a crime. Its hero is not a paragon of heroic virtue, but the archetypal sinner.[38]

*Paradise Lost* is thus rightly called "the Anatomy of Failure."[39]

The most likely influence on this aspect of Milton's epic is the Old Testament Epic of the Exodus. It, too, exposes human failing and reserves its praise for God. God is the chief actor in the deliverance of the nation of Israel. He appears as a divine warrior and is described in terms appropriate to epic heroes. The human characters, by contrast, are consistently portrayed as failures.

*Paradise Lost* likewise accentuates the disproportion between divine greatness and human weakness. Milton thoroughly assimilated the Exodus motif of human waywardness when he wrote the vision of future history in the last two books of *Paradise Lost.* This epic motif was supposed to praise the poet's nation. Milton transforms it into a nightmare of human vice and depravity, relieved only by occasional instances of solitary figures who exhibit moral heroism. In Milton's own words, it is a vision of "supernal grace contending / With sinfulness of men" (XI. 359-360).

*The Spiritual Epic.* A final part of Milton's anti-epic strategy was to transform into a spiritual mode epic motifs that in the inherited tradition had been conceived in physical terms. Thus in *Paradise Lost* warfare is not the armed battles of earthly nations but a spiritual battle between good and evil. The decisive event does not occcur on the battlefield, as classical epic would have it, but within the soul of Adam and Eve. The epic battle in Milton's story is elevated beyond the earthly sphere to a celestial battle conducted by angels instead of human warriors. It is not won through military means but by the spiritual power of the Son.

The transformation of the earthly into a spiritual mode is most evident in Milton's handling of epic heroism. In the received tradition, the hero was the conquering warrior who excelled others in physical strength and who was motivated by the desire for fame, success, and power. Milton replaced the warrior as hero with the Christian saint as hero.

This spiritual conception of the hero takes several forms. Before the Fall it consists of Adam and Eve's life of pastoral perfection and their obedience to God. Dominion, in other words, consists of ruling a garden and one's own soul. After the Fall, heroism is still spiritual and consists of Adam and Eve's repentance, mutual forgiveness, and coming to believe in the Son as Savior.

This spiritual emphasis is well illustrated by the moment of epiphany (climactic insight) toward which the whole poem moves near the end. It comes after the preview of fallen history and just before the expulsion from Paradise. Adam expresses a heroic ideal that is solidly Christian and spiritual in nature (XII. 561-573):

> *Henceforth I learn that to obey is best,*
> *And love with fear the only God, to walk*
> *As in his presence, ever to observe*
> *His providence, and on him sole depend,*
> *Merciful over all his works, with good*
> *Still overcoming evil, and by small*
> *Accomplishing great things . . . .*
> *Taught this by his example whom I now*
> *Acknowledge my Redeemer ever blest.*

Where did Milton learn to write a spiritual epic? From the whole Bible, no doubt, but chiefly from the New Testament book of Revelation. Here is where he saw such epic motifs as battle, conquest, dominion, and glory raised to a heavenly and spiritual level. Here, too, is his model for a Christocentric epic, for there is no doubt that the Son is the greatest example of virtue and the most powerful agent of good in *Paradise Lost*.

*Summary.* The classical tradition gave Milton the epic genre in which he wrote *Paradise Lost*. But various epics within the Bible influenced him to write a domestic and pastoral epic, a satiric epic that elevates God and exposes human failing, and a spiritual epic in which human motifs are given a spiritual identity.

## Notes to Chapter 4

[1]I have taken all my quotations from *Paradise Lost* from Douglas Bush's edition of *The Complete Poetical Works of John Milton* (Boston: Houghton Mifflin, 1965).

[2]Charles Williams, *Reason and Beauty in the Poetic Mind* (Oxford: Oxford UP, 1933), p. 5.

[3]C.S. Lewis, *A Preface to Paradise Lost* (New York: Oxford UP, 1942), p. 40.

[4]Lewis, p. 49.

[5]Barbara Lewalski's book *"Paradise Lost" and the Rhetoric of Literary Forms* (Princeton: Princeton UP, 1985) is rather definitive on the individual genres within *Paradise Lost*. Lewis' *Preface to Paradise Lost* is still the best introduction to Milton's epic genre.

[6]Northrop Frye, *Anatomy of Criticism* (Princeton: Princeton UP, 1957), p. 316.

[7]T. R. Henn, *The Bible as Literature* (New York: Oxford UP, 1970), p. 258.

[8]C.S. Lewis, *The Literary Impact of the Authorized Version* (Philadelphia: Fortress, 1963), p. 15.

[9]Clifford Geertz, "Ritual and Social Change: A Javanese Example," *American Anthropologist* 59 (1957): 33.

[10]Northrop Frye, *The Secular Scripture: A Study of the Structure of Romance* (Cambridge, MA: Harvard UP, 1976), p. 14.

[11]The techniques by which Milton portrays the ideal supernatural (Heaven and Paradise) is the subject of my book *The Apocalyptic Vision in "Paradise Lost"* (Ithaca: Cornell UP, 1970).

[12]James H. Sims, *The Bible in Milton's Epics* (Gainesville: University of Florida, 1962), pp. 9-10.

[13]Lewis, *A Preface to Paradise Lost*, p. 130.

[14]Kester Svendsen, *"Paradise Lost* as Alternative," *Humanities Association Bulletin* 18 (1967): 39.

[15]C.M. Bowra, *From Virgil to Milton* (London: Macmillan, 1965), p. 199.

[16]William Haller, *The Rise of Puritanism* (New York: Harper, 1938), p. 288.

[17]The best discussion of the importance of hierarchy in *Paradise Lost* is Chapter 11 of Lewis' *Preface to Paradise Lost*.

[18]Joseph Addison, *Spectator Paper* No. 369 on *Paradise Lost*, as reprinted in *Milton: The Critical Heritage*, ed. John T. Shawcross (New York: Barnes and Noble, 1970), p. 219.

[19]Douglas Bush, *Paradise Lost in Our Time* (Ithaca: Cornell UP, 1945), pp. 29-30.

[20]John R. Knott, Jr., *Milton's Pastoral Vision: An Approach to Paradise Lost* (Chicago: University of Chicago, 1971), pp. xiii, xv.

[21] This is the conclusion of J.M. Evans, *Paradise Lost and the Genesis Tradition* (Oxford: Oxford UP, 1968), pp. 246-249, 268.

[22] J.B. Broadbent, *Some Graver Subject* (New York: Schocken, 1967), p. 186.

[23] Stanley Fish, *Surprised by Sin: The Reader in Paradise Lost* (New York: St. Martin's, 1967), pp. 86-87.

[24] T. S. Eliot, *On Poetry and Poets* (New York: Farrar, Straus and Cudahy, 1957), p. 177.

[25] The tradition of Adam and Eve as the first Christians is noted by C.A. Patrides, *Milton and the Christian Tradition* (Oxford: Oxford UP, 1966), pp. 127-128.

[26] Bowra, p. 224.

[27] Fish's book *Surprised by Sin* is a sequential reading of the poem slanted around the idea of the guilty reader. The result is a full-scale Christian reading of *Paradise Lost.*

[28] Sims, pp. 170-181, documents all these biblical associations for Satan.

[29] Georgia B. Christopher, *Milton and the Science of the Saints* (Princeton: Princeton UP, 1982), p. 61.

[30] Hugh M. Richmond, *The Christian Revolutionary: John Milton* (Berkeley: University of California, 1974), p. 132.

[31] Lewis, *A Preface to Paradise Lost*, pp. 102-103. Lewis has an utterly engaging chapter on the realistic portrayal of the psychology of evil as we see it in the demonic council in Book 2.

[32] A.J.A. Waldock, *Paradise Lost and Its Critics* (Gloucester, Mass.: Peter Smith, 1959), p. 100.

[33] Erich Auerbach, *Mimesis: The Representation of Reality in Western Literature*, trans. Willard R. Trask (Princeton: Princeton UP, 1953, 1968), pp. 14-15.

[34] For a full discussion of the points that I make in abbreviated form in the pages that follow, see my essay *"Paradise Lost* and Its Biblical Epic Models," in *Milton and Scriptural Tradition: The Bible into Poetry*, ed. James H. Sims and Leland Ryken (Columbia: University of Missouri, 1984), pp. 43-81.

[35] Harold E. Toliver, "Milton's Household Epic," in *Milton Studies IX*, ed. James D. Simmonds (Pittsburgh: University of Pittsburgh Press, 1976), pp. 105-120.

[36] Michael Wilding, "The Last of the Epics: The Rejection of the Heroic in *Paradise Lost* and *Hudibras*," in *Restoration Literature: Critical Approaches*, ed. Harold Love (London: Methuen, 1972), p. 117.

[37] The best treatment of the pastoral element in *Paradise Lost* is Knott's book *Milton's Pastoral Vision.*

[38] John M. Steadman, *Milton and the Renaissance Hero* (Oxford: Oxford UP, 1967), p. v.

[39] Richmond, p. 129.

# Chapter 5

*Poetry and the Christian Life*

## How to Succeed with Poems

❋

1   *The Lord is my shepherd, I shall not want;*
2     *He makes me lie down in green pastures.*
3   *He leads me beside still waters;*
4     *he restores my life.*
5   *He leads me in right paths*
6     *for his name's sake.*
7   *Even though I walk through the valley of deepest darkness,*
8     *I fear no evil;*
9   *for you are with me;*
10     *your rod and staff comfort me.*
11   *You prepare a table before me*
12     *in the presence of my enemies.*
13   *You anoint my head with oil,*
14     *my cup overflows.*
15   *Surely goodness and mercy shall follow me*
16     *all the days of my life;*
17   *and I shall return to the house of the Lord*
18     *as long as I live.*[1]

❋

As I planned this book, I was from the beginning determined to include a chapter on the form of literature that typically gets omitted from discussions of the classics—lyric poetry. Poems are the neglected genre in most people's reading repertoire, yet they stand ready to offer all that

I have ascribed to the classics in my introductory chapter. As my entry into this realm of gold, I have selected the poem that for me has long been the supreme lyric poem of the world, Psalm 23.

*The Form and Content of Poems.* To enjoy poetry, we need to come to it with the right expectations. If we read poetry looking for the same things we expect in a story, we will be endlessly frustrated. Poems are different from stories in both form and content.

At the level of content, for example, a lyric poem is brief. This means that it makes no attempt to cover as much of human experience as a story does. In Psalm 23, the poet wants to make us feel the contentment that comes from resting in the sufficiency of God's provision. That is the only aspect of experience that the poem covers. Because of its brevity, a poem is a moment of awareness, insight, or feeling, not a comprehensive picture of life.

A second feature of the content of a poem is that it consists of either ideas or feelings. Another way of saying this is that a poem is either meditative or affective, either reflective or emotive. A poem might contain snatches of narrative, or it might hint at a story, but it does not (with occasional exceptions) *tell* a story. Psalm 23 catalogs the activities that a shepherd performs for his sheep during the course of a typical day, but it does not follow the format of a story. Instead the psalmist mediates on God's three-fold role as provider, guide, and protector, with a view toward awakening feelings of security and contentment.

The distinctive content of poetry produces its own structure. The basic pattern is theme-and-variation. The theme is the dominant idea, feeling, or situation that unifies the entire poem. The variations on that theme consist of the progressive topical or imagistic units by which the poet develops the theme. The scheme of theme and variation works wonders for our understanding of a poem. It is a lens that brings the whole poem into focus as a unified whole. It also provides an analytic tool as we begin to articulate exactly how each unit contributes to the unifying theme.

Applying this scheme to Psalm 23, we see that the unifying theme is providence—God's provision for his creatures. This theme is announced in the opening line: "The Lord is my shepherd, I shall not want." Because the poet compares God to a shepherd and people to sheep, the basis for his variations is a progression of images that picture a shepherd's daily activities.

The poem begins with the midday resting of the sheep in a lush, shady area (lines 2-4) and is a picture of various types of restoration that God provides for people—physical, emotional, and spiritual. The next six lines develop a journey motif: lines 5-6 are a picture of the shepherd's guidance and lines 7-10 of protection in the midst of the fearful "dark valleys" of life. Provision of food and physical sustenance appears in lines 11-12 in the picture of the prepared table. The last six lines portray a shepherd's activities back at the sheepfold at the end of the day.[2]

Theme-and-variation is the universal pattern that organizes poems. In addition, it may prove useful to know that lyric poets can choose from among four different ways of elaborating their subject. The simplest poems employ repetitive form, maintaining a single principle under different guises with different words and images. Most poems are organized as a contrast or system of contrasts. The catalog or list is a common organizational pattern in poems. Finally, some poems are based on a principle of association in which the poet branches out from an initial subject to one or more related ones. Psalm 23 is a catalog of the shepherd's acts of provision for his sheep, and it implicitly contrasts the shepherd's acts of provision to the dangers that beset the sheep.

*The Language Poets Use.* I have already implied that poets speak a language all their own. An element of strangeness thus characterizes poetry. Poetry employs a tighter syntax than prose does. The poetic idiom is different from ordinary discourse. Poets rearrange the normal order of words, so that (as Owen Barfield puts it) poetry is "a realm of human experience in which such an expression as 'prophets old' may . . . 'mean' something quite different from 'old prophets'."[3] At one level, then, poetry involves what a literary critic calls "the making of un-reality."[4] It creates a world in which empirical fact gives way to things that are not literally true—a world in which God is a shepherd and people are sheep, for example.

Above all, poets think in images (words naming concrete things or actions). In the words of C.S. Lewis,

From Homer, who never omits to tell us that the ships were black and the sea salt, or even wet. . . , poets are always telling us that grass is green, or thunder loud, or lips red. . . . To say that things were blue, or hard, or cool, or foul-smelling, or noisy, is to tell how they affected our senses.[5]

Often the images of poetry are comparisons in the form of either metaphor (an implied comparison, such as "the Lord is my shepherd") or simile (which uses the formula "like" or "as"). In both, A is said to be like B, and it is up to the reader to discover the points of correlation. Stephen Spender, in his famous essay "The Making of a Poem," claimed that "the terrifying challenge" facing the poet is always, "Can I think out the logic of images?"[6]

Interpreting the logic of the imagery is the chief obligation that poetry imposes on a reader. It makes us ask questions like these: Why did the poet use this image for this subject or experience? How is A like B? What meanings do the images and comparisons communicate? These questions are an invitation to discover the meaning that the poet has entrusted to the reader. If poets did not think this a risk worth taking, they would not speak in image and metaphor. A poem is a close relative of the riddle—a curiosity that invites us to unravel its mystery.

The poetic idiom enables poetry to be the most compressed form of discourse. Poetry communicates much more per line than prose of any type does (whether expository or narrative). The recurrent unit in a story or play is the episode or scene. In poetry it is the image, figure of speech, or picture. The recurrent syntactic unit in prose is the sentence; in poetry it is the line—a much shorter unit. The need to unpackage the meaning of individual words and images makes reading poetry a meditative or contemplative act in a way that reading a story is not. Poetry requires slow reading, in contrast to the faster pace of narrative. Instead of hurrying to find out what happens next, we must, as we read Psalm 23, stop to consider what kinds of human provision are embodied in such metaphoric pictures as sheep resting in green pastures beside still waters or being led on safe ("right") paths.

The greater concentration of meaning that poetry contains is matched by its higher proportion of artistry. The usual elements of artistic form—unity, balance, symmetry, progression, pattern, design, intricacy—appear in more compressed form in poetry than in other forms of writing. Psalm 23, for example, is written in the verse form known as parallelism—thought couplets or triplets in which two or more lines written in similar grammatical structure form a unit. The pattern of theme-and-variation and the terse catalog of the shepherd's activities provide more artistic beauty per passage than other types of writing do, just as a Persian carpet has more artistic form per square foot than other carpets have.

*Is Poetry Elitist?* From all that I have said, it may appear that poetry is a difficult and unnatural form of discourse. There is a sense in which this is true. Poetry is a specialized use of language. But so are other forms of discourse. Poetry is simply less common to most people and harder to compose. At least a third of the Bible is written in poetic form. Its prevalence shows that God wants people to understand and enjoy it.

Poetry is not elitist. It is as capable of being folk literature as stories are. In virtually every ancient culture except the Hebraic, poetry preceded prose as an accomplished form of discourse. As Northrop Frye has observed, "In the history of literature we notice that developed techniques of verse normally preceded, sometimes by centuries, developed techniques of prose. How could this happen if prose were really the language of ordinary speech?"[7] Even the strange diction of poetry was once close to the folk mentality. Barfield notes that most words were originally poetic (imagistic or metaphoric):

> If we trace the meanings of a great many words . . . as far back as etymology can take us, we are at once made to realize that an overwhelming proportion, if not all, of them referred in earlier days to one of these two things—a solid, sensible object, or some animal (probably human) activity. Examples abound on every page of the dictionary.[8]

In an earlier discussion of fantasy I noted that the love of fantasy is a taste that one either has or does not have. Some people will never see the point of a story about talking animals or a one-eyed monster. Poetry is not in quite the same category. It is an acquired taste in the sense that one needs to learn the conventions of poetry in order to understand

and enjoy it, but once one has mastered those conventions, poetry becomes a necessary staple in any literary person's diet. I have never met a person who claims that he or she *used* to like poetry.

To become a lifelong lover of poetry, one needs only to learn to read it. It is different from other forms of literature, and this difference should be relished as part of its beauty, delight, and power. Poetry is like turkey on Thanksgiving Day—something different from the ordinary, but not unexpected or unmanageable once we understand that it is a special ritual. Poetry is language on its best behavior.

Once we open ourselves to what poetry offers us, we will find that it particularly meets one of the criteria of a classic that I mentioned in the opening pages of this book—the quality of being irreplaceable by any substitute, of creating a hunger that only it can satisfy. This, in fact, is the specific slant that I wish to give this chapter that discusses poetry— the idea that among the various types of literature, poetry offers a unique kind of beauty and insight.

### Poetry and the Common Life

One of the qualities that defines a classic is that it touches upon life powerfully. The fact that poets speak a language all their own should not obscure that poetry is about recognizable human experience. As M.L. Rosenthal puts it,

> Poetry [is] a natural human activity and state of awareness. . . . Too often poetry is thought to be impossibly far apart from ordinary human existence. Anyone's mind is a teeming gallery of sensations and memories. . . . We all know the taste of things sweet or bland or sour, we all have known rage. . . . A rich confusion of awareness underlies all human feeling, and the language for it surges all around us. The poet reaches into that rich confusion toward the wellspring of the surging speech of life. That is why all real poetry, even when difficult or complex, has so much to say that comes from the depths of normal life. It is always in touch with the intrinsic music of our everyday world.[9]

Of course a poem's brevity means that it covers less of human experience than a play or story does. When we read a poem we relive a fragment of experience and a moment of awareness, not the whole experience that narrative allows us to relive. A poem is a moment of heightened feeling or insight, expressed in heightened language. In a day when the media have accustomed us to short bytes, a poem should seem natural to us. Of course a poem differs from a one-minute television segment by inviting us to go back to it, to look at it carefully in search for more and more levels of artistry or meaning, to memorize it.

For all its far-flung language, poetry deals with recognizable human experience just as thoroughly as Homer's *Odyssey* or Shakespeare's *Macbeth* does. To illustrate, I begin with a sad poem about Lucy written by William Wordsworth two centuries ago:

*She dwelt among the untrodden ways*
    *Beside the springs of Dove.*
*A maid whom there were none to praise*
    *And very few to love;*

*A violet by a mossy stone*
    *Half hidden from the eye!*
*—Fair as a star, when only one*
    *Is shining in the sky.*

*She lived unknown, and few could know*
    *When Lucy ceased to be;*
*But she is in her grave, and, oh,*
    *The difference to me!*

Several common human experiences merge here. The first two stanzas capture the experience of loneliness. The very images used to portray Lucy are examples of this. She is compared to the obscure origin of a river, a violet (which grows in the shade), moss (which also grows in relative darkness), and a solitary star in the sky. In the final stanza the poem moves to the ultimate loneliness, death. The final experience that the poem expresses is grief and a sense of loss.

Human love has been a natural subject for poetry through the centuries. The Victorian poet Dante Gabriel Rossetti wrote the following poem on this experience:

*Your hands lie open in the long fresh grass—*
    *The finger-points look through like rosy blooms;*
    *Your eyes smile peace. The pasture gleams and glooms*
*'Neath billowing skies that scatter and amass.*
*All round our nest, far as the eye can pass,*
    *Are golden kingcup-fields with silver edge*
    *Where the cow-parsley skirts the hawthorn hedge.*
*'Tis visible silence, still as the hourglass.*
*Deep in the sun-searched growths the dragonfly*
*Hangs like a blue thread loosened from the sky—*
    *So this winged hour is dropped to us from above.*
*Oh! clasp we to our hearts, for deathless dower,*
*This close-companioned inarticulate hour*
    *When twofold silence was the song of love.*

Poetry is always an interpretive presentation of experience, not an objective portrayal of it. It is a distillation of experience, not a recording of everything that happens. In this poem, Rossetti has distilled the serenity and contentedness of love.

Several other strategies of poetry are evident in the poem. One is the impulse to show rather than tell. In other words, the poet lavishes his attention on concrete description, not on explanation or abstraction. On the surface the poem is more of a nature poem than a love poem. This suggests that poetry achieves its effects by a certain indirectness. The poet here speaks a language of nature, intending that we transmute our sentiment for nature into romantic sentiment. Poetry is also an affective medium. Rossetti channels his efforts into making us feel the serenity of happy love. The result is a moment of heightened awareness about romantic love.

Nature is as common a subject for poetry as romantic love. Here is how William Wordsworth expressed the experience of a sunrise on Westminster Bridge in London:

*Earth has not anything to show more fair:*
*Dull would he be of soul who could pass by*
*A sight so touching in its majesty;*

*This city now doth, like a garment, wear*
*The beauty of the morning; silent, bare,*
*Ships, towers, domes, theaters, and temples lie*
*Open unto the fields, and to the sky,*
*All bright and glittering in the smokeless air.*
*Never did sun more beautifully steep*
*In his first splendor, valley, rock, or hill;*
*Ne'er saw I, never felt, a calm so deep!*
*The river glideth at his own sweet will:*
*Dear God! the very houses seem asleep;*
*And all that mighty heart is lying still!*

We notice first the poet's ability to paint a scene with words. This is part of the magic of poetry. We notice again the impulse to be affective—to make us feel a certain way toward the subject. In fact, this poem alternates back and forth between expression of feeling (lines 1-3 and 9-11) and description of the scene (lines 4-8 and 12-14).

But most poetry is more than affective. It also conveys an insight into the experience that the poet has chosen to portray. Wordsworth's poem is built around an implied paradox—that the city can also be a part of nature. We share a moment of surprised discovery with the poet. The mechanical, frenzied city for once is naturalized. The key line in this regard is the one that describes the city as being "open unto the fields, and to the sky." I return to my point that poetry is a fragment of experience, a moment of perception. For a moment life is captured, as with a camera click, and we understand a tiny part of it.

Because poetry is affective and subjective, one of its richest subjects is the inner weather of the human feelings and thoughts. In this it shows its superiority to narrative, which generally looks at experience from the outside. Here, for example, is how Emily Dickinson captures the paralysis of feeling that accompanies grief or shock more generally:

*After great pain, a formal feeling comes—*
*The Nerves sit ceremonious, like Tombs—*
*The stiff Heart questions was it He, that bore,*
*And Yesterday, or Centuries before?*

*The Feet, mechanical, go round—*
*Of Ground, or Air or Ought—*
*A Wooden way*
*Regardless grown,*
*A Quartz contentment, like a stone—*

*This is the Hour of Lead—*
*Remembered, if outlived,*
*As Freezing persons recollect the Snow—*
*First—Chill—then Stupor—then the letting go—*

Here, surely, is what grief *feels* like, both emotionally and physically. To communicate that feeling, the poet builds her poem around images of hardness, numbness, and parts of the human body.

By focusing on specific experiences and insights, poetry is able to delight us by uncovering corners of human experience that ordinarily escape our awareness and that we might not expect to find expressed in literature. Consider this poem that John Keats entitled "On First Looking into Chapman's Homer"—a poem that actually deals with something much more universal than simply the occasion named in the title:

*Much have I traveled in the realms of gold,*
    *And many goodly states and kingdoms seen;*
    *Round many western islands have I been*
*Which bards in fealty to Apollo hold.*
*Oft of one wide expanse had I been told*
    *That deep-browed Homer ruled as his demesne;*
    *Yet did I never breathe its pure serene*
*Till I heard Chapman speak out loud and bold:*
*Then felt I like some watcher of the skies*
    *When a new planet swims into his ken;*
*Or like stout Cortez when with eagle eyes*
    *He stared at the Pacific—and all his men*
*Looked at each other with a wild surmise—*
    *Silent, upon a peak in Darien.*

The poem is not about Homer or Chapman's translations of Homer or even Keats' reading of that translation. It is about the rapture of discovery, and the concluding similes make sure that we will thus universalize the experience that occasioned the poem. This is what it feels like to discover something for the first time.

*Summary.* I have presented specimens of the kinds of experience that poems can add to our lives. Poems should be relished for the individual insights and experiences they give us, no matter how small and no matter how specialized their subject matter may be. Robert Frost stated the case for the importance of such writing very well: "A poem . . . ends in a clarification of life—not necessarily a great clarification, such as sects and cults are founded on, but in a momentary stay against confusion."[10] Mathew Arnold has a similarly good description of the kind of delight and profit that such literature can afford:

> The grand power of poetry is its . . . power of so dealing with things as to awaken in us a wonderfully full, new, and intimate sense of them, and of our relations with them. When this sense is awakened in us, . . . we feel ourselves to be in contact with the essential nature of those objects, to be no longer bewildered and oppressed by them, but to have their secret, and to be in harmony with them.[11]

### The Artistry of Poetry

I said earlier that poetry possesses the elements of artistic form in a more concentrated manner than even a story or play does. It invites a purely artistic response to its beauty. C.S. Lewis rightly speaks of the "phrase-by-phrase deliciousness" of poetry.[12] Christian poet Gerard Manley Hopkins claimed that the beauty of poetry exists "for its own sake and interest even over and above its interest of meaning."[13]

As Exhibit A, we can consider Tennyson's famous poem of resignation entitled "Crossing the Bar":

> *Sunset and evening star,*
> *And one clear call for me!*
> *And may there be no moaning of the bar,*
> *When I put out to sea,*

But such a tide as moving seems asleep,
    Too full for sound and foam,
When that which drew from out the boundless deep
    Turns again home.

Twilight and evening bell,
    And after that the dark!
And may there be no sadness of farewell,
    When I embark.

For though from out our bourne of Time and Place
    The flood may bear me far,
I hope to see my Pilot face to face
    When I have crossed the bar.

The subject of this poem is the anticipation of death and what lies beyond it. Tennyson wrote the poem on the inside of a used envelope during the twenty-nine-minute ferry crossing from Lymington to the Isle of Wight at the age of eighty. Although the poem "came in a moment," its artistry is amazing.

To begin, the poem is built around a controlling image or metaphor. The poet compares his anticipated death to a ship that is crossing a sand bar as it moves from a harbor or river to the ocean. Since the sand bar is the crucial point in such a navigational feat, the speaker in the poem expresses his desire for a peaceful death by picturing a tide that is so full that the water moves imperceptibly over the sand bar, allowing the boat to make a smooth transition. Every stanza in the poem makes some reference to this controlling navigational metaphor.

The organization of the poem reveals a careful symmetry. The first two lines set the scene and introduce the controlling metaphor, while the next six state the speaker's prayer for a peaceful death. Stanza 3 repeats this same pattern of situation followed by prayer, with each getting a pair of lines. The final stanza ends the poem on a note of resolution by offering the reason for the speaker's calm acceptance of his approaching death.

Balancing the controlling metaphor is a series of striking individual metaphors, each one of them an archetype filled with evocative associations. The end of life is a sunset, evening, darkness. Death is a vast, unknown sea. Life is a journey and God a pilot. The life beyond is a home. All of these archetypal images work together to give the poem its affective power.

The indirectness of the poem is part of its artistry. The subject of the poem is never named but only hinted at through the images. The result of this understatement is an even greater mood of sadness, mystery, and submission.

Finally, the verse form of the poem is part of its perfection. The verse form—quatrains whose alternate lines rhyme—remains constant throughout the poem. But Tennyson plays this element of sameness off against a pattern in which the number of poetic feet per line varies in each stanza (3, 3, 5, 3 in the first stanza; 5, 3, 5, 2 in the second stanza; 3, 3, 5, 2 in the third stanza; 5, 3, 5, 3 in the final stanza).

Tennyson's classic poem of resignation shows an important feature of lyric poems, namely, that the simple is also a form of the beautiful. Compared to the grandness of the other works that I discuss in this book, a poem might seem too small to be truly impressive. But the very concentration of artistic form in a poem can make it just as much a classic at the level of artistic beauty as a longer work is.

A poem entitled "Virtue," by the Renaissance Anglican poet George Herbert, illustrates this well:

*Sweet day, so cool, so calm, so bright,*
*The bridal of the earth and sky;*
*The dew shall weep thy fall tonight,*
    *For thou must die.*

*Sweet rose, whose hue angry and brave*
*Bids the rash gazer wipe his eye;*
*Thy root is ever in its grave,*
    *And thou must die.*

*Sweet spring, full of sweet days and roses,*
*A box where sweets compacted lie;*
*My music shows ye have your closes,*
    *And all must die.*

> *Only a sweet and virtuous soul,*
> *Like seasoned timber, never gives;*
> *But though the whole world turn to coal,*
>    *Then chiefly lives.*

The theme of Herbert's seemingly simple poem is that the virtuous soul is the only earthly thing that is permanent. Around this conventional religious sentiment Herbert creates an artistic masterpiece that conceals its artistry under an ostensibly simple surface.

The big structural principle in the poem is contrast. For three stanzas Herbert conducts a eulogy for nature—a lament in which three personified representatives for nature prove weak opponents against time and mutability. These three stanzas could stand as a self-contained poem, but in the final stanza the poet introduces the real subject of the poem. The nature stanzas turn out to be part of a foil that heightens the poem's real subject—the permanence of the virtuous soul.

Progression is also a part of the artistry of the poem. For three stanzas we conduct a process of elimination in which three distinguished spokespersons for nature are weighed in the balance and found wanting. The fourth stanza states a quiet exception and brings the growing tension to a resolution. Another pattern in the poem is that time is measured in progressively larger units, as we move from a day to the life span of a rose to an entire spring season to eternity.

Most intricate of all is the symmetry that pervades the stanzas. The equivalent line in each stanza serves an identical purpose. The opening line names a conventional subject and declares it "sweet." The second line of each stanza develops the image further. The third line delivers a message of doom. And the final line of each stanza announces a prophecy—three times a prophecy of death, the last time a prophecy of life.

The versification of poetry is also part of its artistry. Herbert's poem follows a simple *abab* rhyme scheme. The "b" sound is carried forward throughout the first three stanzas, but it is dropped in the final stanza, just as the content of this stanza is a reversal from the previous three stanzas. In addition simply to striking us as a clever handling of language, the ryhme scheme of the poem highlights the central contrast of the poem, as in successive stanzas we see the juxtaposition of the words "bright" and "night," "brave" and "grave," "roses" and "closes," "soul" and "coal."

I have chosen two simple poems to illustrate the artistry that poems possess. Poems contains a concentration of artistic form that other forms of literature do not regularly possess. The American poet Edgar Allen Poe said that beauty is "the province of the poem," and he defined poetry as "the rhymical creation of beauty."[14]

## The Poetry of Protest

Literature as a whole presents a double vision. It is a picture of the world that the human race fears and is trying to get away from, and a picture of the world for which it longs and toward which it aspires. We can organize the content of poetry around this double vision. On one side, therefore, the voice of protest is strong in poetry.

Because poetry is so replete with artistic form and beauty, people have sometimes gotten the impression that poetry avoids the negative side of life. This is untrue. Poetry expresses the tragic spirit as powerfully as a tragic drama does, though on a smaller scale. Here, for example, is how John Keats expressed the tragedy of human life in a stanza of one of his great odes ("Ode to a Nightingale"). As he addresses the nightingale, the poet expresses the desire to

Fade far away, dissolve, and quite forget
   What thou among the leaves hast never known,
The weariness, the fever, and the fret
   Here, where men sit and hear each other groan;
Where palsy shakes a few, sad, last gray hairs,
   Where youth grows pale, and specter-thin, and dies;
     Where but to think is to be full of sorrow
      And leaden-eyed despairs,
   Where Beauty cannot keep her lustrous eyes,
     Or new Love pine at them beyond tomorrow.

A poem like this is the product of dissatisfaction crossed with longing. It expresses the fears and anxieties of the human spirit. This is part of the truthfulness of poetry.

Usually the protest of poetry is more specific than such a generalized protest against the sheer misery of human existence. Not surprisingly, war has been a major subject of protest poetry. Randall Jarrell expressed that protest in a poem entitled "The Death of the Ball Turret Gunner":

*From my mother's sleep I fell into the State*
*And I hunched in its belly till my wet fur froze.*
*Six miles from earth, loosed from its dream of life,*
*I woke to black flak and the nightmare fighters.*
*When I died they washed me out of the turret with a hose.*

Unlike an editorial denouncing war, this poem expresses its protest in images and metaphors. The soldier in the ball turret of the plane is portrayed as a fetus in a womb. The objects of protest include the impersonal power of the State (note that the word is capitalized) over a person's life, the barbarism of war, the denial of youthful dreams, the terror of attack, and the loss of identity as well as life in the soldier's death.

Many protest poems are variations on the theme of the failure of life to match the ideal. Regardless of the specific subject—hopeless or lost love, depression of spirit, loss of religious faith—the more general theme is that life does not satisfy the human longings that it arouses. Matthew Arnold's poem "Dover Beach" is a classic example of this poetry of disaffection, made all the more poignant when we know that the occasion of the poem was Arnold's honeymoon trip to the Continent, when he and his bride stayed overnight in a sea-front hotel in Dover:

*The sea is calm tonight.*
*The tide is full, the moon lies fair*
*Upon the straits; on the French coast the light*
*Gleams and is gone; the cliffs of England stand,*
*Glimmering and vast, out in the tranquil bay.*
*Come to the window, sweet is the night-air!*
*Only, from the long line of spray*
*Where the sea meets the moon-blanched land,*
*Listen! you hear the grating roar*
*Of pebbles which the waves draw back, and fling,*

*At their return, up the high strand,*
*Begin, and cease, and then again begin,*
*With tremulous cadence slow, and bring*
*The eternal note of sadness in.*

*Sophocles long ago*
*Heard it on the Aegean, and it brought*
*Into his mind the turbid ebb and flow*
*Of human misery; we*
*Find also in the sound a thought,*
*Hearing it by this distant northern sea.*

*The Sea of Faith*
*Was once, too, at the full, and round earth's shore*
*Lay like the folds of a bright girdle furled.*
*But now I only hear*
*Its melancholy, long, withdrawing roar,*
*Retreating, to the breath*
*Of the night-wind, down the vast edges drear*
*And naked shingles of the world.*

*Ah, love, let us be true*
*To one another! for the world, which seems*
*To lie before us like a land of dreams,*
*So various, so beautiful, so new,*
*Hath really neither joy, nor love, nor light,*
*Nor certitude, nor peace, nor help for pain;*
*And we are here as on a darkling plain*
*Swept with confused alarms of struggle and flight,*
*Where ignorant armies clash by night.*

Three of the four stanzas begin on a positive note and then reverse the mood later in the stanza. The result is to make us feel betrayed by the dreams that life seems to offer and then withdraws from us.

We might ask how a Christian reader should assimilate this poetry of protest. Such poetry says part of what a Christian, too, would want to say. Within a doctrinal framework of God's creation of the world as good in principle and the human fall as something that brought death and sin into the world, a Christian also protests against much that happens in the world.

But a Christian reader will often find that the poetry of protest does not tell the whole truth about life. Protest poetry often assigns misery to the wrong cause. A poem like "Dover Beach" even asserts the inadequacy of the Christian faith. More customary is the tendency of protest poetry to imply that there is no consolation or escape from the misery and fallenness of life, whereas Christianity postulates an eternal spiritual realm that is available to people both now and in a life to come. But even when the poetry of protest fails to tell the whole truth, it serves an invaluable role for a Christian reader: it clarifies the human situation to which the Christian faith speaks.

## The Poetry of Human Consolation

In its highest reaches, poetry combines beauty of poetic form and fragments of human insight with the Christian faith. But poems do not have to reach that height to be a treasure in a Christian's life. Christians are members of the human race as well as citizens of a heavenly kingdom. They live not only by the ultimate consolation (God and eternal life), but also by the earthly consolations that bind them to the human race.

Nature is surely one of these consolations. It has been a frequent subject of poetry, as in the opening stanzas of Matthew Arnold's poem "Lines Written in Kensington Gardens":

*In this lone, open glade I lie,*
*Screened by deep boughs on either hand;*
*And at its end, to stay the eye,*
*Those black-crowned, red-boled pine trees stand!*

*Birds here make song, each bird has his,*
*Across the girdling city's hum.*
*How green under the boughs it is!*
*How thick the tremulous sheep-cries come!*

*Sometimes a child will cross the glade*
*To take his nurse his broken toy:*

*Sometimes a thrush flit overhead*
*Deep in her unknown day's employ.*

*Here at my feet what wonders pass,*
*What endless, active life is here!*
*What blowing daisies, fragrant grass!*
*An air-stirred forest, fresh and clear.*

Nature poets can make moments immortal, as Wordsworth does at the beginning of one of his sonnets:

*It is a beauteous evening, calm and free,*
*The holy time is quiet as a Nun*
*Breathless with adoration; the broad sun*
*Is sinking down in its tranquillity;*
*The gentleness of heaven broods o'er the Sea.*

The effect of such poetry is to awaken our longing for the beauty of nature.

The idea of longing is an important part of what I mean by the human consolation that poetry expresses. We might say that it is a major function of poetry to awaken such human longings. Wordsworth, for example, in a passage that asserts that "the thought of our past years in me doth breed / Perpetual benediction," has this metaphoric description of the strength that can come from positive images from childhood:

*Hence in a season of clam weather*
*Though inland far we be,*
*Our souls have sight of that immortal sea*
*Which brought us hither,*
*Can in a moment travel thither,*
*And see the Children sport upon the shore,*
*And hear the mighty waters rolling evermore.*

Of course poetry cannot by itself satisfy the longings that it awakens. Such satisfaction can come only from the Great Consolation. But if it is true that humans are the "wanting creatures" in the dual sense of desiring and lacking, poetry can uniquely express some of the deepest human desires and needs.

Human love has rivalled nature as the human consolation to which the human race turns. Shakespeare's sonnet 116 celebrates the permanence and reliability of true love or friendship:

*Let me not to the marriage of true minds*
*Admit impediments. Love is not love*
*Which alters when it alteration finds,*
*Or bends with the remover to remove.*
*Oh no! It is an ever-fixed mark*
*That looks on tempests and is never shaken.*
*It is the star to every wandering bark,*
*Whose worth's unknown, although his height be taken.*
*Love's not Time's fool, though rosy lips and cheeks*
*Within his bending sickle's compass come.*
*Love alters not with his brief hours and weeks,*
*But bears it out even to the edge of doom.*
  *If this be error and upon me proved,*
  *I never writ, nor man ever loved.*

As the poetry of human consolation shows, poetry is a great bonding agent for the human race, not only in the sense that it puts us in touch with the concrete surfaces of everyday experience, but also because it is faithful to the common experiences of the heart and mind. This is a kind of knowledge and affirmation that is important for Christians, too.

### The Poetry of Christian Devotion

We come, finally, to the type of poetry that is likely to hold a very treasured place in any Christian reader's experience. I call it the poetry of Christian devotion, even at the risk of conjuring up images of "devotional verse" that afflicts some religious periodicals and greeting cards. By "devotional poetry" I mean great poetry that expresses devotion to God or the truths of the Christian faith. Its purpose is to give fresh expression to the timeless truths of the Christian faith and to incarnate some aspect of Christian experience in a form in which we can share it.

As is true of poems generally, a poem of Christian devotion can be either reflective or affective. Milton's sonnet on his blindness is a reflective poem in which the poet reenacts his thought process in poetic form:

*When I consider how my light is spent,*
*Ere half my days, in this dark world and wide,*
*And that one talent which is death to hide*
*Lodged with me useless, though my soul more bent*
*To serve therewith my Maker, and present*
*My true account, lest he returning chide,*
*"Doth God exact day-labor, light denied?"*
*I fondly ask. But Patience to prevent*
*That murmur, soon replies: "God doth not need*
*Either man's work or his own gifts; who best*
*Bear his mild yoke, they serve him best. His state*
*Is kingly: thousands at his bidding speed,*
*And post o'er land and ocean without rest;*
*They also serve who only stand and wait."*

This poem contains Milton's response to his blindness (which became total when Milton was forty-four). It is based on a principle of a problem and its solution. The umbrella concept in the poem is acceptable service to God, with the key word "serve" appearing three times.

The premise in the first seven and half lines is that God requires active service. In elaborating this thought, the poet draws heavily on the parables in Matthew about the day-workers in the vineyard and about the master who entrusted his money (in the form of talents) to three stewards. In the concluding movement of the poem, the speaker finds an alternate type of acceptable service—a service of submission and worship. Milton's poem is the most famous poem of submission in the English language. Although that submission focuses on a specific person facing a specific crisis, the biblical allusions and Christian attitudes in the poem ensure that the experience is also universalized. Any reader can "walk" into such a poem and make it personally applicable.

The recognizable Christian experience embodied in John Donne's poem "Batter My Heart" is the longing for sanctification:

*Batter my heart, three-personed God, for you*
*As yet but knock, breathe, shine, and seek to mend;*
*That I may rise and stand, o'erthrow me, and bend*
*Your force to break, blow, burn and make me new.*
*I, like an usurped town, to another due,*
*Labor to admit you, but oh, to no end;*
*Reason, your viceroy in me, me should defend,*
*But is captived, and proves weak or untrue.*
*Yet dearly I love you, and would be loved fain,*
*But am betrothed unto your enemy:*
*Divorce me, untie, or break that knot again,*
*Take me to you, imprison me, for I*
*Except you enthrall me, never shall be free,*
*Nor ever chaste, except you ravish me.*

The Christian experience lying behind the poem is what Paul in the New Testament calls the struggle between the flesh and the spirit, but within the logic of the poem the combatants are the speaker and Satan. Unable to win the battle on his own resources, the speaker utters his poetic prayer to God to enter the fray on his behalf and win the battle for him. This is a poem about grace, built around the rescue motif.

The poet develops his theme in a three-part movement. For four lines he petitions God to "make me new." Six lines then describe the speaker's current situation. The final four lines return to the petitionary mode, with the kernel idea being "take me to you."

Like any true poet, Donne embodies his argument in images and metaphors. In the first four lines he speaks the language of a metal tinker mending pots and pans. Then for four lines he compares himself to a besieged city. From that we move to the imagery of courtship and marriage. We conclude with the violent imagery of imprisonment and rape. The paradoxes at the end (the speaker will never be free unless God imprisons him, never chaste or pure in his loyalty unless God rapes him) are rooted in the paradoxical language of the New Testament. Perhaps we can catch in this a hint of the role that Christian poetry can play in a reader's life. God commands us to sing a new song. The Christian poet expresses the timeless truths and experiences of the

Christian faith in a new form, thereby rescuing them from the inattention that always threatens something that has become overly familiar.

For a final illustration of Christian devotional poetry I have selected a poem entitled "God's Grandeur," written by the Victorian poet Gerard Manley Hopkins:

> The world is charged with the grandeur of God.
>> It will flame out, like shining from shook foil;
>> It gathers to a greatness, like the ooze of oil
> Crushed. Why do men then now not reck his rod?
> Generations have trod, have trod, have trod;
>> And all is seared with trade; bleared, smeared with toil;
>> And wears man's smudge and shares man's smell; the soil
> Is bare now, nor can foot feel, being shod.
> And for all this, nature is never spent;
>> There lives the dearest freshness deep down things;
> And though the last lights off the black West went
>> Oh, morning, at the brown brink eastward, springs—
> Because the Holy Ghost over the bent
>> World broods with warm breast and with ah! bright wings.

The topic of the poem is the permanent freshness of nature. The specific theme is that nature thus declares the grandeur of God. The structure of the poem is again a three-part movement: four lines assert God's grandeur in nature, four more lines contrast that grandeur to the weariness and barrenness that people have introduced into the world, and the final six lines return to a description of how God's Spirit creates a perpetual freshness in nature.

This conventional subject matter becomes a classic through the poem's imagery and sound effects. To say that nature is "charged" with the grandeur of God, for example, makes three simultaneous claims: (1) nature is energized by the granduer of God; (2) nature actively assaults people with the grandeur of God as an army charges an opponent; (3) nature carries the responsibility to declare the glory of God. This sense of brilliant discharge of energy is continued in the picture of light glinting or flaming out from a piece of gold foil. Balancing this charged imagery is the picture of richness that slowly grows on a person, "like the ooze of oil crushed" from olives.

Equally memorable is the picture of human devastation of nature in the middle of the poem. The repetition of the clause "have trod" weighs us down with sheer monotony. In contrast to the brilliant light of the first two lines of the poem, we now have the imagery of things being bleared, smeared, and smudged. Internal rhymes and alliteration in lines six and seven reinforce the impact of the utterance. A key allusion to Moses at the burning bush climaxes the charge against the human race: the world of nature is holy ground, but the human race refuses to take off its shoes in reverence before that holiness.

The concluding movement reasserts God's control over nature. Echoing Genesis 1:2, the poet paints a picture of the Holy Spirit as creator of the continuing freshness of nature. The world is "bent," not only physically, but also morally—a crooked and perverse world. But with each sunrise the Holy Spirit broods over the world just as surely as it brooded on the face of the deep at the beginning of God's creation of the world.

*Summary.* As I conclude this chapter, I do so in an awareness of how lightly I have touched the surface of a great topic. My goal has been to plant in my reader's mind the possibility that poems, too, can be small classics, and that our reading experience is impoverished without a steady diet of poetry.

When the Renaissance poet Sir Philip Sidney found himself called to defend poetry against its detractors, he cited biblical poetry as a sign that God wants us to have poetry in our lives. He then concluded that if people will simply inquire into the nature of poetry they will conclude that it is something that "deserveth not to be scourged out of the Church of God."[15] Sidney was right: poetry is one of God's richest gifts to the human race and to the church.

## Notes to Chapter 5

[1] I have provided my own translation of Psalm 23.

[2] For a complete reading of Psalm 23 that explains my brief outline of the poem here, see my book *Words of Delight: A Literary Introduction to the Bible* (Grand Rapids: Baker, 1987), pp. 169-176.

[3]Owen Barfield, *Poetic Diction: A Study in Meaning* (New York: McGraw-Hill, 1964), p. 41.

[4]Roger Cardinal, *Figures of Reality: A Perspective on the Poetic Imagination* (London: Croom Helm, 1981), pp. 34-44. This entire book is an excellent study of the mingled reality and unreality of poetry.

[5]C.S. Lewis, *Christian Reflections* (Grand Rapids: Eerdmans, 1967), pp. 131-132.

[6]Stephen Spender, "The Making of a Poem," in *Critiques and Essays in Criticism 1920-1948*, ed. Robert Wooster Stallman (New York: Ronald, 1949), p. 23.

[7]Northrop Frye, *The Well-Tempered Critic* (Bloomington: Indiana UP, 1963), p. 18.

[8]Barfield, pp. 63-64.

[9]M.L. Rosenthal, *Poetry and the Common Life* (New York: Oxford UP, 1974), pp. 3, 10.

[10]Robert Frost, "The Figure a Poem Makes," in *Writers on Writing*, ed. Walter Allen (Boston: The Writer, Inc., 1948), p. 22.

[11]Matthew Arnold, "Maurice de Guerin," as excerpted in *The Norton Anthology of English Literature*, 4th edition, ed. M. H. Abrams (New York: W. W. Norton, 1979), 2:1423.

[12]C.S. Lewis, "Edmund Spenser," in *Major British Writers*, ed. G.B. Harrison (New York: Harcourt, 1959): 1:102.

[13]Gerard Manley Hopkins, "Poetry and Verse," as quoted in *Gerard Manley Hopkins: The Major Poems*, ed. Walford Davies (London: J. M. Dent and Sons, 1979), p. 38.

[14]Edgar Allen Poe, "The Poetic Principle," in *Criticism: The Major Statements*, ed. Charles Kaplan (New York: St. Martin's, 1975), p. 388.

[15]Sir Philip Sidney, "An Apology for Poetry," in *Criticism: The Major Statements*, ed. Kaplan, p. 113.

# Chapter 6

## Hawthorne's The Scarlet Letter:
## What Is a Christian Classic?

### "As if the Universe Were Gazing at a Scarlet Token"

✳

*It was an obscure night of early May. . . . The town was all asleep. There was no peril of discovery. . . .*

*While standing on the scaffold, in this vain show of expiation, Mr. Dimmesdale was overcome with a great horror of mind, as if the universe were gazing at a scarlet token on his naked breast, right over his heart. On that spot, in very truth, there was, and there had long been, the gnawing and poisonous tooth of bodily pain. . . .*

*[Hester] silently ascended the steps, and stood on the platform, holding little Pearl by the hand. The minister felt for the child's other hand, and took it. The moment that he did so, there came what seemed a tumultuous rush of new life, other life than his own, pouring like a torrent into his heart . . . .*

*The wooden houses, with their jutting stories and quaint gable-peaks; the doorsteps and thresholds, with the early grass springing up about them; the garden-plots, black with freshly turned earth; the wheel-track, little worn, and, even in the market-place, margined with green on either side—all were visible. . . . And there stood the minister, with his hand over his heart; and Hester Prynne, with the embroidered letter glimmering on her bosom; and little Pearl, herself a symbol, and the connecting link between the two. . . .*

*[Dimmesdale] was . . . aware that little Pearl was pointing her finger towards old Roger Chillingworth, who stood at no great distance from the scaffold.*[1]

✳

This excerpt comes from the middle chapter of *The Scarlet Letter*. It is the scene in which Rev. Dimmesdale, overcome by guilt about his sins of adultery and concealment, goes to the scaffold on which Hester had been publicly humiliated to conduct a nighttime vigil of penitence.

Hawthorne's story is the great American classic. It was published in 1850, at the high tide of the Romantic movement in American literature. Yet it combines this Romantic strand with the influence of the Puritan past.

The story is set two centuries before the time of its writing, in the mid-seventeenth century. The physical setting is Puritan New England, specifically Boston. We are constantly aware of the small Puritan village on the edge of the wilderness. The second paragraph of the novel introduces us to the prison, cemetery, and church, symbolizing the Puritan drama of sin, death, and redemption.

Purtain beliefs and institutions are also important in the story. The story accepts the reality of such basic Christian doctrines as God, sin, judgment, forgiveness, salvation, and the spirit world of angels and demons. The Puritan institutions of church, minister, governor, city magistrates, and the pillory (place of punishment) are the social world of the story. The Puritan institution of the public confession of sin figures prominently in the climax of the story.

The very title of the story draws attention to the fact that the story is about sin and its punishment. The sin, as everyone knows, is adultery, but this is not a story about sex or adultery. There are no erotic scenes. The focus of this crime and punishment story is the moral and psychological consequences of the adultery in the lives of the characters in the story. It is a story of the consciousness of sin.

The scene of the midnight vigil on the scaffold includes all four principal actors in the drama. Hester Prynne, wearer of the scarlet letter in punishment of her adultery, is the protagonist of the first half of the story. Hers is a story of revealed sin that wins a humanistically conceived penitence and renewal.

Her partner in the adultery, Rev. Arthur Dimmesdale, becomes the protagonist of the second half of the story. His is a story of concealed sin that leads to spiritual and psychic collapse. Pearl, the offspring of the adultery, represents inherited sin. And Chillingworth, husband of

Hester and demonic tormenter of his medical patient and housemate Dimmesdale, is a picture of the unpardonable sin of coldheartedness.

The social environment in which these four actors play their parts is in effect a fifth character. It consists of a mass of nameless characters who make up the Puritan community, plus three named characters who step forward briefly to function as representatives of various aspects of the community—Governor Bellingham (secular authority), Rev. John Wilson (the church), and the witch Mistress Hibbins (evil and rebellion inside the community).

The ineffectual nighttime "confession" of Dimmesdale points to another leading feature of the story, that its real subject is concealment. Hawthorne is interested in the psychological, moral, and spiritual effects of concealed sin. He writes a story in which concealment itself becomes the chief sin.

The story is rich in psychological portrayal and insight. Dimmesdale's nighttime return to the scaffold, for example, adheres to the real-life psychological phenomenon of the criminal returning to the scene of the crime (in this case the crime of Dimmesdale's refusal to share Hester's suffering when she was exposed on the scaffold). The theme of concealment also leads to a dominant image pattern of darkness (concealment) and light (revelation).

A final part of Hawthorne's genius illustrated in the excerpt is his descriptive ability. To read this story for the plot line—to find out what happens next—is to invite endless frustration. It is a story where the journey itself is everything. A large part of that journey consists of such things as the set-piece description, the meanderings of the narrator (often into moral or psychological reflection), and the charm of the writer's archaic language and style. Worldmaking is one of Hawthorne's most evident talents as he transports us to another time and place.

## Five Fallacies about What Makes a Classic Christian

*The Scarlet Letter* lends itself to a consideration of exactly what makes a classic Christian in identity, partly because the history of the story's interpretation shows that this is a controversial issue. As a way into the subject, we should clear the air of five prevalent misconceptions.

*Fallacy 1.* **The Scarlet Letter** *is Christian if most readers and critics say it is.* Faced with the variability of interpretation that surrounds any major work of literature, it may be tempting to use a Gallup poll approach to settle the debate about whether a work is Christian in orientation. But majority opinion is no guarantee of correct interpretation.

*The Scarlet Letter* stands as a prime instance. It is probably the most widely misinterpreted of all the classics. It is commonly mistaught in literature courses. The misrepresentation comes from a naive equation of the Puritans portrayed in the story with Christianity, accompanied by a suppression of the Christian elements late in the story. It is a particular pity that most people's ideas of what the Puritans were like come from Hawthorne's story.

Christian classics are particularly prone to misinterpretation in a secular and debunking age. Current trends in literary criticism highlight this problem. Leading critics deny that works of literature can express a definite meaning, and Christian interpretations are thereby rejected as invalid. Other critics scorn Christian readings of literature, not because they can prove these interpretations to be wrong, but simply because Marxist and feminist approaches are the currently fashionable ones.

On the other hand, the fact that critics of earlier eras regarded *The Scarlet Letter* as a Christian classic does not make it such. The text itself must reveal the Christian allegiance of Hawthorne's masterpiece.

*Fallacy 2.* **The Scarlet Letter** *is Christian because it is well written.* The view that any piece of literature or art that is done well brings glory to God and is therefore in some sense Christian has always appealed to a small group of enthusiasts for the arts. But the view is based on false premises.

For one thing, not all good art brings glory to God. Aaron's golden calf, fashioned "with a graving tool" (Exodus 32:4), led people into idolatry. Romans 1:21-23 describes how pagans "exchanged the glory of the immortal God for images resembling mortal man or animals or reptiles." The art itself was exquisite, as we can see in art galleries that have a section of ancient art. But superior artistry does not make it Christian.

The theory that superior artistry is inherently Christian also makes an elementary failure to distinguish between form and content in literature. As Francis Schaeffer correctly insisted, "There is no such thing as a godly or an ungodly style."[2] The religious element in literature is found primarily in the attitude that a work takes toward the human experiences that it portrays.

*Fallacy 3. To know whether* **The Scarlet Letter** *is Christian we need to know whether its author was a Christian.* Wrong again. The fact that an author is a believing Christian does not guarantee that what he or she writes embodies a genuinely Christian viewpoint. Even more emphatically, it is possible for an unbeliever to embody a Christian viewpoint in his or her writing. The Renaissance dramatist Christopher Marlowe was an atheist who wrote a very Christian play *(Dr. Faustus)*. Shakespeare was probably not a Christian believer, but his works show a Christian allegiance at many turns. The principle that we need to follow was stated succinctly by D. H. Lawrence: trust the tale, not the teller.[3]

What we know about the life of Nathaniel Hawthorne is decidedly inconclusive on how he stood toward Christianity. He was not a member of the institutional Christianity of his day. Yet his notebooks show him to be, in the words of one critic, "more than any other writer of his time . . . a God-centered writer" and a person who "was innately religious."[4] Here is a specimen entry in Hawthorne's journal:

> I look out of the window and think, "O perfect day! O beautiful world! O good God!" And such a day is the promise of a blissful eternity. Our Creator would never have made such weather, and given us the deep hearts to enjoy it, above and beyond all thought, if he had not meant us to be immortal. It opens the gates of heaven and gives us glimpses far inward.[5]

We must also remember the cultural situation in which Hawthorne wrote. He had two intellectual traditions within which to place himself—transcendentalism, with its optimistic view of human nature, and Christianity. Given Hawthorne's pessimistic view of human sinfulness, he naturally aligned himself with Christianity.

That is why Amos Wilder describes Hawthorne as a writer "freely at home in the Hebraic-Christian tradition."[6] Someone else calls him a Protestant writer and considers *The Scarlet Letter* the nearest American equivalent to the novels of the French Catholic writer Francois Mauriac.[7] Austin Warren's analysis of Hawthorne's theology finds it to be a "nameless and indisputatious" Calvinism or Puritanism, "arrived at by experience and insight."[8]

These Christian leanings do not, however, prove that *The Scarlet Letter* is Christian in its viewpoint. For one thing, the biographical data about Hawthorne's attitude to the Christian faith is too inconclusive. Furthermore, not everything that a Christian writer produces is genuinely Christian in nature.

*Fallacy 4.* **The Scarlet Letter** *is Christian because it contains Christian situations, terms, and allusions.* Given the definition of "Christian fiction" that prevails in some circles, *The Scarlet Letter* can't miss being a Christian work. Its protagonist is a minister. The other characters are parishioners. The story is filled with references to churchgoing, sermons, catechism, confession, and such like.

Some scholars would make similar claims for the Christian or biblical allusions in the story. The language in which Hawthorne writes is reminiscent of the style of the King James Bible, for example. Hawthorne names the illegitimate daughter in the story "Pearl," thereby alluding to the pearl of great price in Jesus' parable and drawing attention to the way in which Pearl is of great worth to her mother while at the same time costing her everything in terms of social standing. Some of Hawthorne's epithets for God, such as "Providence" or "Eternal Justice," allude to the attributes of the Christian God.

But none of these things by themselves prove a Christian allegiance for the work as a whole. The most that we can say is that they are points at which the work intersects with the Christian faith and accordingly where a Christian context is necessary to a full understanding and experience of the book. The reason we must not overstate the degree to which Christian allusions prove a work to be Christian is that such allusions commonly appear also in works that are not Christian.

The Christian element in a story is ultimately measured by the work's implicit ethical and philosophic patterns. Christian situations and allusions are often a signpost to, or vehicle for, a Christian world view, but they are not the final test of Christianity in literature.

*Fallacy 5.* **The Scarlet Letter** *is Christian because it deals with profound issues.* When the "religion and literature" movement was in the ascendancy two or three decades ago, the definition of what made a work religious was broad enough to include virtually any work that dealt with serious issues. It was not uncommon to see the claim that such literature was not simply religious but also Christian.

The fact that *The Scarlet Letter* is concerned with such issues as sin, guilt, prejudice, moral responsibility, and forgiveness does not make it Christian. It only means that the story deals with issues to which the Christian faith speaks. Whether Hawthorne's story is Christian in orientation depends on how the work deals with these issues.

*Summary.* The case for *The Scarlet Letter* as a Christian classic must rest on a sure foundation. That many critics regard it as Christian, that it is well written, that its author had discernible Christian inclinations, that it contains Christian references and deals with issues of religious interest are not enough to make it a Christian classic. There are, however, other reasons for reaching such a conclusion.

### The Artistry of *The Scarlet Letter*

Although superior artistry does not make *The Scarlet Letter* a Christian classic, one thing that needs to be asserted strongly is that a Christian classic is first of all a classic, meeting the same criteria of excellence as other classics meet. A Christian vision in literature is not a substitute for literary excellence. Christian writers are first of all writers who have mastered the craft of writing.

*The Structure of the Book.* The structure that Hawthorne created for his masterpiece is one of its artistic excellences. The very content of the story possesses an inner structure. The story is organized as a cause and its effects. The original cause is a moral sin, adultery. But Hawthorne borrows a technique from epic and begins his story "in the middle of things." The adultery is long past. Only the effects remain to be dealt with.

For Hester the effects are exposure, suffering, isolation, greater sympathy for the human situation, and eventual social acceptance. For Pearl, the undeserving victim of sin, the sin leads to alienation from the human community. For Dimmesdale it leads to concealment, hypocrisy, physical and spiritual decay, and finally to confession and conversion. For Chillingworth the results are hatred and a spirit of revenge. For the Puritan community the sin is the occasion to display censure, sadism, social ostracism, and self-righteousness.

Hawthorne's carefully contrived plot enhances the shapeliness of the story. The book has twenty-four chapters, lending a sense of completeness that reminds us of Homer's *Odyssey* and *Iliad*, Virgil's *Aeneid*, and Milton's *Paradise Lost* (all of which are divided into multiples of twelve).

The first chapter is a prologue to the story and sets the scene for the action. The last chapter is an epilogue in which the author conducts a fireside chat with the reader about the action that reached its resolution in the preceding chapter. The middle twenty-two chapters fall into two sections of eleven chapters each. Within this block of chapters, the first, middle, and last ones (2, 12, 23) constitute the three major climaxes of the story. All three, moreover, are staged in the same setting—the scaffold on which the pillory stands. It is here that Hester is exposed to public shame, that Dimmesdale makes his ineffectual nighttime "confession," and that Dimmesdale is finally saved.

The two halves also follow a symmetrical pyramid of rising and falling action. Chapters 2-8 narrate the rise of Hester's fortunes from her original ignominy to her gradual victory over social prejudice. The next four chapters trace the decline of Dimmesdale and bring him, nearly demented, to his visit to the scaffold. From this low point we ascend to the emotional ecstasy of the forest meeting of Hester and Dimmesdale, where they plan to escape together to Europe. But this is followed by the dashing of those hopes as Dimmesdale deteriorates still further and finally dies. Of course the physical death on the scaffold is balanced by the spiritual life that Dimmesdale attains.

All of this is to say that Hawthorne approached his story as a craftsman with a high regard for artistic pattern and design. His story possesses the time-honored qualities of unity, coherence, and emphasis.

*Storytelling Technique.* Hawthorne displays equal skill with other aspects of his craft. He is a master dramatist, for example. In a manner remniscent of biblical storytellers, Hawthorne tells his story as a series of dramatic scenes, linked together with narrative summaries. *The Scarlet Letter* stays in our memory with its staged scenes. We remember Hester's exposure on the scaffold, meeting Chillingworth in prison, defending her right to retain custody of Pearl at the governor's house, talking with Dimmesdale in the forest. We remember Dimmesdale on the scaffold at midnight, delivering the election day sermon in church, and making his climactic confession on the scaffold.

Hawthorne is also adept as a symbolist. In fact, his symbols are so powerful that they become virtual actors in the story. Chief among them is the scarlet letter that Hester wears on her bosom. It appears on the average more than once every two pages. It is a developing symbol that first identifies Hester's sin but later comes to mean "Able," in testimony to the self-generated renewal that Hester manages to win for herself.

Dimmesdale's placing his hand over his heart is a symbolic gesture that recurs some thirty times. It, too, is a developing symbol. First it identifies Dimmesdale as the guilty sinner. Then it comes to picture physical, psychological, and spiritual deterioration.

The rose symbolizes nature. Darkness and light have their archetypal meanings of evil and goodness, though in this story they also mean concealment and exposure. Red variously symbolizes the passionate and the demonic. Instead of making the forest and the town simple images, as most writers do, Hawthorne makes both of them ambivalent. The forest is the place of both moral error and natural freedom and love. Similarly, the town is a place of both social oppression and the Christian experience of divine grace and forgiveness.

In short, Hawthorne writes as a moral symbolist. He writes about moral reality by means of the technique of symbolism.

Hawthorne also manipulated the standard devices of plot. *The Scarlet Letter* is one of the world's great suspense stories. For the handful of people who come to the story without having absorbed the plot line by cultural osmosis, the story is a detective story in which we piece together the clues about who Hester's partner in the adultery is. Then we wonder about a series of further questions—whether Hester will stay in the community and if so under what conditions, whether Chillingworth will discover that Dimmesdale is his rival and if so what he will do about the discovery, what will happen to Dimmesdale, and whether the guilty lovers will successfully escape together.

Other plot devices also abound. The story is one of almost unbearable conflict. On every reading after the first, the story is permeated with dramatic irony, as we know the hidden significance of details of which characters in the story are ignorant. On subsequent readings we also catch the richness of Hawthorne's foreshadowing. The great reconciliation scene between Pearl and Dimmesdale in the climactic confession scene is carefully set up by the rush of new life that Dimmesdale experiences when he takes Pearl's hand on the scaffold in the nighttime vigil and by this statement from the narrator: "She wanted [lacked] . . . a grief that should deeply touch her, and thus humanize and make her capable of sympathy. But there was time enough yet for little Pearl!" Some of these very words are repeated in the scene of grief that brings this moment of foreshadowing to its fulfillment in the final confession scene.

Hawthorne's skill at two additional features of narrative is legendary. One is his ability to describe scenes and characters. Another is his expertise at character portrayal, especially his ability to create characters about whose destiny we are made to care, to take us inside a character's mind and feelings, and to show a character's evolving development.

*Summary.* Before a work can be a Christian classic, it must be a classic. As such, it must display superior artistry that moves us to admiration and amazement. Hawthorne's story is, like the other stories I discuss in this book, one of the best-told stories the world has known.

### Truthfulness to Human Experience

The writer's task is threefold: to create literary form and beauty, to present human experience for our contemplation, and to interpret human experience. The first two are the skills of the writer regardless of his or her philosophic perspective. They are unlikely to yield much that is distinctively Christian.

In keeping with the emphasis of the preceding section on artistry, I want to insist that a Christian classic meets the criterion of truthfulness to reality and experience, even though this does not constitute the distinctively Christian aspect of a Christian classic. The writer of a

Christian classic, like the writer of every classic, is a sensitive observer of life. *The Scarlet Letter* has so much recognizable human experience in it that my selection of examples is representative rather than extensive.

*Social Reality in* **The Scarlet Letter.** An obvious category of human experience portrayed in the story is social reality. The lives of the four principal actors in the story are lived out in the social context of the Puritan community. This narrative situation allows Hawthorne to portray key social issues as they are actually lived out in any person's life.

Foremost among these issues is the conflict between the individual and society. American literature has made much of this conflict. In Hawthorne's story we see it chiefly in the lives of Hester and Dimmesdale. Their behavior and desires bring them into conflict with community values and mores at every turn.

For Hester, whose sin has been exposed and condemned by the community, the conflict is external. For Dimmesdale, whose sin remains hidden inside his own consciousness, the battle is all internalized. In both cases, the characters buckle under the pressure of societal norms, but in contrasting ways. Hester concedes outward conformity only, while Dimmesdale experiences inner conviction. In all of this, Hawthorne has accurately captured the tensions everyone feels between individual desires and actions on the one hand and the demands of society on the other.

Hawthorne is also truthful in his portrayal of society's judgment against the individual. If we want to see how a society mobilizes itself against an individual offender, all we need to do is read the second chapter of *The Scarlet Letter*. Here Hester steps out of the prison as the solitary figure exposed to a crowd of judgmental spectators who have the law as well as their own self-righteousness and vindictiveness to fuel their oppression. Here, in glaring fullness, is an anatomy of how society victimizes an individual.

A related experience that the career of Dimmesdale embodies is the false judgments that a society reaches. Because his sin is hidden from public view, Dimmesdale's parishioners idolize him. Minutes before Dimmesdale confesses his sin, the narrator says of him, "He stood, at this moment, on the very proudest eminence of superiority." Simply because Hester's sin was known, she was an outcast. It is no wonder that there is a note of rebuke to the Puritan community in Dimmesdale's speech from the platform:

> *Ye that have deemed me holy!—behold me, here, the one sinner of the world! . . . Lo, the scarlet letter which Hester wears! . . . But there stood one in the midst of you, at whose brand of sin and infamy ye have not shuddered!*

In short, one of the reasons people resonate with *The Scarlet Letter* is that it accurately captures the contours of certain social experiences that all people have had.

*Moral Experience in* **The Scarlet Letter.** When we look at Hawthorne's portrayal of moral reality, we also understand why the book makes such an impact. The battle between good and evil in the world and within the individual human soul is expressed with gripping power. From the start of the story to the end we feel with heightened clarity that good and evil are not simply abstractions but realities in the world in which we live. I would note in passing that in the moral universe of Hawthorne's story, moral evil is more strongly felt than moral good.

Hawthorne accurately depicts the way in which moral sin produces consequences in people's lives. At almost every turn in the story we see how the main characters' lives have been tainted by the adultery that Hester and Dimmesdale committed. Hawthorne wrote a story that illustrates a principle that he elsewhere phrased thus: "Every crime destroys more Edens than our own."[9] As the narrator of the story says when Hester binds up her hair after having let it down during the forest meeting, "So it ever is, whether thus typified or no, that an evil deed invests itself with the character of doom."

Hawthorne is also adept at portraying the reality of moral dilemmas. When Hester and Dimmesdale meet in the forest, for example, we are led to feel simultaneously the validity of the romantic dream of wanting to escape from an oppressive society and the voice of duty that propels the couple back to the community. "A Flood of Sunshine," Hawthorne entitles the chapter in which we share the exhilaration of the couple over the prospect of their escape from oppression. But as this pyramid-shaped sequence of four chapters descends back into the world of reality, we feel equally how illusory the dream of escape had been.

Hawthorne not only *portrays* moral reality in his story—he also devised an ingenious way to make the reader a *participant* in the moral action of the story. It is known as the technique of the guilty reader. This means that Hawthorne induces readers initially to sympathize with characters, events, and viewpoints that they later come to see as wrong. Throughout most of the story we sympathize with Hester and the Romantic viewpoint that she embodies. Late in the story we progressively see the deficiency of our original sympathies.

**Psychological Experience in The Scarlet Letter.** Towering above all the other types of experience portrayed in *The Scarlet Letter* is what Hawthorne managed to do with psychological experience. A century before modern psychology gave us the terms by which to name the experiences, Hawthorne portrayed them in such a way as to make us see and understand them.

To some degree Hawthorne embodied specific psychological experiences in specific characters. Hester enacts the experience of shameful exposure and isolation stemming from social ostracism. The story portrays how the human psyche responds to these twin traumas. We reenact the thoughts and feelings that accompany them, the coping mechanisms that Hester develops, the resistance to her status in the community and her simultaneous resignation to it as inevitable, her development of a pattern of deception in which she conforms outwardly but rebels inwardly.

Chillingworth's story is based on the psychology of revenge. His actions in the story give us an ever-expanding vision of how revenge works in a person's life. It begins with an overpowering sense of grievance toward a specific person. It then propels the perpetrator of the revenge to hatred, intrigue, obsession, cruelty, the desire to harm the object of hatred, and the refusal to forgive. In the case of Chillingworth, the final phase is the loss of purpose in life once the victim of the revenge is gone.

The greatest psychological feat in the story is the portrayal of Dimmesdale. It is primarily an anatomy of how guilt affects a person's inner life. The source of Dimmesdale's guilt is not only his adultery. More troublesome to him (and to the reader) is his cowardice in not shouldering responsibility for his share in the adultery and his hypocrisy stemming from his concealment of his sin while his congregation reveres him in his saintly role as pastor.

This journey into guilt stemming from deception is laden at every turn with psychological analysis. Foremost in the picture is self-laceration, as Dimmesdale loses his self-esteem and turns to self-punishment as a defense against the guilt. We observe the futile attempts to escape from the deception and guilt—the elaborate plans to rectify the problem that is producing the guilt followed by the feeble acquiesence in the status quo. We see how conscience plagues a guilt-haunted psyche, how weak will keeps the prison door locked, how the guilty person sends out hidden cries for help, and how guilt produces psychosomatic symptoms. Among the psychological experiences portrayed after Dimmesdale's forest meeting with Hester is Hawthorne's dramatization of how "no man, for any considerable period, can wear one face to himself, and another to the multitude, without finally getting bewildered as to which may be the true."

In addition to these psychological experiences that are specific to the individual characters, Hawthorne portrays the shared experience of suffering. Here, too, we are made to feel the reality of the thing itself and its way of crushing the human spirit. We observe a range of defenses that characters evolve to cope with it. And we see characters destroyed by suffering and triumphing over it.

*Summary.* A Christian classic achieves that identity partly by doing what any classic does at the level of content: it touches upon life powerfully at many points (to borrow the formula of the Victorian literary critic Matthew Arnold). One level of truthfulness in *The Scarlet Letter* is truthfulness to human experience in the social, moral, and psychological realms.

## The Interpretation of Life in *The Scarlet Letter*

In addition to portraying human experience, literature offers an interpretation of that experience. As novelist Joyce Cary puts it, a novelist "can give only . . . truth with an angle."[10] From works of literature we can infer a series of themes or comments about life. It is common to regard these ideas as constituting a world view.

*Toward a Definition of World View.* The simplest way to conceive of a world view in literature is to identify what value is elevated to a position of supremacy. This value also becomes an integrating force, so that all aspects of life are defined in terms of it. This central value is what Nathan Scott calls the work's "ultimate concern"—some "fundamental hypothesis about the nature of existence which . . . introduces structure and coherence . . . into the formless stuff of life."[11]

In addition to a central integrating value, a world view consists of basic premises about God, people, and the universe. The imagined world that a piece of literature presents is offered to us as the author's picture of reality—of what is and what ought to be. To identify a world view in literature, therefore, we can ask such questions as these: According to this picture, what really exists? What is the exact nature of these things? What consitututes good and evil behavior? What is valuable and worthless? What is the good life?

An additional useful tool of analysis is to regard the major characters in a story (especially the protagonist) as undertaking an experiment in living. A character's experiment in living is tested during the course of a story, and its successful or unsuccessful outcome is an implied comment on its adequacy or inadequacy.

The Christian allegiance of a work is seen chiefly in its world view. A Christian novel, claimed Flannery O'Connor, is not identifiable by its subject matter but is instead a story "in which the truth as Christians know it has been used as a light to see the world by." It is Christian by virtue of "what it assumes about human and divine reality."[12]

*The Scarlet Letter* is a special case in regard to world view. It gives full coverage to three distinct world views. The Christian element is evident partly in the story's rejection of two of these world views.

*Puritan Legalism in* **The Scarlet Letter.** The first world view to emerge in the story is that of the Puritan community. Its great experiment in living is to exalt a moral code to supremacy. The narrator describes the Puritans as "a people amongst whom religion and law were almost identical." They define people in terms of their moral law. In their eyes Hester is not a person but "the figure, the body, the reality of sin." They themselves are the self-righteous keepers and guardians of the moral law.

It is important to note that the Puritans' legalism is not Christian behavior. The simplistic equation of these two is at the heart of the prevalent misinterpretation of the novel. The Christian ideal is to forgive and restore a sinner, not simply to judge as guilty. Christ forgave the woman taken in adultery (John 8:2-11). He did not excuse her, but he restored her with the words, "Go, and do not sin again" (v. 11). Galatians 6:1-2 paints a similar picture: "If a man is overtaken in any trespass, you who are spiritual should restore him in a spirit of gentleness. Look to yourself, lest you too be tempted. Bear one another's burdens, and so fulfil the law of Christ."

*The Scarlet Letter* shows a Christian allegiance, then, when it rejects the Puritan community's experiment in living. The Puritans are consistently portrayed as unsympathetic in their behavior, even though the story ultimately affirms their Christian doctrine as truthful. As readers we have no difficulty in condemning the Puritans' bigotry, self-righteousness, sadism, and unforgiving spirit.

**The Romantic World View in The Scarlet Letter.** Romanticism is the world view that revolutionized Europe and America at the beginning of the nineteenth century and has been influential ever since. It elevates emotion, nature, impulse, and individual freedom from civilized restraints as the highest values.

Hester is the great proponent of Romanticism in *The Scarlet Letter*. In her experiences we are repeatedly made to feel what it would be like to view the world as a Romanticist does. The early scene in which Hester steps out of the dark prison into the sunlight to be exposed on the scaffold is vintage Romanticism. It reenacts the archetypal Romantic situation of the solitary figure victimized by a hostile society.

Hester is the Romantic rebel in the story. We read that she looks from an "estranged point of view at human institutions, and whatever priests or legislators had established; criticizing all with hardly more reverence than the Indian would feel for the clerical band, the judicial robe, the pillory, the gallows, the fireside, or the church."

The plan of escape that Hester urges in the forest meeting is based on Romantic premises. The evil from which the couple must escape is not within, in this view, but is located in the society that torments them. Once beyond "the white man's tread," they are "free." The decision has the sanction of nature—"that wild, heathen Nature of the forest, never subjugated by human law, nor illumined by higher truth" (that is, Christian revelation).

Hester's attitude toward the adultery also exhibits a Romantic ethic based on feeling. She whispers to Dimmesdale, "What we did had a consecration of its own. We felt it so!"

Early in the story, when Hester and the Puritan community are the only obvious combatants on the scene, we sympathize rather whole-heartedly with Hester's Romantic world view. But this is part of Hawthorne's technique of the guilty reader. As the story progresses, we come to revise our initial assessment.

The last third of the story traces what one critic calls "the progressive moral dereliction of Hester."[13] Already evident in the forest meeting, this deficiency becomes clearest in the climactic confession scene, where the Christian world view is juxtaposed to Hester's Romanticism. Dimmesdale asks whether the salvation he is in the process of attaining "is not . . . better . . . than what we dreamed of in the forest." Hester, who conceives of happiness as an escape from civilized restraints, replies, "I know not! I know not!"

*Summary.* The Christian interpretation of experience in *The Scarlet Letter* consists partly of how the story gets us to share the writer's negative assessment of the Puritan and Romantic world views. Using the affective strategies of the storyteller, Hawthorne influences us to disapprove of the Puritan community's behavior throughout the story and Hester's Romantic values in the late stages of the story.

### The Triumph of Grace in *The Scarlet Letter*

To merit the title of Christian classic, a work must do more than portray a Christian viewpoint on a chosen aspect of experience. It must also give a convincing presentation of what is most important in Christian experience—the triumph of God's saving grace in the forgiveness of a sinner. Stated another way, a Christian classic portrays a protagonist who attains belief in salvation and eternal life.

Hawthorne's hero does so in the great confession scene in the next-to-last chapter of *The Scarlet Letter*. There is no more thrilling conclusion in all the annals of literature. Since I do not have the space to conduct a sequential reading of this drama, I will extract the strands of Christian belief that are intertwined in the account. But this is intended as no more than a lens through which the story itself can be brought into focus as one reads it.

To recall the action for a moment, Reverend Dimmesdale, having preached his greatest sermon ever, joins the Election Day procession as it winds its way from the church through the town to the town hall. As Dimmesdale passes the scaffold on which the pillory stands, he mounts the scaffold with the premonition of death on him. With the Puritan community looking on as spectators, and with Dimmesdale, Chillingworth, Hester, and Pearl serving as the principal actors, Hawthorne stages his climactic scene. I use the word "stages" consciously, for Hawthorne himself uses dramatic imagery in the chapter, speaking of "spectators," "drama," "actors," and "closing scene."

*The Confession of Sin.* The very fact that this chapter is customarily called the confession scene in the novel attests the centrality of confession in this drama of redemption. The confession begins not with words but with a gesture: Dimmesdale "turned towards the scaffold, and stretched forth his arms. 'Hester,' said he, 'come hither! Come, my little Pearl.' " This acknowledgement of relationship is Dimmesdale's first confession of his twin sins of adultery and concealment.

Dimmesdale makes his confession of sin explicit as the scene proceeds. He tells Hester, "Let me make haste to take my shame upon me!" He calls himself "the one sinner of the world" and speaks of his hidden "brand of sin and infamy." "God's eye beheld it," he says of his guilty heart. The climax of his speech to the onlookers, just before he rips the clothing from his breast to make his revelation, is the statement, "Stand any here that question God's judgment on a sinner? Behold! Behold a dreadful witness of it."

The narrator reinforces this element of judgment against sin. He speaks of "the judgment which Providence seemed about to work." The clergyman, he says, "stood out from all the earth to put in his plea of guilty at the bar of Eternal Justice."

*The Acceptance of Grace.* Along with his confession of sin, Dimmesdale accepts God's grace. Several distinct strands make up this experience. One is Dimmesdale's conception of God as a God of mercy as well as judgment. Joseph Schwartz has shown how Dimmesdale's "fundamental weakness" through most of the story "is not his sin, nor even his hypocrisy, but his failure to recognize that God is a God of love. . . . The central fact of [Dimmesdale's] nature is indecision about the nature of God."[14] In his forest conversation with Hester, Dimmesdale speaks only of God's judgment, telling Hester, for example, "The judgment of God is on me. It is too mighty for me to struggle with!"

With this as the background, certain statements by Dimmesdale in the confession scene leap out as evidence that he has solved his theological confusion. He tells Hester that he is at last confessing his sin "in the name of Him, so terrible and so merciful, who gives me grace. . . ." "God is merciful," Dimmesdale tells Hester in response to one of her nonsense statements in the scene. In response to another of Hester's nonsense statements, Dimmesdale replies that "God . . . is merciful. He hath proved his mercy, most of all, in my afflictions." He follows this with a catalog of God's mercies, which is of course a key literary genre of the Bible.

In keeping with this new attitude toward God, Dimmesdale attributes the change that is occurring in his life to God's power. Even as Dimmesdale asks Hester to assist him with her strength, he adds, "but let it be guided by the will which God hath granted me!" "Thanks be to Him who hath led me hither!" Dimmesdale tells Chillingworth. In his catalog of God's mercies, Dimmesdale claims that God has shown his mercy "by bringing me hither, to die this death of triumphant ignominy before the people."

A final ingredient in Dimmesdale's experience of God's grace is the clear emphasis on salvation from guilt and judgment. The imagery of escape is prominent. Dimmesdale tells Chillingworth early in the scene, "With God's help, I shall escape thee now!" Late in the scene, Chillingworth mumbles repeatedly, "Thou hast escaped me!" And echoing the language of the Bible, Dimmesdale comments that if any of his "agonies had been wanting, I had been lost for ever!"

Dimmesdale's very last words follow immediately: "Praised be his name! His will be done! Farewell!" The sinner saved by grace thus dies praising God and echoing Christ's words in Gethsemane. As Randall Stewart puts it, "Thus in his profoundest character-creation, and in the resolution of his greatest book, Hawthorne has employed the Christian thesis: 'Father, not my will, but thine be done.' "[15]

*Human Reconciliation.* Reconciliation with God produces reconciliation with people in the story's climactic scene. The drama is filled with gestures of human reconciliation—arms outstretched, motions of physical assistance, a child's clasping of her arms around her father's knees, a kiss on the lips, a head resting on a beloved's bosom.

Dimmesdale's efforts at reconciliation with Chillingworth and Hester are largely unreciprocated. Chillingworth, whose revenge gave purpose to his life, plays a satanic role (he is repeatedly called "old Roger Chillingworth") and tries to snatch Dimmesdale's soul away from God. Dimmesdale rebuffs the temptation, and his final words to his tormenter are reminiscent of the dying words of Christ and Stephen: "May God forgive thee!"

Dimmesdale's efforts at reconciliation with Hester are scarcely more successful. Hester withers in this scene. She moves in a daze. She is caught off guard by the reversal of her and Dimmesdale's plans of escape. Her responses to Dimmesdale's cogent statements to her are singularly inappropriate to what is happening. In the great drama of redemption, she remains the archetypal refuser of festivities—a foil to Dimmesdale's sudden ascent. Hester's slowness on the draw cannot be attributed to Dimmesdale, who extends repeated invitations to her to participate with the movement of his own soul.

The great triumph of reconciliation—and one of the great moments in the story—is Dimmesdale's reconciliation with Pearl. Throughout the book, Pearl has remained "the wild infant" outside the human community. But a key statement of foreshadowing sets up the scene of reconciliation: "She wanted . . . a grief that should deeply touch her, and thus humanize her and make her capable of sympathy. But there was time enough yet for little Pearl."

This prophecy is fulfilled as Dimmesdale addresses Pearl with "a sweet and gentle smile over his face":

> *Pearl kissed his lips. A spell was broken. The great scene of grief, in which the wild infant bore a part, had developed all her sympathies; and as her tears fell upon her father's cheek, they were the pledge that she would grow up amid human joy and sorrow, nor for ever do battle with the world, but be a woman in it.*

Here is the great scene of grief, a rite of passage for both Pearl and her dying father. Someone writes that once the sin of Pearl's "birth has been acknowledged, a psychic transformation overtakes her. When Dimmesdale reveals himself, the long search for the father is ended. . . . All the latent human emotions rise up in this crisis to overwhelm that wildness that had linked her to nature."[16]

*Summary.* The salvation of Dimmesdale resolves the plot conflict and completes the action. It now becomes apparent that the protagonist and hero of the story is Dimmesdale, not Hester. His struggle of conscience and quest for salvation overshadow Hester's conflict with the community, which is largely resolved by the midpoint of the novel. "The protagonist of the novel is Arthur Dimmesdale," writes James Ellis, and "the progress of the novel is the working out of Dimmesdale's redemption."[17]

To accentuate the Christian vision, Hawthorne uses the technique of a foil between Hester and Dimmesdale. In the words of one commentator, Hawthorne "reserves for Hester the accents of fear and doubt" and pictures in Dimmesdale the life of a sinner "irresistibly drawn into the protective blaze of salvation."[18] The final scene on the scaffold is "the acknowledgement . . . of God's power and the confirmation of God's mercy—which Hester has dimly glimpsed, but which she cannot hope to comprehend."[19] The most plausible explanation of why Hawthorne's wife reacted to a reading of this chapter of the novel with one of her customary headaches is that she "must have been dumfounded by the stark and uncompromising revelation of her husband's beliefs."[20]

I said earlier that to merit the title "Christian classic," a work must portray the heart of the Christian gospel. *The Scarlet Letter,* as someone notes, "is a complete vision of salvation."[21]

## Notes to Chapter 6

[1] All quotations from *The Scarlet Letter* have been taken from *The Scarlet Letter and Other Tales of the Puritans,* ed. Harry Levin (Boston: Houghton Mifflin, 1960).

[2] Francis Schaeffer, "Some Perspectives on Art," in *The Christian Imagination: Essays on Literature and the Arts,* ed. Leland Ryken (Grand Rapids: Baker, 1981), p. 92.

[3] D.H. Lawrence, *Studies in Classic American Literature* (Garden City, NY: Doubleday, 1923, 1951), p. 13. Lawrence's specific formulation is, "Never trust the artist. Trust the tale."

[4] Joseph Schwartz, "Nathaniel Hawthorne, 1804-1864: God and Man in New England," in *American Classics Reconsidered: A Christian Appraisal,* ed. Harold C. Gardiner (New York: Charles Scribner's Sons, 1958), pp. 126-127.

[5] *American Notebooks*, as quoted in John Cline, "Hawthorne and the Bible," dissertation, Duke University, 1948, 83. This entire dissertation contains information relevant to any consideration of the Christian element in Hawthorne's fiction.

[6] Amos Wilder, *Modern Poetry and the Christian Tradition* (New York: Charles Scribner's Sons, 1952), p. 30.

[7] Louis O. Rubin, Jr., *The Teller in the Tale* (Seattle: University of Washington, 1967), p. 30.

[8] Austin Warren, "Introduction" to *Nathaniel Hawthorne* (New York: American Book Company, 1934), p. xxiv.

[9] Quoted by Darrel Abel, *The Moral Picturesque: Studies in Hawthorne's Fiction* (West Lafayette: Purdue UP, 1988), p. 198.

[10] Joyce Cary, *Art and Reality: Ways of the Creative Process* (Garden City: Doubleday, 1961), p. 134.

[11] Nathan N. Scott, Jr., "The Modern Experiment in Criticism: A Theological Appraisal," in *The New Orpheus: Essays toward a Christian Poetic*, ed. Scott (New York: Sheed and Ward, 1964), pp. 156, 163.

[12] Flannery O'Connor, *Mystery and Manners*, ed. Sally and Robert Fitzgerald (New York: Farrar, Straus & Giroux, 1957), pp. 174, 196.

[13] Abel, p. 181.

[14] Schwartz, p. 131.

[15] Randall Stewart, *American Literature and Christian Doctrine* (Baton Rouge: Louisiana State UP, 1958), p. 88.

[16] Chester E. Eisinger, "Pearl and the Puritan Heritage," *College English* 12 (1952): 327-328.

[17] James Ellis, "Human Sexuality, the Sacrament of Matrimony, and the Paradox of the Fortunate Fall in *The Scarlet Letter*," *Christianity and Literature* 29, no. 4 (Summer 1980): 53.

[18] Hugh N. Maclean, "Hawthorne's *Scarlet Letter*: 'The Dark Problem of This Life,'" *American Literature* 27 (1955-56): 13, 22.

[19] Ibid. 22.

[20] Ibid. 22.

[21] W. Stacy Johnson, "Sin and Salvation in Hawthorne," *Hibbert Journal* 50 (1951): 44.

# Chapter 7

## Dickens' Great Expectations
## and Literature as Recreation

### "Toiling Home Barefoot from Distant Travel"

※

*Within a quarter of an hour we came to Miss Havisham's house, which was of old brick, and dismal, and had a great many iron bars to it. Some of the windows had been walled up; of those that remained, all the lower were rustily barred. . . .*

*Upon leaving I was so humiliated, hurt, spurned, offended, angry, sorry . . . that tears started to my eyes. The moment they sprang there, the girl looked at me with a quick delight in having been the cause of them.*

※

*As I had grown accustomed to my expectations, I had insensibly begun to notice their effect upon myself and those around me. Their influence on my own character, I disguised from my recognition as much as possible, but I knew very well that it was not all good. . . .*

*Concerning the influence of my position on others, I . . . perceived—though dimly enough perhaps—that it was not beneficial to anybody.*

※

*The June weather was delicious. The sky was blue, the larks were soaring high over the green corn, I thought all that countryside more beautiful and peaceful by far than I had ever known it to be yet. . . . They awakened a tender emotion in me; for my heart was softened by my return, and such a change had come to pass that I felt like one who was toiling home barefoot from distant travel, and whose wanderings had lasted many years.*[1]

✳

These excerpts epitomize the three main phases of Dickens' classic story about an orphan boy whose life was transformed by the generosity of a criminal who became his anonymous benefactor. First published in 1861, *Great Expectations* traces Pip's character development from age seven to his mature acceptance of the human condition at age thirty-four or thirty-five.

The first phase of the story portrays Pip's childhood in the village. It is governed by the child's point of view as Pip tells his own story. Pip is an abused child, terrorized by virtually every adult in the village except his stepfather, the gentle blacksmith Joe Gargery, who relates to Pip more like a brother than a parent. The opening excerpt describes Pip's first visit to the dwelling of the psychotic Miss Havisham, where the coquette Estella begins her career as tormenter of Pip.

Already we can see some of Dickens' preoccupations in the story. He is interested in human psychology—in how characters (especially the narrator-protagonist) respond to events. Dickens is also a writer of social protest, though the heavy issues raised in his writing are consistently lightened by Dickens' prevailing humor. Finally, it is obvious that Dickens is interested in romantic love as a literary theme.

The middle phase of the action is set in London. Once Pip has come into his great expectations, he becomes a gentleman. His manners rise as his morals decline. Not that he becomes a highly immoral person. But he becomes a snob, useless to society and shallow as someone cut off from human suffering. Dickens' novel is a study in what money can to do to a person's values. As the second excerpt quoted above shows, here, too, Dickens keeps the focus on the inner story of Pip's mental development and on the element of social protest.

The second phase of the story comes to a close with the crash of the "great expectations" of Pip, who is now twenty-three. When Magwitch, the criminal who had been Pip's anonymous benefactor, shows up on Pip's doorstep on a rainy night and makes his revelation, Pip is forced to acknowledge the false premises on which he has based his life. Miss

Havisham is not (as he thought) his benefactor. Estella is not destined for him after all. And Pip faces the need to forge a new identity for himself. The coma into which Pip lapses and his eventual recovery symbolize the death and rebirth that provide a transition to the final phase of the story.

That phase is a return to some of the values of Pip's childhood. In fact, when Pip describes himself as "toiling home barefoot from distant travel," he becomes in our imaginations another prodigal son returning home after a journey to a "far country" of squandered money and moral bankruptcy.

We should not over-romanticize the village to which Pip returns, though. In the first third of the story, the village has been a place of almost unmitigated horror for the youthful Pip. At the end it seems ideal only by contrast to the evil of London and because Dickens keeps the focus on the virtuous Joe and Biddy. Pip himself does not settle down in the village, despite some critics' misleading comments about Pip's emulating Joe and embracing rural values. Pip becomes a clerk in Herbert's shipping firm in the East. Pip thus embraces a life of modest usefulness and lives by a modified success ethic, as summarized in a key statement at the end of the next-to-last chapter: "We were not in a grand way of business, but we had a good name, and worked for our profits, and did very well."

The presence of the circular story of the prodigal son in Dickens' novel illustrates the prominence of archetypes in Dickens' fiction. Dickens is a writer of universal human experience, and the prevalence of archetypes in his books is an index to that fact. *Great Expectations* is replete with the archetypes of our waking dreams—heroes, villains, the evil city, the eerie marsh, the British village with its high street, churchyard, town hall, and inn. Archetypal plot motifs include the journey of initiation and transformation through ordeal.

*Great Expectations* is also typical of Dickens' stories by having affinities with folk literature, fairy tales, and ghost stories.[2] Fairy-tale motifs in the story include the ill-treated child, the wicked stepmother, the proud princess who emerges as a sleeping beauty at the end, and the benevolent god-parent. Ghost story motifs are equally important in a story that features a witch, a haunted house, ghostlike specters, the demonic Orlick (associated with gates and blacksmith's tools), and a sinister swampland. The novel opens in a graveyard at twilight in the dead of winter with a figure of evil springing out from behind a tombstone and capturing a helpless child.

In the excerpt quoted above, Dickens' description of the English countryside in June epitomizes one of his greatest gifts as a writer, that of worldmaking. Dickens is enjoyable to read just for his descriptions of weather and landscape. In his own way he is a nature writer. By the magic of his descriptions he can make us fall in love with things English, including London, the village, the countryside, and even British weather.

Since the focus of my discussion will be the entertainment value of *Great Expectations*, I should conclude these introductory remarks by saying something about the wisdom that the story embodies. Joyce Cary's formula that a storyteller paints a picture of the world and of what is right and wrong in that world is a helpful framework. The world of Dickens' fiction is the world as we know it—of a mingled web, good and evil together, with people capable of both qualities. The blend of optimism and pessimism adheres to the Christian view of the world. As a novel of protest, *Great Expectations* likewise says much that a Christian would want to say.

The morality of the story is broadly Christian as well. The virtues that the novel implicitly affirms include sacrificial love, loyalty, friendship, generosity, contentment, and industriousness. The vices include laziness, self-centeredness, snobbishness, violence, and hypocrisy. Pip's life reenacts the familiar Christian paradox that gaining (in worldly success) is losing, losing is gaining (in terms of moral stature). The story is a warning to avoid false values and embrace true ones.

But although the moral vision of the novel is Christian, its world view is not. One critic writes, "Though the ethical pattern of the novel is Christian, the vision is not, finally, religious: there is no real communication between God and man. There is only the basic communion of men who are related in guilt and sorrow, in forgiveness and in love."[3] The world of the story is alarmingly secular. The church is around as a social institution in the village, but it is not even that prominent in the London of the middle chapters. Nothing in the story suggests that the highest values in life are God, the forgiveness of sins, or eternal life.

## Once upon a Time: Reading as Escape

The appeal of reading literature is based ultimately on the pleasure of being transported from one's immediate physical surroundings to a world merely imagined. We undertake reading in a holiday spirit. Our very posture as we read shows this, as does the timing of it. We read in a relaxed position. We do it, moreover, in the evening, on the weekend, during a break from work, or while on vacation.

The prerequisite to such transport is an attitude of leave-taking from the world of ordinary responsibilities. The very attention that reading demands of us ensures such a relinquishing of ordinary concerns. Self-forgetfulness is an essential ingredient of our best reading experiences.

We are willing to let go like this only if the world of the imagination that beckons us is sufficiently alluring, compelling, and irresistible. That is why the opening paragraph and even the opening sentence or line of a story is so crucial. Our favorite works of literature are ones that create in us a hunger for a world that only that book can satisfy.

Every good reading experience is thus an escape. Since we have been conditioned to respond negatively to the idea of reading as escapist, I want to underscore this. C.S. Lewis has written with his usual good sense that

> all reading whatever is an escape. It involves a temporary transference of the mind from our actual surroundings to things merely imagined or conceived. This happens when we read history or science no less than when we read fictions. All such escape is *from* the same thing: immediate, concrete actuality. The important question is what we escape *to*. . . . Escape is not necessarily joined to escapism.[4]

*The Worldmaking of Dickens.* Part of the genius of Dickens is his ability to create a world that compels our entrance into it and that we find enjoyable as we live in it. That world is first of all British. In fact, I know of no better introduction to the land, weather, and temperament of England than *Great Expectations*.

The novel is permeated with a strong sense of place, for example. Pip's hometown, modelled on the river town of Rochester in Kent, is the very epitome of small town England. Half of the novel is set in London, which similarly comes alive in our imaginations. And as for the sense of British weather, a passage such as this speaks for itself:

> *It was a rimy morning, and very damp. I had seen the damp lying on the outside of my little window, as if some goblin had been crying there all night, and using the window for a pocket-handerkchief. Now, I saw the damp lying on the bare hedges and spare grass. . . . On every rail and gate, wet lay clammy; and the marsh-mist was so thick, that the wooden finger on the post directing people to our village . . . was invisible to me until I was quite close under it.*

The physical properties of the world of the story are thoroughly British. All roads—and especially all railroads—run to London. The world of the story is small and provincial, just as the island country of England is. The village of the novel is replete with pub, inn, church, and town hall, as every British village is.

The customs of the world of the story are equally British. Class consciousness is much in evidence. In one of the great comic scenes in the novel, the simple blacksmith Joe Gargery finds it virtually impossible to know how to relate to Pip when he visits the gentlemanly Pip in London. Joe chases his constantly falling hat when it periodically slides from its perch. For his part, Pip views the village where he grew up with contempt once he comes into money and becomes a member of the leisure class.

The British formality, reserve, and love of privacy are also evident throughout the story. Pip learns virtually by accident that his friend Herbert Pocket is engaged. John Wemmick, clerk of the criminal lawyer Mr. Jaggers, keeps his private and work worlds totally separate. As he walks to work and progressively leaves his house behind, he "by degrees . . . got dryer and harder as we went along, and his mouth tightened into a post-office again." The subtlety of humor in *Great Expectations* is also vintage British, as is the richness in eccentric characters.

In short, one of the chief pleasures of Dickens' story is its ability to transport us to the world of nineteenth-century England. Once transported to that delightful world, we are made to care about the destiny of the characters who inhabit it.

*The Refreshment Value of Literature.* What is the value of entering a world so remote from our own? That question is usually answered by asserting the usefulness of the venture. Having entered the world of *Great Expectations,* the argument runs, we return to our own world with renewed understanding of it. This is true, but for the moment I want to defend our excursions into imagined worlds as a pleasure that leaves us refreshed.

Reading is an act of leisure, and leisure is essential to life.[5] People who ignore their need for freedom from work and obligation end up impoverished, if not with physical or emotional breakdowns.

The essence of leisure is its dual status as a break from necessity and something that gives pleasure. The very word *leisure* can be traced back to two root words that show this. One is the word from which we get our word *license.* It implies the idea of freedom—in this case, freedom from work or obligation. The other word (the Latin *schola)* carries the idea "to halt or cease," implying time in which we call a halt to work and duty. In other words, leisure is a temporary escape from ordinary obligations. This gets us back to the subject of reading literature as a beneficial escape from burdensome reality.

The God-intended balance between work and leisure is a clear theme in the Bible. After God performed the work of creation, "he rested, and was refreshed" (Exodus 31:17). The same rhythm of work and rest reappears in the fourth commandment of the Decalogue: "Six days you shall labor, . . . but [on] the seventh day . . . you shall not do any work" (Exodus 20:9-10).

The example of Jesus confirms this rhythm. Jesus did not confine life to ceaseless work and evangelism. He warned against the tyranny of the utilitarian in his discourse on anxiety, where he commands us to "consider the lilies of the field" (Matthew 6:25-34). He directed his disciples away from their busy ministry to the crowds and told them to "rest a while" (Mark 6:30-32). Christians should not feel guilty when they relax. They should instead feel guilty when they do not take time to relax.

Leisure is part of the stewardship of life. Christians should want to be all that they can be, in this sphere of life also. Because most Christian assume that leisure is frivolous and therefore fail to dignify it with their best thinking and with conscious choice, by default they gravitate to mediocrity in their leisure. They are content to pass the time with simply any diversion (usually television) that puts itself in their path.

But leisure pursuits can be more enriching than this, which brings us to the pleasures of reading a classic like *Great Expectations*. What does reading good literature have to commend it over turning the television knob or randomly reading the latest printed matter that catches our eye?

Reading literature awakens our minds and imaginations and makes us participants in experiences that are worth sharing. It puts us in touch with human experience at a significant level. Reading literature gets us beyond ourselves and enlarges our range of experience. It introduces us to characters and places that we find delightful and that always stay with us.

Part of the superiority of reading good literature as a leisure activity is that it provides an experience of beauty. In a day when mass entertainment often reinforces the cheapness and tawdriness of our society, the classics by their sheer artistry and excellence give us images of greatness. They dignify the human spirit.

*Summary.* Reading literature is, as T.S. Eliot aptly called it, "superior amusement."[6] It does more for us than help to pass the time. It begins in delight and ends in wisdom. Paul Elmen, in his book *The Restoration of Meaning to Contemporary Life*, analyzes the triviality that afflicts people in our society and is especially evident in their leisure pursuits: boredom, the search for distraction, the fear of spending time alone, sensuality, violence, and the appeal of horror ("the fun of being frightened").[7] The classics offer a better way. Mass entertainment is eminently forgettable; great literature is unforgettable and sometimes life-changing. It is a permanent possession.

## Lost in a Story: How Stories Please Us

My point of departure in discussing what makes a story entertaining is an incidental comment made by C.S. Lewis. In remarking that the English poet Edmund Spenser did not always rank as a difficult writer, Lewis puts him in the category of writers like Homer, Shakespeare, and Dickens, who speak "to every reader's imagination."[8] What things make up the popular imagination? I have been led to wonder.

*Getting Started.* Storytellers begin their task at a disadvantage: they have to interest their readers in the action before the readers know where the story is headed or even what it is about. To solve the problem, storytellers resort to several time-honored strategies.

One is to introduce an engaging central figure into the action. This person is in some loose sense of the term the hero of the story. In *Great Expectations* this role is obviously filled by Pip, the narrator of his own story who at once treats the reader as a confidant. Pip is a person who is interesting in himself and about whose destiny we care.

For the hero of the story to attract our initial interest, he must be in trouble. Pip emphatically is. We are barely into the story when Pip is turned upside down at twilight in a graveyard by an escaped convict. It is a scene of horror and resembles the opening of a ghost story. From the opening pages, we are plunged into a world of conflict, tension, and fear.

When Pip arrives back home after his encounter with the convict, there is no relief from the terror. Pip is an abused child. A seven-year-old orphan, he is being raised by his older sister, the archetypal shrewish wife who afflicts both Pip and her husband. Pip quickly wins our sympathy and interest as the archetypal underdog. He is afflicted by the adult world at every turn—by the pompous Uncle Pumblechook, the sadistic recluse Miss Havisham, and the coquette Estella (whom Miss Havisham has fashioned to avenge herself on men for having been jilted).

A hero cannot carry a story alone. Storytellers thus keep adding to the cast of characters as the opening chapters unfold. They do so almost reluctantly, knowing that they have to sustain our interest over a long read. The cast of characters needs to have sufficient range to be interesting and to do justice to the fullness of life as know it. Often these characters are foils to each other: the kindly Joe and his oppressive wife, the solid but unnoticed Biddy and the attractive but heartless Estella, the bombastic Uncle Pumblechook who has a shop on High Street and the terse Miss Havisham with her prison-like decaying house on a side street.

External action is of course the backbone that supports the characters. The reading public at large wants exciting external action, and Dickens obliges. His story is an adventure story. The homey village where the first third of the story is set has a misleadingly calm exterior. Just beyond the village are the convict ships, and from the opening chapter Pip finds himself enmeshed in a world of criminals. He is also quickly drawn into the world of the witch-like Miss Havisham and her haunted house. Like other adventure stories, *Great Expectations* is a kaleidoscopic journey into danger, the exotic, the unexpected, the mysterious. It is a world of narrow escapes and heightened terror.

But of course the strain cannot be unrelieved. Stories are built on the principle of rhythm. We swing back and forth between safety and threat as we progress through the early chapters of *Great Expectations*. The humor of Dickens is likewise a constant counterbalance to the evil. We never feel trapped as we progress through the story.

Another rhythm that wins us early in the story is the way we swing between the familiar and the strange as we read. To interest us, literature must portray recognizable human experience. But it must also be sufficiently striking to make an impact. Every child has known the experience of secretly taking food from a cupboard, but Pip's stealing food for the convict before daybreak is a heightened version of it.

Christmas dinner with invited guests is a common event in all of our lives, but who of us has ever experienced it in the form we find in Chapter 4 of *Great Expectations*, with the Gargerys, Mr. Wopsle, Uncle Pumblechook, and Mr. and Mrs. Hubble? Many Christmas dinners have been marred by some minor table mishap, but what can compare with the spectacle that ensues when Mr. Pumblechook takes a swig of the tar water that Pip substituted for the brandy:

> *Instantly afterwards, the company were seized with unspeakable conster-*
> *nation, owing to his springing to his feet, turning round several times in*
> *an appalling spasmodic whopping-cough dance, and rushing out at the door;*
> *he then became visible through the window, violently plunging and expec-*
> *torating, making the most hideous faces, and apparently out of his mind.*

As we read such a passage, we find familiar experience defamiliarized. Our attention is fixed and our interest aroused. We sense that we are participating in something more interesting and entertaining than real life.

*The Middle of the Story.* By the time we reach the middle of a story, we have a better idea of what it is really about. This means that the storyteller can draw upon a larger repertoire of narrative ingredients.

As we conclude Part One of *Great Expectations,* we do not yet know precisely what kind of story it is going to be. It might simply be a "slice of life" story about life in a British village. Alternately, because of the emphasis on the victimization of Pip, we could imagine that it is headed in the direction of a story of social protest.

But when Pip inherits wealth and moves to London to begin his life as a gentleman, we quickly sense that the story is going to raise the issue of values. Pip becomes a developing character, and the writer no longer has to interest us in him solely as a personality. Now Pip's moral development absorbs our attention. Pip's manners improve as his morals decline. He becomes the complacent snob, self-absorbed and isolated from the broader world of human suffering. He strikes us as shallow and frivolous, not so much immoral as a moral nonentity.

New forms of external action take center stage with the shift from the village to London. The main narrative strategy is to create a brave new world of trivial socializing. The chief action for seven chapters is Pip's meeting new people, being invited various places for dinner, and settling into his apartment and new routine. The problems of the village seem a hundred miles away, even though the proximity of the village to London results in one of the brilliant strokes in the novel—the constant back and forth movement between the two worlds.

Whenever a story enters a new phase, the cast of characters expands. As always, Dickens' mastery of characterization generates its own interest. In a story where power and its abuse are a preoccupation, the towering figure is the criminal lawyer Jaggers. More interesting as a person is his clerk Wemmick, whose tiny home that he shares with his deaf father (called "the Aged") is a charmingly literal version of the English saying that "a man's home is his castle." Pip's apartment mate Herbert Pocket, the romantic dreamer and naive optimist about his own financial future, is another evidence of one of Dickens' greatest gifts—his inventiveness.

Readers like suspense in a story, and again we can see why *Great Expectations* wins us. Early in the story we wonder how Pip will fare with the convict, as well as who attacked Pip's sister and left her paralyzed. In the middle of the story, we wonder about such matters as how Pip's life will turn out now that he is affluent, who Pip's benefactor is, and whether his continuing infatuation with Estella will ever be reciprocated.

Readers expect a romantic love interest in a good story. *Great Expectations* is a full-fledged love story. In the first third of the novel Pip's youthful infatuation with Estella is mainly an extension of his suffering. But in the middle phase Pip's love is an adult passion. In his own words, "I loved her with the love of a man."

Storytellers love recognition scenes in which a secret is unmasked. Chapter 39, in which the convict Magwitch sits in Pip's apartment and announces that he has been Pip's benefactor, ranks with the best (including the homecoming of Odysseus and Joseph's revelation of himself to his brothers in Egypt). The action alternates between the convict's rambling series of disclosures and Pip's internal responses of horror as he listens. The interview unmasks the false premises on which Pip has based his life. His great expectations come crashing down as we conclude the middle phase of the story.

*Final Developments.* With the collapse of Pip's great expectations, a whole new action takes over. The story now comes to focus on Pip's struggle to establish a new identity without benefit of wealth, and to help his benefactor escape from England (where he is subject to arrest because he returned from his exile as a convict). Pip's whole earthly security is stripped away from him, including even Estella, who marries the villainous Drummle.

Storytellers often infuse an abundance of new external action into their story in the last phases, and *Great Expectations* illustrates the strategy. The conventions of the suspense thriller take over as Pip lives with constant fear while planning the convict's escape. The earlier narrative questions, What happened? and, What happened next? now give way to, How did it turn out? Readers like chase scenes, so in *Great Expectations* we have the thwarted attempt to smuggle Magwitch out of England by boat.

Heroism and villainy reach new heights in this phase of the story. Pip rises in our estimation as he renounces the shallowness of his affluent life and embraces human suffering. Virtuous Joe, who nurses Pip back to health after his coma, continues to fill the role of virtuous hero. Good stories need villains as much as they need heroes, though, and *Great Expectations* obliges us with three ideally villainous characters—Orlick, Drummle, and Compeyson.

Other favorite story elements also make an appearance. The rescue motif is one of them. It makes its most notable appearance when Pip is snatched from the drunken Orlick's claws in the sluice-house on the marshes. Storytellers love reunion scenes because of their emotional potential. And so we are given moving emotional reunions between Pip and Joe, Pip and Biddy, and Pip and Estella. Surprises are also sprung on us: the criminal who terrorized Pip in the churchyard revealed as his benefactor, that same criminal as the father of Estella, Compeyson as the man who jilted Miss Havisham. Dickens also keeps the romantic love interest high by gradually marrying off the couples who have emerged—Wemmick and Miss Skiffins, Joe and Biddy, Herbert Pocket and Clara Barley, and (at the very end) Pip and Estella.

Stories normally end with poetic justice, meaning that good characters are rewarded and evil ones punished. In *Great Expectations*, Compeyson is killed, Herbert establishes a successful business (Pip regards his efforts to help Herbert financially as "the one good thing" that he accomplished during the era of his great expectations), Drummle dies in an accident, Pumblechook's house is broken into and Pumblechook is punched in the nose, Orlick ends up in prison, Estella is purified by her suffering and is at last worthy of Pip's affection.

Suffice it to say, the popular taste prefers a happy ending. *Great Expectations* gives us a muted happy ending. Pip is now thirty-five. He will always bear the scars of his suffering. But he enjoys a modest success as a clerk in Herbert's shipping company in the East. Dickens was virtually forced to rewrite the ending of his story, moreover. In the first version, Pip encounters Estella on a London street, where they part for the last time. In the revised version, Dickens created a magnificent twilight love scene in which Pip and Estella, both maimed but renewed characters, leave the ruined garden of Satis House to enter a new life together.

*Summary. Great Expectations* has virtually all of the ingredients that readers want in a story. It has heroes and villains, vivid characters and scenes, adventure and atmosphere, conflict and suspense, scenes of reunion, rescue, surprise, and recognition. It has both sadness and a happy ending.

## The Pleasures of Characterization

At the simplest level, said T.S. Eliot, a story invites interest in its plot.[9] At the next step up the ladder of sophistication, a story engages our interest with its characterization. The characters we meet in literature are one of the chief pleasures that we derive from literature. Dickens, as everyone knows, is famous for his powers of characterization. What do we mean when we praise a writer for the ability to portray character?

*Universal Characters.* Writers known for their character creations possess the ability to portray universal character types. When we meet such people in literature, we at once feel that we have also met them in life. The element of recognition is high. These characters are already part of our circle of acquaintances.

Pip, for example, begins the story as the archetypal child. His longings and fears are instantly recognizable. We ourselves have known them. His childish miscalculations are equally familiar, as when he irrationally concludes that Uncle Pumblechook must be a happy man because he has so many drawers in his seed store. Later Pip becomes the indolent teenager, and still later the adult chastened by suffering—the person for whom life has been disillusioning and tragic but somehow dear.

Other characters are equally recognizable. Joe Gargery's wife is the shrewish wife and tormenting older sibling. Biddy is "the girl next door"—the person of wisdom and virtue, but unnoticed because she lacks sparkle and sex appeal. Pumblechook is the archetypal windbag and fatso, Mrs. Coiler the smothering flatterer. Estella is the coquette or flirt or tease. The Pocket children, who "were not growing up or being brought up, but were tumbling up," are the typical undisciplined children who can be found in anyone's nighborhood or home church. Herbert Pocket is the naive optimist, the person who, "having already made his fortune in his own mind," acted as though it were an accomplished fact. Trabb's boy is the jealous mocker and Miss Havisham the reclusive spinster. Pip's life of rising and falling fortunes is strewn with fair-weather friends. Orlick, like a certain strain of student, never "seemed to come to his work on purpose, but would slouch in as if by mere accident."

*Unique Characters.* Balancing these universal characters are the unique characters that we encounter only in literature. Here the appeal is not the familiarity but the strangeness of the person.

Miss Havisham is an example. She may belong to a recognizable type (the recluse), but where in real life have we met anyone who fits that type in this form? She stopped her clocks at twenty minutes to nine of her scheduled wedding day. She has barricaded herself in her decaying house ever since, wearing her wedding dress to keep the memory of her ill-fated wedding day alive. The wedding cake is still on the table and features "speckled-legged spiders with blotchy bodies running home to it, and running out from it."

Other characters also stand out from the pages of *Great Expectations* resplendent in their eccentricity and idiosyncracies. An example is Mr. Jaggers' routine of washing his hands (and in particularly extreme cases gargling as well) to rid himself of the taint of his criminal clients. Wemmick, his clerk, lives by the motto that every person's purpose in life is to get his or her hands on "portable property" (money). He lives in a castle-like house without parallel in the annals of life or literature. Clara Barley's father, Old Gruffandgrim, stays in our memory as the one who growls and pounds as he paces the floor overhead. Magwitch, the generous convict, is himself unique.

Sheer vividness in description can make a character come alive with unique individuality. The opening description of Pumblechook is a classic: "a large hard-breathing middle-aged slow man, with a mouth like a fish, dull staring eyes, and sandy hair standing upright on his head, so that he looked as if he had just been all but choked, and had that moment come to." Sometimes the speech pattern associated with a character makes the character distinctive. Dickens was so captivated by Joe Gargery that he created a new vocabulary and syntax for him.

*Characters Who Elicit Reader Involvement.* Storytelling is an affective art in which storytellers manipulate our sympathies and aversions. This is most evident in the attitudes that a writer induces toward characters.

We have a predictable sympathy for the underdog, for example. This is why we identify so strongly with Pip in the opening and closing phases of the story. Villains are equally effective in activating a reader. Thus we react strongly to Drummle, Orlick, and Compeyson. We also like attractive or exemplary characters who fulfill our ideals, and the simple but virtuous Joe Gargery is accordingly one of our favorite characters in the story.

Writers who are known for their character portrayal are usually satirists adept at portraits that make us laugh at characters' foibles or loathe them for their vices. Many of Dickens' characters are satirically exposed, usually in the laughing mode but sometimes in a more scathing way.

*Summary.* Our favorite stories do more than excite us with a fast-moving plot that makes us want to know what happens next. They also absorb us in the characters who perform the actions. It is the characters who give depth and substance to the events that occur.

### The Enjoyment of Technique

In the lone book of literary theory that C.S. Lewis wrote, he suggested that we can judge books by how readers read them. Some books ask to be read only to find out what happens. Others invite us to enter a whole world of the imagination and enjoy its features, including the characters. Books that display superior technique go beyond even this and allow us to relish not only what is portrayed but how it is portrayed. Lewis comments that "every episode, explanation, description, dialogue—ideally every sentence—must be pleasurable and interesting for its own sake."[10]

*The Shape of the Story.* All the narrative ingredients that I discussed earlier might appear in a clumsily told story. Part of the greatness of *Great Expectations* is the skill with which Dickens structured it. The organization is multiple.

The simplest structural principle is choronological. We follow the protagonist from his earliest moments of self-awareness at the age of seven to his mature adulthood at the age of thirty-five. Pip is twenty-three when his life falls apart. At the center of all the action is the hero, whose commanding presence is reinforced by the fact that he tells the story in his own voice.

The story is also divided into three clear phases of the hero's development. First we see Pip in his childhood and adolescence in the village.

It is a spectacle of moral innocence but limited horizons and thwarted potential. The middle phase is the period of Pip's great expectations. During his life in London, he becomes a better educated and more interesting person, but his morals decline. His final phase is a synthesis of the preceding ones. In terms of external standing, Pip retains his new friends and contacts and does not rebuild his life from scratch in the village. But his values represent a return to the childhood values he absorbed from Joe. These values include work, loyalty, and self-sacrifice.

The profundity of this pattern emerges if we stop to note its universality. It is the prodigal son story. One critic notes that "variants of such a narrative are found in the myths of many heroes."[11] The ingredients in the pattern are tragic choice, initiation into suffering, transformation through ordeal, and wisdom through suffering.

*The Comic Genius of Dickens.* An additional avenue by which we can enjoy the "how" of Dickens' performance is the comedy of *Great Expectations*. In the first half of the book, Dickens consistently regales us with his humor (while in the second half of the story the comic element virtually drops out of sight).

The story is filled with moments of situation comedy. The fight between Pip and Herbert Pocket in Miss Havisham's garden is an example, as Herbert puts on an elaborate show with his preparations for the fight but is easily quelled by Pip. Its sequel, when the two recognize each other at the door of the apartment they will share in London, is equally hilarious. Other typical specimens include the mockery that Trabb's boy inflicts on Pip when the latter returns to the village in all his splendor, the scene in which Drummle and Pip stand elbowing each other in front of the fireplace at the Blue Boar Hotel, and the initial visit of Pip to the mismanaged Pocket household.

Comedy arising from character also greets us at every turn. Wemmick's obsession with "portable property" and his eccentric domestic life are richly comic. So is the inconsistency involved when Mr. Pocket, father of a family in shambles, goes about lecturing as an expert on family management. Pip is held up to satiric ridicule during the middle phase of the story, as when he devises elaborate rituals of self-deception on evenings when he and Herbert tally up their debts.

*The Portrayal of Human Psychology.* Another thing that makes a Dickens story enjoyable in itself is the psychology with which Dickens laces the story. On the eve of his leaving the village and moving to London, for example, the youthful Pip finds that "all night there were coaches in my broken sleep, going to wrong places instead of to London, and having in the traces, now dogs, now cats, now pigs, now men— never horses." As the seven-year-old Pip runs out to the marsh with the vittles that the convict had frightened him into bringing, "every board upon the way, and every crack in every board, [called] after me, 'Stop thief!' "

Elsewhere it is not the inner response of the narrator that embodies the psychology but simply the experiences about which Dickens writes. The impact of Pip's first visit to Miss Havisham's house, for example, is delineated in detail. Pip walks away "deeply revolving that I was a common labouring-boy." As for the formative effect that such an event can have on a person's mind, we read, "That was a memorable day to me, for it made great changes in me. But, it is the same with any life. Imagine one selected day struck out of it, and think how different its course would have been."

**The Beauty of the Style.** A final feature of *Great Expectations* that makes us delight in how the story is told is the beauty of Dickens' language. A literary critic rightly speaks of "the sheer beauty of much of the book."[12] Novelist Graham Greene praised the novel for its "delicate and exact poetic cadences."[13]

Dickens' way with words also accounts for much of the humor of the book. Consider the description of what Pip observes on a visit to Wemmick's house during the era when Wemmick is courting Miss Skiffins:

> As Wemmick and Miss Skiffins sat side by side, . . . I observed a slow and gradual elongation of Mr Wemmick's mouth, powerfully suggestive of his slowly and gradually stealing his arm round Miss Skiffins's waist. In course of time I saw his hand appear on the other side of Miss Skiffins; but at that moment Miss Skiffins neatly stopped him with the green glove, unwound his arm again as if it were an article of dress, and with the greatest deliberation laid it on the table before her. Miss Skiffins's composure while she did this was one of the most remarkable sights I have ever seen. . . . Taking the table to represent the path of virtue, I am justified in stating that during the

*whole time of the Aged's reading, Wemmick's arm was straying from the path of virtue and being recalled to it by Miss Skiffins.*

The subtlety of Dickens' humor is achieved by stylistic means. He is a master of understatement, for example. On Pip's first meeting with Miss Skiffins, he "judged her to be possessed of portable property." "Your sister is given to government," Dickens makes Joe Gargery say to the youthful Pip. Overstatement is equally a part of Dickens' style. Pip mocks himself for his self-deception when he tallied up his over-spending when he claims, "I established with myself on these occasions the reputation of a first-rate man of business—prompt, decisive, ener-getic, clear, cool-headed."

The descriptions of Dickens are a continuous fountain of delight. Again it is his inventiveness with words that works the magic: "A cold silvery mist had veiled the afternoon, and the moon was not yet up to scatter it. But, the stars were shining beyond the mist, and the moon was coming."

With linguistic feats like this, Dickens can make ordinary experiences unforgettable. When, for example, has a breakfast roll ever had the following degree of immortality conferred upon it: "Mr Trabb had sliced his hot roll into three feather beds, and was slipping butter in between the blankets, and covering it up."

*Summary.* The pleasures of literature are heightened when we can read not only to find the story material and characterization that we like but also to delight in the writer's flaunting of technique. *Great Expectations* makes the expression itself so enjoyable that we would read the book for how it expresses its content even if we did not equally love the content.

## "Richly All Things to Enjoy": The Christian Endorsement of Recreation

It remains to say something about how the recreative function of litera-ture relates to the Christian life. Doing so will take us to a cluster of biblical themes, including creativity, beauty, and enjoyment.[14]

*Creativity.* Human creativity that produces an inventive story like *Great Expectations* is rooted in divine creativity. People create because

God created first. Genesis 1 is the foundational text in this regard. According to Genesis 1, God is the original creative artist. He created people in his image, moreover, and this assures us that they share his ability to create and invent.

The relevance of this to the artistic enterprise is obvious. It validates human creativity as good in principle. Christian poet Chad Walsh has said that the writer "can honestly see himself as a kind of earthly assistant to God. . . , carrying on the delegated work of creation, making the fullness of creation fuller."[15]

This same endorsement of creativity extends to readers who enter into the creativity of others. To delight in literary creation can be a way of valuing the image of God in people, of celebrating the worth of human creativity, and of honoring the God who gave the gift of creativity to the human race.

*Beauty.* Much of what we mean by the recreative aspect of literature is also encompassed by the aesthetic idea of beauty. Beauty consists of the elements of artistic form (such as unity, variety, contrast, balance, symmetry, repetition, progression) and the pleasurable response that we feel toward artistry and aesthetic form.

We know from the Bible and our senses that God values beauty. He created a beautiful universe. When God formed paradise, the perfect human environment, he "made to grow every tree that is pleasant to the sight and good for food" (Genesis 2:9). God's design for life, in other words, is aesthetic as well as utilitarian. Theologian Abraham Kuyper wrote that "as image-bearer of God, man possesses the possibility both to create something beautiful, and to delight in it."[16]

If God values the beautiful as well as the utilitarian, so can we. We do not need to defend our love of literature solely on a didactic basis. The human capacity for beauty is God-implanted. One way to read literature to the glory of God is to relish its artistic beauty, recognizing God as the ultimate source of the beauty we enjoy.

*Enjoyment.* The Bible also endorses enjoyment. Some of the best proofs are the God-centered passages in the Old Testament book of Ecclesiastes. Here is one of the passages:

> I know that there is nothing better for [people] than to be happy and enjoy themselves as long as they live; also that it is God's gift to man

that every one should eat and drink and take pleasure in all his toil (3:12-13).

The writer of Ecclesiastes extended this to his philosophy of writing as well, telling us that he "sought to find pleasing words," or "words of delight" (Ecclesiastes 12:10).

The example of Jesus confirms this positive attitude toward enjoyment. According to the Gospel accounts, one of Jesus' habitual activities was attending dinners and parties. He turned water into wine to keep a party going (John 2:1-10) and by this example consecrated pleasure and enjoyment.

To this we can add Paul's instructions to Timothy regarding the wealthy. The command includes the statement that "God . . . giveth us richly all things to enjoy" (1 Timothy 6:17, KJV). The way to show gratitude for a gift is to enjoy it.

*Summary.* All of this biblical data may seem like a long way from Dickens' *Great Expectations*, but it is not. The biblical endorsement of creativity, beauty, and pleasure means that we are free to value our reading of literature for these qualities. *Great Expectations* exists for more than our enjoyment, but it does not exist for less than that.

## Notes to Chapter 7

[1] I have used the Penguin edition of *Great Expectations*, ed. Angus Calder (Harmondsworth: Penguin, 1965).

[2] One of the best books on Dickens' fiction deals with these very qualities: Harry Stone, *Dickens and the Invisible World: Fairy Tales, Fantasy, and Novel-Making* (Bloomington: Indiana UP, 1979).

[3] Ruth M. Vande Kieft, "Patterns of Communication in *Great Expectations*," in *Assessing Great Expectations*, ed. Richard Lettis and William E. Morris (San Francisco: Chandler, 1960), p. 179.

[4] C.S. Lewis, *An Experiment in Criticism* (Cambridge: Cambridge UP, 1961), pp. 68-69.

[5] For more on the subject of leisure than I can provide here, see my book *Work and Leisure in Christian Perspective* (Portland: Multnomah, 1987).

[6] T.S. Eliot, "Preface" to *The Sacred Wood* (London: Methuen, 1920, 1960), p. viii.

[7] Paul Elmen, *The Restoration of Meaning to Contemporary Life* (Garden City: Doubleday, 1958).

[8]C.S. Lewis, "Edmund Spenser," in *Major British Writers*, ed. G.B. Harrison (New York: Harcourt, Brace and World,1954), 1: 97.

[9]T.S. Eliot, *The Use of Poetry and the Use of Criticism* (Cambridge, MA: Harvard UP, 1933), p. 146.

[10]Lewis, *An Experiment in Criticism*, p. 84.

[11]G. Robert Stange, "Expectations Well Lost: Dickens' Fable for His Time," in *Assessing Great Expectations*, ed. Lettis and Morris, p. 75.

[12]Angus Calder, Introduction to *Great Expectations* (Harmondsworth: Penguin, 1965), p. 17.

[13]Graham Greene, as quoted in Calder, p. 17.

[14]For more on these subjects than I can say here, see my book *The Liberated Imagination: Thinking Christianly about the Arts* (Wheaton, Ill.: Harold Shaw, 1989).

[15]Chad Walsh, "The Advantages of the Christian Faith for a Writer," in *The Christian Imagination: Essays on Literature and the Arts*, ed. Leland Ryken (Grand Rapids: Baker, 1981), p. 308.

[16]Abraham Kuyper, "Calvinism and Art," in *Calvinism* (Grand Rapids: Eerdmans, 1943), p. 142.

# Chapter 8

## Tolstoy's The Death of Ivan Ilych
## and the Truth of Fiction

## "Most Ordinary and Therefore Most Terrible"

✳

*"Gentlemen," he said, "Ivan Ilych has died!"*

*"You don't say so!"*

*"Here, read it yourself," replied Peter Ivanovich, handing Fedor Vasilievich the paper still damp from the press. . . .*

*Ivan Ilych had been a colleague of the gentlemen present and was liked by them all. He had been ill for some weeks with an illness said to be incurable. . . . So on receiving the news of Ivan Ilych's death the first thought of each of the gentlemen in that private room was of the changes and promotions it might occasion among themselves or their acquaintances. . . .*

*The dead man [as he appeared in the coffin] . . . was much changed and had grown even thinner since Peter Ivanovich had last seen him, but, as is always the case with the dead, his face was handsomer and above all more dignified than when he was alive. The expression on the face said that what was necessary had been accomplished, and accomplished rightly. Besides this there was in that expression a reproach and a warning to the living. . . .*

*Ivan Ilych's life had been most simple and most ordinary and therefore most terrible.*[1]

✳

These sentences come from the first several pages of *The Death of Ivan Ilych*, published by the Russian fiction writer Leo Tolstoy in 1886, midway through his writing career. Following his conversion at the age of fifty-one, Tolstoy became an influential prophet who espoused a radical and unorthodox form of Christianity. Based on a literal reading of the Gospels, its tenets included nonviolence, sexual abstinence, communal property, asceticism, and a rejection of organized religion and government.

The plot of Tolstoy's story about Ivan Ilych (the Russian equivalent of John Doe) is simple. It opens with the last event in the story—the death of the protagonist and its effect (actually a lack of effect) on his surrounding society (represented by Ivan's family and colleagues). The rest of the story traces the life of Ivan Ilych before and after the accident that caused his terminal illness.

The story is a quest in which we follow the hero's search for salvation. The narrator's comment that "what was necessary had been accomplished" lets us know from the start that Ivan's quest was successful, but we have to follow him through his life to see exactly what this means. The story is structured like a detective story in which we step-by-step solve the mystery of how Ivan's life can possibly end with things "accomplished rightly." Tolstoy prolongs the suspense by withholding the solution of the protagonist's life problem until two hours before his death.

Part of the power of the story is its portrayal of pain, suffering, and the process of dying. There is nothing quite like it anywhere else in literature. Yet as I told someone who responded to my account of the story with the comment that "it must be a depressing story," the truthfulness of the story and the correctness of its value system actually make it refreshing to read. It has the ring of truth that produces an effect very much the same as reading the Bible does. Its exposure of the falseness by which most people in the modern world live is a disinfectant.

Other features of the story are also suggested by the quoted excerpt. The genre of the work is obviously realistic fiction. The premise is that we are being given a "slice of life." The realistic writer aims to create the effect of everyday reality. The easy-reading prose style is part of this strategy. So is the inclusion of realistic details, such as the mention of the paper "still damp from the press." Realistic fiction gives us the concreteness and apparent randomness of everyday life. Of course writers of such fiction work just as hard to create their effects as do writers of fantasy.

Nearly everything in the opening excerpt shows that this is a story of social protest. It is a work of satire in which Tolstoy exposes what is wrong with our own valueless society. For the most part, Tolstoy relies on his selectivity of material to make us *see* the moral deficiency of our society—its selfishness, its isolation from human suffering, its denial of death, its materialism and triviality.

But in addition to this straightforward portrayal, Tolstoy creates a narrator who orchestrates our journey through the story. He tells the story from the detached, third-person point of view. This distances him from the action and conveys the impression that he is looking down on the characters in the story from a perspective of moral superiority. The narrator speaks with unusual authority, reminiscent of the effect of the Bible. He is obviously a reliable narrator whose simple, matter-of-fact style strikes us as both honest and unsettling in its probing of every corner of our lives. We come to perceive the utter sarcasm of his comments on the lifestyle of the characters in the story. The most famous of all such assessments is the one that begins Chapter 2: "Ivan Ilych's life had been most simple and most ordinary and therefore most terrible."

As that sentence reveals, *The Death of Ivan Ilych* is a subversive story. It aims to undermine established attitudes and to make us distrustful of the way we live our lives. It does so by challenging the values by which most people live. Like the Old Testament book of Ecclesiastes, the story touches all the bases as it pursues the myriad ways people try to find satisfaction in life while avoiding the deeper issues. Like the Bible as a whole, Tolstoy's story is marvelously adept at relentlessly getting beneath the surface of life to the real issues. The biblical effect is reinforced by the style—concrete but unembellished, simple and elemental, an evocative outline into which we pour our own experiences.

In an era when realism is almost synonymous with a secular viewpoint, it is refreshing to note that Tolstoy's masterpiece goes beyond simply analyzing social problems to become that rarity of modern literature—a work that accurately and from a Christian perspective tells us how to live. Paradoxically, it tells us how to live by showing us how not to live. The story raises the most basic of all questions: what is the goal of life, and how ought people to conduct their lives in the light of that goal? The answers offered are Christian.

It goes without saying that the world of Tolstoy's story is a Russian world. It has all the earmarks of Russian fiction: the strange names, the foreign geography, the bureaucratic milieu. It is a remote world—as remote as the world of myth. It requires of us the willingness to be transported to a strange place. Once transported, we also find ourselves in a world of familiar human experience.

Tolstoy's story is a case study in how realistic fiction works, and this is how I propose to explore it. My particular interest is the types of truth that fiction can express.

## "I Want Truth Rather than Fiction": Why Fiction Is Suspect in Some Circles

Conversations with Christian bookstore proprietors have alerted me to how widespread the bias against fiction is in some Christian circles. Clerks in such stores tell me of customers who carry books to the counter wanting to know if the books are fictional or whether they "really happened." What precisely is the case against fiction?

*Usefulness vs. Pleasure.* For some people the case against fiction is really an objection to pleasure. If one is going to spend one's time reading, the argument runs, one should at least read something useful. The equation of fiction reading with time wasting is very old and persistent in the Christian tradition.

My response is twofold. One is to defend the pleasure principle. Where do we get the idea that it is wrong to spend one's time doing something pleasurable? Surely not from the Bible, which (as I noted in the preceding chapter) endorses pleasure in principle. People who cannot enjoy things in life suffer from an aberration that psychologists call *anhedonia*—the inability to experience pleasure.

In the second place, it is untrue that fiction is nonutilitarian. The uses of fiction are synonymous with the uses of literature. They include refreshment, clarification of life, self-awareness, expansion of our range of experiences, and enlargement of our sense of understanding and compassion for people. Like literature generally, fiction is a form of discovery, perception, intensification, expression, beauty, and understanding. If it is all these things, the question of whether it is a legitimate use of time should not even arise.

*Fact vs. Illusion.* A second objection to fiction is concerned not with use of time but with the ontological status of fiction. In this scheme fiction is suspect because it is deficient in the facts that prevail in our world of time and space. It is merely imagined instead of being tangible like the computer in front of me.

But so are the facts that appear in *any* book. The words on the page of a history book or newspaper are in themselves intangible and exist only in the reader's mind. When we speak of them as being factual, we mean that the words name things that exist in the actual world.

Having said that, it is obvious that fictional writing is also factual. Its details are the details of the real world. "You have to give them something to write about," Robert Frost once said about his teaching of writers. What he meant is that writers must be sensitive observers of reality. When they are, their writing is filled with the facts of life around us. Poet John Ciardi once remarked that "the lofty . . . acreages of poetry are sown to fact. . . . Even so mystical a poet as Gerard Manley Hopkins . . . is gorgeously given to the fact of the thing. . . . A writer is a [person] who must know something better than anyone else does."[2]

When Tolstoy wrote *The Death of Ivan Ilych*, the facts of existence were all that he had for his story material. Facts are the very stuff of fiction. Consider a random specimen:

> *[Ivan] found a delightful house, just the thing both he and his wife had dreamt of. Spacious, lofty reception rooms in the old style, a convenient and dignified study, rooms for his wife and daughter, a study for his son—it might have been specially built for them. Ivan Ilych himself superintended the arrangements, chose the wallpapers, supplemented the furniture, and supervised the upholstering.*

The passage is filled with the facts of the experience being portrayed. On the physical side we observe the architectural facts of a house and of the activities required to move a family into a house, as well as a knowledge of what needs to be done in the process of redecorating. But the genius of literature is that it also gives us the human or psychological facts of life, in this case the human dreams that arise in us whenever we move into a new place of residence or new phase of life.

The attempt to set fiction against fact is doomed to defeat. Fiction does not give us illusions. It consists of facts that we can see in the world around us. Fiction writer Flannery O'Connor commented, "I'm always highly irritated by people who imply that writing fiction is an escape from reality. It is a plunge into reality."[3]

**Truth vs. Falsehood.** A third objection to fiction centers around the dichotomy of truth and falseness. Put simply, the argument is that fiction is lies. Tolstoy tells us what Ivan Ilych did when moving into his new residence, but we know that Ivan never literally lived and that the house Tolstoy describes is merely imagined. Fiction claims things that are literally false.

But the argument that fiction therefore misleads people is frivolous. By its very nature, the genre of fiction includes the understood convention that the events portrayed are pretended events. Sir Philip Sidney, whose defense of the fictional element in literature remains one of the best, said simply that the imaginative writer "nothing affirms, and therefore never lieth."[4] In other words, the writer of fiction makes it clear from the outset that the characters and events are merely imagined rather than things that actually existed.

As Sidney goes on to observe, it is writers of nonfiction who are guilty of misleading people. They do so because people expect everything that such writers say to be completely truthful, and we know that no one has the omniscience to give total and objective truth about a matter. That is why textbooks and history books are always in need of revision, while literature is permanent.

The question of the truthfulness of fiction is a bigger subject than simply refuting the charge that fiction misleads people. Exploring it will occupy the remainder of this chapter. Although my focus will be on fiction, the principles that I cover apply to all imaginative literature, including poetry.

**Summary.** People who say they have no use for fiction tell a lie. Everyone spends part of every day living in the world of daydreaming or fantasy. We relive the events of the day (or of our childhood) and preview the events that we expect to happen. We conduct imaginary conversations of a meeting that lies ahead or that we just had. Obviously fiction *does* have a use in everyone's life. That is why G.K. Chesterton could claim that "literature is a luxury; fiction is a necessity."[5]

## Levels of Truth in Fiction

Does fiction tell the truth? Discussions where I have heard this question debated have usually been conducted on a false premise. The premise is that the question yields a simple yes-or-no answer. But it doesn't. It all depends on what *type* of truth we are talking about. Fiction has the potential to embody four types of truth. A given work might tell the truth at some levels and not at others.

*The Truth about Human Longings, Fears, and Values.* At the broadest possible level, fiction is a repository of human values. Simply at the level of subject matter, the world of fictional literature shows us what people long for and what they fear. In the words of Northrop Frye, human fictions embody "man's views of the world he wants to live in, of the world he does not want to live in, of his situation and destiny and heritage, of the world he is trying to make and of the world that resists his efforts."[6] Fiction tells us the truth about human aspirations and anxieties regardless of its specific philosophic slant.

Tolstoy's story illustrates this level of fictional truth. As we follow the life of Ivan Ilych and see his experiences reinforced by other characters in the story, it is easy to see what the human race fears. It fears death, first of all—so much so that everyone in the story except Ivan at the end denies the reality of death. Tolstoy's story gives shape to the fear of suffering, of being isolated from others, of being deceived. We are also forcibly reminded of our fear of physical pain and illness, especially terminal illness.

We see even more clearly what the human race longs for as we read this piece of fiction. One of these longings is the longing for life. When an inner voice asks the dying Ivan, "What is it you want?" his immediate answer is, "To live and not to suffer." In Ivan's experience we see the human longing for a faith to die by, for forgiveness, for reconciliation, for a meaning to life that goes beyond physical comfortableness.

All of these are noble longings. But the story also shows us the inferior longings that, while not bad in themselves, are insufficient as a basis for life. They include professional success, material prosperity, sexual fulfillment, a harmonious family (for which we are made to long by the portrayal of its absence), physical health and comfort, and human compassion (which we see especially in the behavior of the butler's assistant Gerasim).

From what I have said about fears and longings, it is obvious that fiction like this tells us the truth about human values. It forces us to think about what matters most and what matters least. Despite its brevity, *The Death of Ivan Ilych* portrays a host of human values. These remind us of what it means to be a member of the human race. Fiction tells us the truth about what is important in human experience.

From this it is easy to see one of the important benefits of reading fiction: it nurtures human values and raises our awareness of them. It calls us to an ideal world and reminds us of the obstacles that prevent us from attaining it. This is one of the types of knowledge most worth having, for it leads to an understanding of both ourselves and the world in which we live.

*The Reality Principle.* A second level of truth to which fiction almost universally rises is representational truth—truthfulness to the way things are in the world. In the whole history of thinking about fiction, no principle has been so consistently asserted as the correspondence between fiction and life. The oldest version of the theory belongs to the Greeks, who spoke of fiction as *mimesis*—an imitation of life. Beginning with the Romantic era in the nineteenth century, people decided that the idea of imitation did not do justice to the creative element in literary composition, so the word *image* became the standard term by which to signify that fiction is a picture of human experience. The English poet Shelley sounded the keynote when he called literature "the very image of life expressed in its eternal truth."[7]

Henry James' essay "The Art of Fiction" can be taken as an important modern statement of the theory of imitation.[8] "The only reason for the existence of a novel," writes James, "is that it does attempt to represent life." "The supreme virtue of a novel" is "the air of reality" that it conveys. The effectiveness of a piece of fiction is "the success with which the author has produced the illusion of life" and the resulting impression we have that the author has been able "to render the look of things, the look that conveys their meaning, to catch the colour, the relief, the expression, the surface, the substance of the human spectacle." Fiction is based on "an immense and intricate correspondence with life."

It is exactly here that we see the genius of Tolstoy as a fiction writer. In *The Death of Ivan Ilych* he holds the mirror up to life. Passage after passage captures the reality of physical illness and suffering, for example: "The pain in his side oppressed him and seemed to grow worse and more incessant, while the taste in his mouth grew stranger and stranger." As we follow the progress of Ivan's illness, we reenact the whole sickening process as it happens in real life, from the early uncertainty of the diagnosis, through the emotional roller coaster of wondering how serious the illness is, then to the self-deceptions surrounding the seriousness of the prognosis, and finally to the stage where the illness becomes the only reality.

To say that this fictional account is untruthful is preposterous, as anyone who has confronted serious illness can confirm. Here is the reality of the experience as we have all known it: "all the way home he was going over what the doctor had said, trying to translate those complicated, obscure, scientific phrases into plain language and find in them an answer to the question: 'Is my condition bad? Is it very bad? Or is there as yet nothing much wrong?'" Such writing seems untruthful only to someone who has not seen enough of life. For the patients visited by Robert Coles on his rounds in the hospital, Tolstoy's story had the ring of truth.[9]

Tolstoy portrays with equal reality the experience of coming to grips with human mortality. We see it chiefly in the progress of Ivan's response to his own terminal illness, but the responses of Ivan's family and acquaintances reinforce it. The most common response in the story, as in life, is to distance the death as a form of denial. When the news of Ivan's death first hits the office, it "aroused, as usual, in all who heard of it the complacent feeling that, 'it is he who is dead and not I.' " Ivan's wife tries to sidestep the seriousness of the illness by taking refuge in the ability of medicine to solve her husband's problem: "Mind now to take your medicine regularly."

Only Ivan manages to move beyond denial as his illness forces him to confront his own mortality. He begins with full-scale denial: "The pain did not grow less, but Ivan Ilych made efforts to force himself to think that he was better." Again, "He recalled all the doctors had told him of how [a floating kidney] detached itself and swayed about. And by an effort of imagination he tried to catch that kidney and arrest it and support it."

Ivan's next stage is to accept the fact that he is dying: "I think of the appendix—but this is death!" At first even this is surrounded with misunderstanding: "Ivan ILych saw that he was dying, and he was in continual despair. In the depth of his heart he knew he was dying, but not only was he not accustomed to the thought, he simply did not and could not grasp it." Eventually death becomes personified as an impersonal *It* that would "stand before him and look at him, and he would be petrified and the light would die out of his eyes."

The deception of people toward each other is another of the experiences that Tolstoy captures accurately. "What tormented Ivan Ilych most," the narrator tells us, "was the deception, the lie, which for some reason they all accepted, that he was not dying but was simply ill." And later, "This falsity around him and within him did more than anything else to poison his last days." The servant Gerasim, who supported Ivan's legs to ease the pain, "alone did not lie."

People's self-centered indifference to the suffering of others is also realistically portrayed. Several scenes portray Ivan's family paying a perfunctory visit to his bedside, irritated that the flow of their lives has been interrupted by his unseemly illness. In one of these scenes, Ivan's daughter "came in in full evening dress, her fresh young flesh exposed, . . . strong, healthy, evidently in love, and impatient with illness, suffering, and death, because they interfered with her happiness." This recalls the wife's statement in the opening chapter that her husband "suffered terribly the last few days. . . . I cannot understand how I bore it."

The dying Ivan is left in emotional isolation: "Apart from this lying, or because of it, what most tormented Ivan Ilych was that no one pitied him as he wished to be pitied." The story illustrates a leading theme of the literature of the past two centuries—the fear of the loss of the power to feel. In a particularly poignant moment of isolation, we read that Ivan "wept on account of his helplessness, his terrible loneliness, the cruelty of man, the cruelty of God, and the absence of God."

Much more could be said about the truthfulness to reality that we find in Tolstoy's fictional story. But my examples show why John Ciardi can write that "poetry and fiction, like all the arts, are a way of perceiving and of understanding the world. Good writing is as positive a search for truth as is any part of science. . . . Good writing always increases the amount of human knowledge."[10]

*General Truth: Social Protest in* **The Death of Ivan Ilych.** In addition to representational truth, fiction expresses ideational truth, or perspectival truth. In other words, writers do more than portray human experience. They also offer an interpretation of that experience. By means of character, setting, and action, fiction writers make implied assertions about reality.

We can arrange these embodied ideas on a continuum from the very general to the very specific. At one end of the spectrum we state the embodied ideas of literature in sufficiently general terms that virtually anyone would accept them as true. I call this general truth. It is part of the common wisdom of the human race and a bond that Christians share with others.

One avenue by which to see the general truth of *The Death of Ivan Ilych* is to explore the element of social protest in the story. Tolstoy's attitude toward his material is satiric. His aim is to expose the failings of the society and characters that he portrays. The story becomes a truthful indictment of modern society.

The portrait of society begins already in the opening chapter, where we observe the reactions of Ivan's colleagues and wife to his death. We see how selfish and unfeeling people are, for example. We observe how our culture denies death. We sense the gap between social rituals (visiting the widow to express condolence) and the feelings of people as they perform these rituals (the colleagues are actually irritated that their visit to the widow will interfere with their weekly card game).

The shallowness of modern society emerges even more clearly once we start to follow Ivan's life story. Until his illness and impending death force him beneath the surfaces of life, his life follows the typical course of the American dream. Ivan begins his life with complete social, professional, and moral conformity. The narrator's vocabulary heaps a crescendo of scorn on Ivan's conformity, as he is said to base his life on such qualities as being *agreeable, correct, decorous, approved of by society.* A sarcastic summary is the narrator's comment that Ivan performed his "duty, that is, to lead a decorous life approved of by society."

Other features of Ivan's life are equally truthful to what we can see around us. Ivan becomes an organization man who makes work the center of life. When he gets married he undergoes a progressive dehumanizing in which he becomes interested in household *things* rather than his work (which had at least involved people). His life becomes increasingly trivial: playing cards and "giving little dinners to which he invited men and women of good social position" become Ivan's "chief pleasure."

Other features of the society portrayed in this fictional world are likewise thoroughly familiar to us. We look on a world that is materialistic, worshipful of success (measured in terms of career and the size of one's house), and enamored of power and prestige. We catch glimpses of social climbing, extreme individualism, breakdown of families, sexual permissiveness, and a loss of relationship. We observe secularism, an unwarranted trust in medical technology (with an accompanying sense of betrayal when it fails to cure the patient), avoidance of suffering, mass identity, alienation, the worship of work, and the trivialization of leisure.

The truthfulness of this fictional portrait of a lost society is not simply a matter of truthfulness to the way things are. In addition to such representational truth, the story offers a satiric perspective on the portrait. This is part of the general truth that the story imparts. One does not need to be a Christian to assent to the narrator's equation of Ivan's life being "ordinary and therefore most terrible." Any good reader is led to see that leading an "ordinary" life as the story depicts it is to miss the true issues of life and death.

**Ultimate Truth: The Realism of Grace in The Death of Ivan Ilych.** In addition to the general insights that a work of fiction asserts are more ultimate claims. Writers, in other words, have a world view as well as common-sense observations about life. This world view consists of basic premises about God, people, and the world. It is a comment not only on how people live but on how they ought to live. Someone has said that all of Tolstoy's books "concern the same theme, the good life."[11] To portray the good life is to assert a world view.

In Tolstoy's story, the attack on how most people live is conducted in terms with which most people can agree. By itself, this portrayal of the deficiencies of modern society contains no strong hints about the writer's philosophic perspective on life. This is not to say that a Christian reader might not resonate more strongly than other readers with the scathing indictment that Tolstoy makes of modern society. But the story's explicit world view emerges clearly only in the latter phases of the story where Tolstoy portrays the solution to the problem of Ivan's "ordinary and terrible" life. Here we increasingly see that the author's vision is religious and finally Christian.

Tolstoy's story shows that there is a realism of grace as well as a realism of carnality. Because the subject of realistic fiction is ordinarily the depravity or disappointments of human life, it is easy to begin thinking that realism is by definition the portrayal of evil in the world. But fictional realism is not bound to just one philosophic viewpoint. Christian fiction writers have proven that there is also a realism of grace. The last four chapters of *The Death of Ivan Ilych* are a crowning example of such realism (and we might note in passing that the chapters become shorter late in the story as the pace quickens near the climax).

Ivan Ilych becomes a latter-day Job as he pursues his quest to find meaning in his suffering. He first acknowledges the reality of God in Chapter 9 (four chapters from the end). "Why hast Thou done all this?" he asks suddenly, with the capitalized "Thou" signalizing that for the first time in the story Ivan has addressed God. This is the minimal but necessary starting point in the quest for salvation. As Hebrews 11:6 puts it, "Whoever would draw near to God must believe that he exists."

The second key event in Ivan's spiritual progress is conviction of sin. The main obstacle to that conviction is complacency. Whenever the thought occurred to Ivan that he had not lived as he ought to have lived, "he at once recalled the correctness of his whole life and dismissed so strange an idea." But in a memorable scene in Chapter 10, pictures of Ivan's past rise before him. In this catalog of memories, the one bright spot is his early childhood, "and afterwards all becomes blacker and blacker." This is enough to start Ivan thinking.

But the real breakthrough comes in the next-to-last chapter as Ivan's suffering becomes more intense. Here is the moment of high drama:

> *His mental sufferings were due to the fact that that night, as he looked at Gerasim's sleepy, good-natured face with its prominent cheek-bones, the question suddenly occurred to him: "What if my whole life has really been wrong?"*
>
> *It occurred to him that what had appeared perfectly impossible before, namely that he had not spent his life as he should have done, might after*

*all be true. It occurred to him that . . . the whole arrangement of his life . . . might all have been false. He tried to defend all those things to himself and suddenly felt the weakness of what he was defending. There was nothing to defend.*

This moment of conviction leads Ivan to lie on his back and "pass his life in review in quite a new way."

As he does so, Ivan is led to make an assessment of the earlier parts of his life that goes beyond what we would have guessed from our reading of the story up to this point. The story has been told in such a way as to make us share the narrator's scorn for the life that is portrayed. But the indictment becomes more specific and more religiously tinged when we read that Ivan now saw that everything he had lived for "was not real at all, but a terrible and huge deception which had hidden both life and death." This is the ultimate deception in a story that has dealt with deception on several levels—deception among colleagues, among family members, between doctor and patient, within people's own being.

Tolstoy saved his best writing for the last chapter. It begins with Ivan's impasse: he knew that "he was lost, that there was no return, that the end had come, the very end, and his doubts were still unsolved and remained doubts." The writing becomes more imagistic, symbolic, and concrete at this point. Death becomes pictured as a black sack into which Ivan is being forced "by an invisible, resistless force." Ivan responds by struggling "as a man condemnned to death struggles in the hands of the executioner, knowing that he cannot save himself." The word "save" is obviously a word charged with Christian meaning.

Then a force struck Ivan in his side and he "fell through the hole and there at the bottom was a light." Not only does Tolstoy use the imagery of the New Testament at this point, but he borrows the technique of analogy from Jesus' parables. Remembering Jesus' formula "the kingdom of heaven is like. . . ," Tolstoy writes, "What had happened to him was like the sensation one sometimes experiences in a railway carriage when one thinks one is going backwards while one is really going forwards and suddenly becomes aware of the real direction." This is the imagery of conversion, even though Tolstoy avoids abstraction in deference to the indirection of analogy and image.

Having fallen "through and caught sight of the light, . . . it was revealed to him that though his life had not been what it should have been, this could still be rectified." The occasion for doing the right thing comes when Ivan's wife and son appear at his bedside. Ivan feels sorry for them. Although he says "forego" when he tried to say "forgive me," Ivan knows "that He whose understanding mattered would understand."

Then things begin to happen in rapidfire succession. The weight that had been physically and spiritually oppressing Ivan "was all dropping away at once from two sides, from ten sides, and from all sides." After truckloads of self-pity, Ivan is sorry for his family and wants to "act so as not to hurt them." The pain that had been Ivan's only reality ceases to tyrannize him: "Yes, here it is. Well, what of it? Let the pain be."

The finale of the story draws heavily upon allusions to the New Testament. New Testament texts that speak of death's being abolished are echoed in the comment that Ivan "sought his former accustomed fear of death and did not find. 'Where is it? What death?' There was no fear because there was no death." Equally biblical is the imagery of the statement, "In place of death there was light" (see 2 Timothy 1:10 and Matthew 4:16). The experience of salvation is experienced as a moment of recognition and joy: " 'So that's what it is!' he suddenly exclaimed. 'What joy!' "

To show that Ivan is participating in the atonement that Christ achieved in his death and resurrection, Tolstoy frames his final chapter with allusions to the passion story of the Gospels. At the beginning of the chapter we read that Ivan's final agonizing suffering lasted for three days. At the end of three days he passes through the darkness and awakens into light. At the very end of the chapter he hears "someone near him" say, "It is finished," repeating one of Christ's sayings from the cross. Ivan himself "heard these words and repeated them in his soul." Ivan's final words are, "Death is finished. It is no more."

In view of this wealth of Christian experience, imagery, and allusion in the last chapter, we must turn a deaf ear to attempts to flatten out the force of the ending and make it fit what I have called general truth. I refer to statements that caution us not to "provide Ivan Ilych's end with an 'uplifting' moral" or that assert that "Tolstoy resists a facile 'religious' conclusion—the light he sees at the bottom of his imaginary sack is not God's love or immortality, but only a release from suffering."[12] It is obvious on the contrary that the story is "a religious work of art,"[13] "on a level with the greatest religious writings of the world,"[14] probably even Tolstoy's "expression of his conversion experience."[15]

*Fictional Truth and Other Forms of Truth.* If we compare these types of fictional truth to the truth of a theology book, history book, news magazine, or biography, some key distinctions emerge. *The Death of Ivan Ilych* embodies the same moral and theological ideas that a sermon or theology book does, but the knowledge that it gives us is an experiential knowledge. Fiction contributes to our understanding by making us relive an experience, just as Jesus told a fictional story instead of giving an abstract definition of "neighbor."

The great advantage of fiction over history or biography is its universality. When we read about a specific person's actual experience, we look at that experience from the viewpoint of a spectator. We may be edified and instructed by the account, but we are conscious that the experience happened to someone else instead of to us.

Fiction, by contrast, is open-ended and personally applicable. We can walk into a fictional world and make it our own. The experience of Ivan Ilych is *our* experience, and his world *our* world, in a way that is never quite true of history and biography. Tolstoy's story is set in nineteenth-century Russia, but Ivan Ilych has been called a typical American.

Fiction also offers the writer more freedom than history and biography. Sir Philip Sidney analyzed this in his great defense of fiction. Writers of history and biography are limited to what actually happened, whereas writers of fiction can be true to the pattern of truth that they are developing. In history and biography that pattern is often obscured by the need to record only the facts. As a result, the truth they give us is partial and local. Fiction is free to be complete. The truth that fiction gives us is the truth not about what *happened* but about what *happens*, a truth that is universally applicable.

When the movie version of Eric Liddell's life came out ("Chariots of Fire"), articles started to appear about the real-life events on which the movie was based. It quickly became obvious that the movie contained fictional elements. Liddell knew long before embarking for France that his race was scheduled for Sunday, but the movie made that moment of crisis occur during the boat trip from England to France. The movie portrayed Liddell's sister as objecting to her brother's running when he should have been doing missionary work, but in real life the confrontation between brother and sister on the hillside overlooking Edinburgh never happened.

Why do script writers rearrange the materials of real life in these ways? Because it allows them to highlight the principles involved in the experience. The movie version of Eric Liddell's life, including its fictional elements, is as truthful a portrayal of the Christian life of Liddell as a biography is. Simon Lesser observes that "while fiction alters the facts of experience, a fundamental purpose of those alterations . . . is the achievement of an imaginary world more lifelike than life itself, more directly and honestly concerned with essential problems, . . . less burdened by distracting irrelevancies."[16]

*Summary.* Fiction is one of the most powerful vehicles for truth that exists. It has the potential to tell us the truth about human values, fears, and longings. It is truthful to human experience as we know it. And it embodies ideas that can be true. People who return fictional books to the bookstore shelf are cutting themselves off from a type of truth that everyone needs.

### Realism as a Form of Literature

In my earlier chapter on Homer's *Odyssey* I explored the virtues of fantasy or myth as a literary form. I need to balance that praise with some concluding comments about what realistic fiction does particularly well.

A brief definition of realism is in order. The standard source on the subject is Ian Watt's book *The Rise of the Novel.*[17] Watt contrasts the realistic novel to its predecessors epic and romance. The novel is based on techniques of "formal realism"—formal in the sense that we can identify a set of narrative devices that create the effect of realism. These devices include originality (as distinct from using a story from existing myth or legend), realism of events (absence of marvelous characters and occurrences), low mode characters (the "ordinary people" principle), realism of characters' names, realism of the social setting, and a realistic style that approximates ordinary speech (as opposed to the poetry of epic).

Fantasy excels in transporting us to an alternate world. The strength of realism is its ability to give us a replica of our own world. Realism thus offers a more direct version of the truth about human experience than fantasy does. Before a one-eyed Cyclops has relevance to our lives, we need to translate the monster into its meaning (the terror of evil). But the picture of Ivan Ilych visiting the doctor and suffering pain requires no such translation. The truth of the picture is ready at hand. One of the virtues of realism is its closeness to lived experience and a resulting sense of immediacy to our own world. Realism is accessible to the ordinary reader's experience in a way that fantasy may not be.

Because realism gives us a replica of ordinary life, it is adept at showing not only the spirit of an age but its daily life as well. Epics like Homer's *Odyssey* or Milton's *Paradise Lost* are a picture of their age largely in the sense of letting us see the ideas, feelings, and values that prevailed in the writer's culture. These mythical stories do not primarily give us pictures of life as it was lived in the author's society. But *The Death of Ivan Ilych* lets us experience life as it was actually lived in the early modern era.

Although mythical stories can portray human psychology, realism is even better at portraying the inner workings of the human mind. In Tolstoy's story we are repeatedly shown the thoughts and feelings of characters as they respond to the events in the narrative. In fact, the story of Ivan's internal life is the focus of the story. The story of his inner development is the main plot.

Fantasy specializes in the extraordinary. Its forte is the excitement of the exceptional. By contrast, realism wins us with its portrayal of the average. Its authority is the authority of the typical. *The Death of Ivan Ilych* is a prime illustration. One critic writes,

> Tolstoy wanted to render a universal experience. . . . The strategy Tolstoy hit upon was to create a figure who, in his absolutely commonplace life and character, would indeed seem universal. . . . All of us share at least some of those trivialities and vanities that make up the bulk of Ivan Ilych's existence. . . . [Chaper One was] composed by Tolstoy with the idea of implicating all of us in the ordinary responses to the ordinary fact of an ordinary man's death.[18]

The strength of realism is its closeness to every reader's experience.

Realism thus implies a whole view of reality that one writer calls "prosaics."[19] In contrast to philosophies that believe history is determined by heroic figures and spectacular, epoch-making events, prosaics believes that it is determined by ordinary people and the ordinary events of their lives. In the words of my source,

> Most historians and philosophers tend to focus on the big events—on wars, revolutions, dramatic incidents, critical choices, and decisive encounters. Individual people, too, tend to tell themselves the story of their lives in terms of exceptional events and big decisions. But what if the important events are not the great ones, but the infinitely numerous and apparently inconsequential ordinary ones, which, taken together, are far more effective and significant? . . . It is often the small items in the background of old photographs that most powerfully evoke elusive memories of the past. . . . The furniture long ago discarded, a spot on the wall, a picture we had long ignored but that now suggests the habitual life we lived beneath it—these small items remind us of how it felt to live in a room.

Realism shares with this prosaic view of life the premise that the most important events are "the most ordinary and everyday ones—events that we do not appreciate simply because they are so commonplace. . . . Cloaked in their very ordinariness, the prosaic events that truly shape our lives—that truly *are* our lives, escape our notice." Literary realism attempts to make sure that these prosaic events do *not* escape our notice.

The accident that causes Ivan Ilych's life-ending illness fits into this view of life. Literary tragedy traces the hero's downfall to a titanic tragic choice that the hero makes. By contrast, Ivan slips on a step-ladder while decorating his house and suffers a minor bruise. From this trivial household accident stems his long slide toward death. His illness remains mysterious to the doctors.

We should also note the artistry of realism. Realism is a didactic genre. We do not ordinarily read realistic fiction like *The Death of Ivan Ilych* because we want to be entertained. We read it because we sense that it tells us something we need to know. This should not be allowed to obscure the artistry that realism possesses and offers for our appreciation and enjoyment.

We should remember first that realistic stories are just that—stories. They possess the same types of narrative artistry that any good story does, including unity, coherence, and emphasis. The usual narrative ingredients of suspense, dramatic irony, foreshadowing, surprise, and climax are all potentially present.

Other narrative techniques seem especially suitable for realism. Writers of realism are usually adept at concrete description, for example. They are skilled at creating realistic dialogue and speech patterns. We usually admire their inventiveness in creating characters and events. My explication of the conclusion of *The Death of Ivan Ilych* shows that realism can also use the time-honored resources of symbol and allusion. Most of all, realistic writers are masters of selectivity—choosing just the right details to embody their sense of life or contribute to characterization.

In other words, we should not allow the fact that realism aims to create the effect of real life to mislead us into thinking that it is devoid of literary artifice. Writers of realism choose and arrange their material and search for the right words just as painstakingly as a poet or fantasy writer does. Tolstoy spent two years creating his sixty-page masterpiece.

*Summary.* Realism is the dominant form of modern literature. Its conventions include choosing story material from everyday life and then treating it in the vocabulary of ordinary speech. The result is that we are put into close contact with everyday experience in a manner that may have more impact than real life ordinarily conveys. Joyce Cary rightly claims that a "reader is often aware of learning more about the world from a book than he gets from actual experience" because the ordering of experience that literature presents can reveal "new orders of meaning" in "what had seemed the mere confusion of . . . daily affairs."[20]

## Notes to Chapter 8

[1]I have used the Aylmer Maude translation of *The Death of Ivan Ilych*, as printed in Leo Tolstoy: *The Death of Ivan Ilych and Other Stories* (New York: Signet, 1960).

[2]John Ciardi, "What Every Writer Must Learn," *The Saturday Review* 15 December 1956: 8.

[3]Flannery O'Connor, *Mystery and Manners*, ed. Sally and Robert Fitzgerald (New York: Farrar, Straus & Giroux, 1957), pp. 77-78.

[4]Sir Philip Sidney, *An Apology for Poetry*, in *Criticism: The Major Statements* ed. Charles Kaplan (New York: St. Martin's, 1975), p. 132.

[5]G.K. Chesterton, "Fiction as Food," in *The Spice of Life and Other Essays*, ed. Dorothy Collins (Beaconfield: Darwen Finlayson, 1964), p. 30.

[6]Northrop Frye, *The Stubborn Structure* (Ithaca: Cornell UP, 1970), p. 18.

[7]Percy Bysshe Shelley, "A Defence of Poetry," in *Criticism: The Major Statements*, ed. Kaplan, p. 360.

[8]I have quoted from Henry James' essay "The Art of Fiction" as it appears in *Criticism: The Major Statements*, ed. Kaplan, pp. 432-449.

[9]Robert Coles, *The Call of Stories: Teaching and the Moral Imagination* (Boston: Houghton Mifflin, 1989), pp. 164-174.

[10]Ciardi, p. 39.

[11]Rene Wellek, introduction to *The Death of Ivan Ilych* in *The Norton Anthology of World Masterpieces*, fourth ed., ed. Maynard Mack (New York: Norton, 1979), 2: 725.

[12]Irving Howe, "Introduction" to *The Death of Ivan Ilych* in *Classics of Modern Fiction: Eight Short Novels*, ed. Howe (New York: Harcourt, Brace and World, 1968), p. 120; and R.F. Christian, *Tolstoy: A Critical Introduction* (Cambridge: Cambridge UP, 1969), p. 237.

[13]G.W. Spence, *Tolstoy the Ascetic* (New York: Barnes and Noble, 1967), p. ix.

[14]"Tolstoy," in *The Encyclopaedia Britannica*, 14th ed. (London: Encyclopaedia Britannica, 1929, 1936), 22: 274.

[15]Mortimer J. Adler and Seymour Cain, *Imaginative Literature II* (Chicago: Encyclopaedia Britannica, 1962), p. 175.

[16]Simon O. Lesser, *Fiction and the Unconscious* (Chicago: University of Chicago Press, 1957, 1975), p. 54.

[17]Ian Watt, *The Rise of the Novel* (Berkeley: University of California, 1965).

[18]Howe, pp. 114-115.

[19]Gary Saul Morson, "Prosaics: An Approach to the Humanities," *The American Scholar* 57 (1988): 515-528. This is a truly outstanding essay.

[20]Joyce Cary, *Art and Reality: Ways of the Creative Process* (Garden City: Doubleday, 1961), p. 155.

# Chapter 9

## Camus' The Stranger *and Modern Literature*

### Life under the Sun

❋

*Mother died today. Or, maybe, yesterday; I can't be sure. The telegram from the Home says: YOUR MOTHER PASSED AWAY. FUNERAL TOMORROW. DEEP SYMPATHY. Which leaves the matter doubtful; it could have been yesterday.*

*The Home for Aged Persons is at Marengo, some fifty miles from Algiers. With the two-o'clock bus I should get there well before nightfall. Then I can spend the night there, keeping the usual vigil beside the body. . . .*

*For the present, it's almost as if Mother weren't really dead. The funeral will bring it home to me, put an official seal on it, so to speak. . . .*

*I took the two-o'clock bus. It was a blazing hot afternoon. I'd lunched, as usual, at Celeste's restaurant. Everyone was most kind, and Celeste said to me, "There's no one like a mother." When I left they came with me to the door. . . .*

*I had to run to catch the bus. I suppose it was my hurrying like that, what with the glare off the road and from the sky, the reek of gasoline, and the jolts, that made me feel so drowsy.*[1]

❋

There is no more striking opening in all of literature than the opening paragraphs of this novel. The reasons for the memorable impact are multiple.

The first is the narrator who speaks to us with such intimate familiarity. The first-person point of view does its usual magic as we are put under the spell of the speaker's consciousness from the first page to the last. Paradoxically, even though the narrator takes us into his inner consciousness, the effect is one of utter objectivity as the narrator dispassionately records details as an automaton might.

Once we become acclimated to the intimacy with which the narrator takes us into his confidence, we begin to notice what he is like. On page five we learn that his last name is Meursault. We are never told his first name. By day he works as an office clerk. Off the job he inhabits an uneventful, humdrum urban existence, breaking the unpleasantness of his life in a bad city neighborhood by swimming, going to the movies, staring in boredom out of his window, and engaging in random conversations with acquaintances who thrust themselves into his life. This is the external story.

Much more important is the interior story. From the opening paragraph we sense the utter unconventionality of the narrator—an unconventionality that initially fascinates us by its sheer unusualness and eventually repels us by its ethical and emotional poverty. Everything carries equal weight for him. The fact that there is no one like a mother is no more important than that he had to run to catch the bus. Part of his unconventionality is his emotional deficiency. We expect a son to be deeply moved by his mother's death, but Meursault displays no sense of grief or personal involvement. In the opening paragraph the narrator's mental energies are devoted solely to trying to decipher the telegraph.

The style of the novel also engages us. It is an example of the art of simplicity. The sentences are terse and self-contained. Connectives are sparse. The tone is matter of fact. Like a camera, the narrator records details meticulously. He speaks a language that is concrete, sensory, and vivid. No book ever obeyed the literary impulse to show rather than tell more effectively than this one. The style itself strikes us as an artistic achievement that merits the old word "beauty" and brings to mind C.S. Lewis's designation "phrase-by-phrase deliciousness."[2]

The opening paragraphs of the book also introduce us to the world of the story and hint at the central action of the plot. The story is set in Algeria, which at once makes the French protagonist who lives there a geographically displaced person—in the words of the book's title, an outsider. The world of the story is a world of death, both literally and figuratively. Indeed, the story is a conventional murder story, complete with shooting and trial scenes. By beginning the story with the mother's funeral, moreover, the storyteller foreshadows the mainspring of the plot. Anyone who has heard anything at all about this novel knows that it is about someone who is convicted for murder, not because he killed someone, but because he failed to weep at his mother's funeral.

Finally, the quoted excerpt hints at the crucial role that the sun and its attendant heat will play in the action. We rather continuously encounter descriptions like these: "The sky was already a blaze of light." "The sun was scorching hot." "The glare of the morning sun hit me in the eyes like a clenched fist." It is no wonder that the Old Testament book of Ecclesiastes provides a helpful interpretive framework for interpreting this novel. In Ecclesiates the phrase "under the sun" appears more than thirty times and denotes life lived on a purely earthly and human level, without recourse to a transcendent world. Like the Old Testament book, *The Stranger* paints a memorable picture of life "under the sun." Camus himself claimed that "at the center of my work there is an invincible sun."[3]

*The Stranger* is the classic modern novel. Its publication in 1942 was an epoch-making literary event that sent shock waves through the intellectual world. It continues to epitomize modern literature, and I have accordingly chosen to discuss it as representing the profit and perils of modern literature for a Christian reader. Despite its brevity, *The Stranger* illustrates almost all of the leading features of the landscape of modern literature. The dominant trends in modern literature include social protest, hedonism, nihilism or despair (including the absurd tradition), naturalism (extreme realism), and existentialism. That Camus could have compressed all of this into 150 pages is astounding.

## The Logic of Camus' Story
*The Stranger* falls into two balanced halves that together display a high degree of symmetry. This should serve to remind us that realistic fiction, despite all its lifelikeness, is a heightened version of reality, highly selective and artfully arranged. In real life, events do not display the high degree of organization that we find in Camus' story.

*Apparent and Hidden Plots in* **The Stranger.** The external action of Part One is Meursault's life until he murders an Arab on a hot Sunday afternoon. Judged by externalities, this life is conventional and prosaic.

Meursault performs adequately on the job and minds his own business. Half of the chapters in Part One are devoted simply to describing life on the block. That life is monotonous and empty, as well as morally and economically impoverished. Meursault's neighbors in the apartment building include Salamano, a lonely widower who abuses his dog, and a pimp named Raymond, who abuses his mistress.

The rest of Part One focuses on the weekend of the funeral of Meursault's mother and its aftermath. Mrs. Meursault is buried on a Saturday. The next day Meursault goes swimming and renews acquaintance with a friend named Marie, with whom he attends a comic movie and initiates an affair. The next weekend Meursault and Marie accompany Raymond to the beach, where Meursault gets entangled in a quarrel that Raymond is having with two Arab men. Meursault ends up shooting one of the Arabs.

Part Two is the story of Meursault's imprisonment and trial. Here the symmetry of the book's organization emerges. Almost every character, event, and detail that we observe in Part One reappears at the proceedings of the trial in Part Two.

What I have said thus far simply summarizes the apparent plot. The more profound story, as always in great literature, is the hidden plot. Part One shows us Meursault's acceptance of immediate physical sensation as the only truth he can grasp. Part Two portrays society's need to explain the events of Part One in terms of conventional logic. The discrepancy between the two results in extended dramatic irony, inasmuch as we know from Part One that Meursault did not experience the events as he is said to have experienced them by the prosecutor at the trial. Meursault, for example, is perplexed when the prosecutor calls Marie his mistress, since to him she is simply Marie.

*The Foundation of the Story: An "Innocent Crime."* Critics have noted the contradictory and implausible nature of the story's postulates. Given Meursault's indifference and boredom with life, he is the last person in the world to write a detailed journal of his experiences such as we find in the novel. In the Algeria in which the story is set, no European would have been condemned to death for murdering an Arab. And since the two Arabs on the beach had provoked the attack, the most serious case that would have been brought against Meursault in real life would have been involuntary manslaughter. Then, too, for all the author's professed admiration of Meursault, Camus in real life did not live like his fictional hero.

These implausibilities are things that we must accept as the "givens" of the story, and we will do so more willingly if we understand what Camus was up to in his novel. Camus' message in the story depends on the paradox of an "innocent" crime. In writing a novel of social protest, it was Camus' purpose to indict the injustices of conventional society and its institutions (as represented especially by the judge, the prosecutor, and the prison chaplain). He wanted to show that society will inevitably persecute someone who threatens the status quo by refusing to play the game of conventional social behavior. Furthermore, because one of the conventions of literature is to heighten the issues, Camus wanted this persecution to be drastic—condemnation to death in a court of law.

But herein lay a problem for Camus. The protagonist of the story is a mousy little office worker whose external life is harmless. It is his *attitudes* that challenge conventional standards and for which he is tried in the second half of the novel. As one critic puts it, "Every detail of the trial adds up to the conclusion that the judges resent the murderer not for what he did but for what he is."[4] Of course Camus was wrong when, in a preface to an American translation of the novel, he asserted, "In our society any man who does not weep at his mother's funeral runs the risk of being sentenced to death."[5] Taken literally, the statement is preposterous, and the novel itself shows that Camus was aware of this.

Camus knew that no jury would have even heard about Meursault solely on the basis of his inner life. Camus' solution was ingenious: he made his protagonist commit an "innocent" murder. Meursault, for example, commits the murder but does not will it. As in any murder story, we are shown the events that lead up to the murder, and what we learn is that the shooting was unpremeditated and without psychological motive. The actual murder is described as a riot of sensations, devoid of human reasoning or feeling. Instead of Meursault's *pulling* the trigger of the gun, we read that "the trigger gave, and the smooth underbelly of the butt jogged my palm." When, at the trial, Meursault tries to explain how he happened to murder the Arab, his explanation is that "it was because of the sun."

In other words, the murder is a pretext to get the protagonist of the story into court. Once there, he is tried and condemned for his attitudes rather than the murder he committed, and Camus has a free hand to make his critique of conventional society while generating sympathy for his rebel hero. Once we are aware of the strategy, the logic of the story falls into place.

We should be in no doubt that Camus himself sympathized with his hero. He made this plain in the preface that I have already mentioned:

*The hero of my book is condemned because he does not play the game. In this respect he is foreign to the society in which he lives. . . . He refuses to lie. . . . He says what he is, he refuses to hide his feelings, and immediately society feels threatened. . . . One would therefore not be much mistaken to read* The Stranger *as the story of a man who, without any heroics, agrees to die for the truth. . . . I have tried to draw in my character the only Christ we deserve. (335-337)*

It is not surprising that in a book that challenges conventional values so thoroughly Camus wrote a parody of the conventional saint's life by portraying a secular and irreligious "martyr."

Of course we are under no obligation to read the story as its author did. In place of Camus' simple reading, I suggest a more complex interpretion. A *double* feeling of judgment builds up as we read—judgment against society (as Camus insists) and against the protagonist. Meursault is (to quote the Christian critic Edmund Fuller) "essentially subhuman, whether Camus conceives him as inherently such, or as reduced to such."[6]

### The Depravity of Life under the Sun: Realism in Modern Literature

The twentieth century is the age of realism in literature. Simply at the level of subject matter, therefore, *The Stranger* can serve as a case study in how a Christian reader might read realistic literature. Modern realism, of course, is of a pessimistic type that sometimes goes by the name of naturalism. Its basic premise is that the rose bush in front of the house is much less real than the garbage can behind the house.

*The World of Modern Realism.* The basic impulse of modern realism is to picture life at its worst in a fallen world. *The Stranger* follows this impulse from start to finish. The world that Meursault inhabits is a dreary one. The landscape itself is oppressive: "Evenings in these parts must be a sort of mournful solace. Now, in the full glare of the morning sun, with everything shimmering in the heat haze, there was something inhuman, discouraging, about this landscape." The city milieu of Meursault's apartment building is no better: "The whole building was as quiet as the grave, a dank, dark smell rising from the well hole of the stairs. . . . Then the dog began to moan in old Salamano's room."

The people who inhabit this depressing world reinforce the sense of misery. The setting of the opening chapter is the home for the elderly where Meursault's mother had lived. "I'd never noticed," writes the narrator, "what big paunches old women usually have. Most of the men, however, were as thin as rakes, and they all carried sticks." In the apartment building where Meursault lives, Salamano and his dog hate each other. The stock in trade of naturalistic fiction is all here, from the compulsory ugly landscape scenes to the mangy dog scene.

The world of realism is also a world of immoral behavior. Sex and violence are conventional preoccupations with writers of realism. Here, too, *The Stranger* is typical. Meursault engages in promiscuity with Marie. His apartment neighbor Raymond is a pimp who beats his mistress and then finds himself engaged in brawls with her Arab protectors. The story is a murder story. What we encounter in the story, in short, is approximately what makes up the daily news.

By contemporary standards, the book is a rather tame version of realism. There are no extended sex scenes, and the book is devoid of profanity. Still, it forces a Christian reader to confront the problems posed by literary realism. What is an appropriate Christian response to the realistic portrayal of depravity?

*A Christian Assessment of Realism.* We should begin by noting that the Bible affirms realism as a literary technique. The Bible depicts the full range of human depravity. It does not shrink back from portraying sexual experience and abuse, violence, lying, thievery, cruelty, and a dozen other immoralities. Realism tells us something we need to know, namely, the sinfulness of the human condition and the misery of a fallen world. The mere portrayal of evil is not something Christians have a right to reject. Its positive purpose is to remind us of the "givens" of life in a fallen world, to spare us from an unwarranted optimism about the world or isolation from it, and to enlarge our sense of compassion for a lost world.

Literary realism tells us part of the truth that we need to know. It is truthful to human experience in a fallen world and as such can raise our consciousness about the plight of people living in that world. It clarifies the human condition to which the Christian faith speaks.

*Meursault as Modern Person.* It is in this regard that we can profitably take a deeper look at the protagonist of Camus' story. He is a heightened version of what we find everywhere around us in a fallen and post-Christian world.

To begin, he is a sensualist and hedonist. The only reality he knows is immediate sensory experience. His highest ecstasy is to feel the water against his body when he swims. He accepts promiscuous sex as though it were as natural as eating a meal. His greatest deprivations while in jail are the lack of cigarettes and women ("I never thought of Marie especially"). He is the slave of his physical sensations and the incurable hedonist who lives for the moment. By his own testimony, he lives only in the sensory present—"too much absorbed in the present moment, or the immediate future, to think back."

This ties in with Meursault's inability to attach meaning to sensory experience. As he records the events of the story, everything carries equal weight. He cannot even rise from his momentary physical pleasure with Marie to a permanent emotion called love. The highest he can attain is existence without commitment.

Meursault is indifferent to life and human relationships. The title of the novel rightly calls him the stranger or outsider. He lacks the normal ambitions of life, so that, for example, when he is offered the chance for a promotion that would allow him to live in Paris, he turns it down on the ground that "one life was as good as another."

The protagonist's indifference is seen most clearly in his lack of normal feelings. He experiences his mother's funeral as a series of physical sensations, and the one ingredient that is conspicuously absent is grief. In fact, the punch line that concludes the chapter describing the weekend following the funeral is the statement, "Really, nothing in my life had changed."

The protagonist's emotional deficiency is also vividly portrayed in the famous conversation with Marie about marriage:

> Marie came that evening and asked me if I'd marry her. I said I didn't mind; if she was keen on it, we'd get married.
> Then she asked me again if I loved her. I replied, much as before, that her question meant nothing or next to nothing—but I supposed I didn't. . . .
> Then she remarked that marriage was a serious matter.
> To which I answered: "No."

Of course this strikes us as unrealistically exaggerated, and it is. But this is how literature works: it heightens issues in order to silhouette a feature of life with the desired degree of clarity.

An extension of Meursault's indifference to life and human relationships is his inability to feel guilt or even regret about the murder he committed. He confides, "I have never been able really to regret anything in all my life." When asked by the examining magistrate whether he regretted what he had done, he replies that "what I felt was less regret than a kind of vexation." He tells the prison chaplain, "I wasn't conscious of any 'sin.' "

Meursault is also the epitome of the secular person. He does not believe in God. His mother "had never given a thought to religion in her life." Meursault tells the prison chaplain that he "had little time left and . . . wasn't going to waste it on God." Literary critics commonly speak of Meursault as Camus' pagan hero—a person who lives life at the level of the physical senses and who affirms the life of nature.

*Modern Literature as Mirror of the Age.* What claim does such a portrayal of life have on a Christian? The answer should be obvious: here is a picture of how many (perhaps most) people in our society live. Meursault is our contemporary unbelieving neighbor. He also represents a fallen part of ourselves to which we are capable of descending and from which we need to be rescued by God's grace. The effect of realism can be redemptive in a reader's experience, though it is not automatically so. As we look "down" at depraved human experience, we are also led to look "up" as we are made aware of something better.

I am claiming that the truth of modern realism is its truthfulness to life in the world in which we live, conveying more interpretive understanding to us than when we see the same experiences portrayed in thirty-second segments on the television news. If Meursault's life reflects how a substantial segment of people in our own society live, we need to understand that way of living.

Of course there are qualifications that need to be made. We do not need to *immerse* ourselves in realistic literature in order to know what is going on around us. In heavy doses, realism can blunt our human sensibilities and numb our sense of horror at evil.

We can also fault extreme realism for falsifying life by its singleminded selectivity of ugliness and misery as its subject. By omitting other aspects of life, it distorts the truth. There is a realism of grace as well as a realism of carnality. Furthermore, realism portrays depravity as the natural condition of the human race, whereas Christianity regards it as a pathological condition that can be corrected. While being truthful in its depiction of how many people live, it is misleading in its implied claim that this is the complete truth about life's possibilities.

### Futility under the Sun: Alien Views in Modern Literature

Realism is one of the problems that Christian readers feel when reading modern literature. The other is the alien world views that are offered for approval. Four of these are particularly evident in *The Stranger* and modern literature generally. I will call them hedonism, naturalism, existentialism, and absurdism.

*Hedonism.* I have already noted that the protagonist of the story is an incurable hedonist. He lives at the level of physical sensation. The highest he can imagine rising is to the plane of physical pleasure. Swimming and sexual gratification are his version of fulfillment. In C.S. Lewis's list of the values that literature as a whole has offered for approval, Meursault lives by the one that dominates modern literature—"liberation of impulses."[7]

Critics and biographers repeatedly speak of the paganism of Camus, by which they mean his substitution of nature for God and his finding of happiness, not in the transcendent God of Christianity, but in natural experience. Camus himself was nurtured under the warmth of the Mediterranean sun. His enjoyment of the sea apparently gave him a happy childhood despite the poverty and suffering he experienced in his home. One biographer comments that Camus' "childhood and youth were devoid of religion except for the unconsciously pagan rites of sun and body worship, swimming and soccer. The sea remained throughout Camus's life the powerful symbol of temporary freedom from the burdens of human ugliness and oppression."[8] Camus seems to have poured much of his own experience into his hero Meursault in this regard. This paganism is of course a form of humanism. When asked by the prison chaplain how he pictures the life after the grave, Meursault replies, "A life in which I can remember this life on earth. That's all I want of it."

*Naturalism.* But this affirmation of natural hedonism is muted when compared with the negative theme of the story. The pessimism of *The Stranger* is the pessimism of a naturalistic world view that we encounter everywhere in modern literature. It is based on three great denials. One is the denial of hope. The experience of Meursault while he is imprisoned in the second half of the novel encapsulates this absence of hope. Deprived of his freedom and condemned to death, Meursault has no future for which to hope. The moment of epiphany toward which the story moves comes on the last page. Following a scene in which Meursault has angrily assaulted the chaplain who visited him, Meursault suddenly concludes, "It was as if that great rush of anger had washed me clean, emptied me of hope, and, gazing up at the dark sky spangled with its signs and stars, for the first time, the first, I laid my heart open to the benign indifference of the universe."

This suggests a second denial of naturalism, the denial of relationship—to God, to society, to self, to nature. The spectacle of loneliness and alienation runs strong in modern literature. Nowhere has it been captured more singlemindedly than in the story of Camus' *Stranger*. Imprisoned within his own consciousness, unable to establish emotional bonds with other characters, disbelieving in God, Meursault tells us in the final sentence of the novel that all that remains for him to hope (a word whose meaning, in this context, has to be ironic) "was that on the day of my execution there should be a huge crowd of spectators and that they should greet me with howls of execration [cursing and loathing]."

Finally, the naturalistic world view espouses a thoroughgoing determinism—in other words, a denial of human choice. This is where the oppressive heat of the sun and the degradation of Meursault's social environment enter the picture. We are led to feel that anyone's life in such an environment is doomed. The determinism is psychological as well as environmental, as characters are victimized by their own irrational impulses. As a prime illustration, we can picture Meursault holding the gun on the fateful Sunday afternoon, impulsively shooting the Arab not once but five times.

In summary, naturalism has a view of the universe and a view of the person. Its view of the universe is that the world is hostile, cruel, impersonal, ugly, deterministic, and self-contained (devoid of the supernatural). It pictures the individual as helpless, determined by environment and physical drives, alone, and seized by irrational impulses. One could not ask for a clearer illustration of these tenets than *The Stranger*.

*Existentialism.* Although Camus claimed not to be an existentialist, his story exemplifies any standard definition of existentialism that we might cite. Existentialism, for example, exalts human subjectivity. Meursault's way of viewing reality is his own, not shared by other characters in the story. His vision of truth is radically personal. His own consciousness and sensations are the only realities in his life.

Existentialism is preoccupied with death, and so is Camus' novel, especially after Meursault is condemned to death. "Nothing, nothing had the least importance," Meursault concludes late in the story. "All alike would be condemned to die one day. . . . And what difference could it make if, after being charged with murder, he were executed because he didn't weep at his mother's funeral, since it all came to the same thing in the end?"

Existentialists also make much of life itself as the goal of existence. They speak of the need to assert oneself in action as a way of authenticating oneself, even when that action is self-destructive. In other words, revolt against conventional values and modes of thought is at the heart of existentialism.

This conception of freedom without responsibility was important to Camus' own interpretation of *The Stranger*, as evidenced by his praise of Meursault in the preface from which I quoted earlier. According to

Camus, Meursault is heroic for refusing to play the game of conventional social rituals. He refuses to lie about his feelings. If he is unmoved by his mother's death, he will not pretend to be moved. If he cannot rise from his momentary pleasure with Marie to a permanent emotion called love, he will simply refuse to say he loves her. In the author's view, this makes him a martyr for truth. By endorsing this vision of radical individual freedom, Camus confirms that he has important affinities with modern existentialism.

*Absurdism.* More important even than the trends I have noted thus far is the novel's embodiment of the spirit of absurdism. An influential twentieth-century literary trend, the absurd tradition is actually part of the line of nihilism and despair. In this tradition, the idea of absurdism is given a philosophic and metaphysical identity. Eugene Ionesco, a playwright who participated in the theater-of-the-absurd movement, defined the concept of absurdity thus: "Absurd is that which is devoid of purpose. . . . Cut off from his religious, metaphysical, and transcendental roots, man is lost; all his actions become senseless, absurd, useless."[9] This is similar to a comment made by Jean-Paul Sartre, whose essay on *The Stranger* helped to make it famous: "Absurdity means divorce, discrepancy. *The Stranger* is to be a novel of discrepancy, divorce and disorientation."[10]

Sharing the absurdist view of life, Camus faced the task of inventing literary forms that would embody his outlook. His effectiveness in doing so is one of the triumphs of the book. His chief means of embodying his absurdist view of the meaninglessness of the universe is the protagonist of the story. If we want to know what it feels like to believe that life is devoid of meaning, all we need to do is enter the consciousness of Meursault.

Several specific things are noteworthy in this regard. One is Meursault's indifference to everything except immediate physical sensations. For him, sensory experience has replaced meaning. Related to this is the way in which Meursault experiences and describes events not as a sequence of logically related things but as a mere succession in which one thing follows another without connection. Meursault is also unable to arrange individual experiences or details into a hierarchy of values. In his distorted thinking, everything carries the same value and importance.

As we read the story we also repeatedly observe the discrepancy within Meursault's mind between events and the meaning that rational logic would ordinarily attach to them. For example, to Meursault the experiences of burying his mother, beginning an affair with a mistress on the day after the funeral, and committing a murder have no logical connections. These same events are related by witnesses at the trial, where they are put in a logical order and explained in a causal way by the public prosecutor. Meursault has the impression that the prosecutor is talking about someone else. Again, Meursault does not love Marie but agrees to marry her. He murders a man and feels no regret. As Sartre truly said, "Absurdity means divorce, discrepancy."

Finally, Camus evokes a picture of a meaningless universe by parodying the first-person narrative point of view. In most novels where there is a first-person narrator, the narrator exhibits a privileged insight into the characters and actions of the story. Such a narrator's task is to enlighten the reader. But Meursault is an obtuse and unreliable narrator. He continuously protests his inability to follow what is happening and to attribute meaning to events. Whereas the reliable narrator implies a meaningful and comprehensible view of the universe, Camus turns that convention upside down. His confiding narrator does not help us interpret experience because he is incapable of providing experience with meaning. His very unreliability, incidentally, subverts any heroism that we might attach to him (and that Camus himself tried to ascribe to him).

Two things in addition to the narrator work to establish the absurdist view of reality. One is the plot, whose very climax, the trial and condemnation of a man, reflects an absurd discrepancy between event and logic. Meursault is condemned for murder, not because he killed an Arab, but because he did not weep at his mother's funeral. Secondly, the style of writing in the novel rests heavily on the short, terse sentence. The effect is one of fragmentation and incoherence. Sartre made much of this:

Each sentence is a present instant. . . . The sentence is sharp, distinct, and self-contained. It is separated by a void from the following one. . . . The world is destroyed and reborn from sentence to sentence. . . . All the sentences of his book are equal to each other, just as all the absurd man's experiences are equal."[11]

*Summary.* Here, then, is the ideological world of Camus' novel and of modern literature. On the surface it is a calculated setup to offend Christian sensibilities. The writer chooses depravity as his subject and then interprets that experience in an offensive manner by offering for approval such alien philosophies as hedonism, naturalism, existentialism, and absurdism. What is an enlightened Christian response to this challenge?

## In Search of Balance: The Profit and Peril of Modern Literature

We can profitably begin by remembering the threefold task of the writer—to entertain us with pleasing artistry, to portray human experience, and to interpret the human experience thus portrayed. Christian readers need not agree with all that a piece of modern literature espouses in order to find the purposes of literature—profit and delight—partially fulfilled.

*Artistry in Modern Literature.* For all that a Christian reader might find objectionable in *The Stranger*, there can be no doubt that the story is skillfully told. Its spare, concrete style is enjoyable to read. The effectiveness with which the first-person narrator makes us want to keep reading is also unsurpassed. And the inventiveness with which Camus managed to embody an absurdist view of life in narrative form is striking. All of this artistry tells us once again something about the image of God in people, namely, their capacity for creativity and beauty.

*The Redemptive Potential of Subject Matter in Modern Literature.* When we move to a consideration of subject matter, we can also begin with partial agreement. In my opening chapter I claimed that a beneficial way to assimilate literature is to allow it to awaken good longings within us. Whether by positive or negative example, *The Stranger* awakens a wealth of such longings—for justice, for love, for relationship, for unity with nature, for meaning in life, for a healthy emotional life.

While the book's vision of life is mainly bleak, there are occasional celebrations of the common experiences of life. One of my favorite passages is the catalog of memories that Meursault experiences while in prison:

> *I heard the tin trumpet of an ice-cream vendor in the street. . . . And then a rush of memories went through my mind—memories of a life which . . . had once provided me with the surest, humblest pleasures: warm smells of summer, my favorite streets, the sky at evening, Marie's dresses and her laugh.*

Even modern literature, in other words, can nurture our sense of beauty and provide the occasion to celebrate the human life that God has given to everyone as a gift.

I have already affirmed the partial truthfulness of the book's realism. Although most of the human experiences portrayed in the book are unpleasant ones, the picture itself is true to human experience in a fallen world. Controlled contact with this truth can have beneficial results in a Christian's experience. It raises our consciousness about how people live in our society. It raises our conscience by enlarging our sense of compassion for people in need. And it enhances our self-understanding as we see some of our own attitudes—bad as well as good—projected onto fictional characters.

*Testing the Spirits of Modern Literature.* Even when we come to assess the themes of the story, we can begin with a measure of agreement. Camus' story seeks to convince us that life under the sun is meaningless. The book of Ecclesiastes says the same thing: "Then I considered all that my hands had done and the toil I had spent in doing it, and behold, all was vanity and a striving after wind, and there was nothing to be gained under the sun" (2:11).

Of course the writer of Ecclesiastes throughout his book offers an alternative to life under the sun, namely, life lived with God at the center. The ancient writer believed, as Camus did not, that "God is in heaven" (5:2), that God "has put eternity into man's mind" (3:11), and that the goal of life is to "fear God, and keep his commandments; for this is the whole duty of man" (12:13).

Christianity, claimed Francis Schaeffer, has a major theme and a minor theme. The minor theme is the fact of sin and fallenness. The major

theme is salvation in Christ. Modern literature gives us truthful variations on the minor theme. Or consider the threefold Christian view of
the person—good as created by God, fallen by virtue of its inclination
toward evil, and capable of redemption. Modern literature tells us the
truth about one of these three.

But partial agreement is not total agreement. While Christian readers
must be on guard when reading any work of literature, they must be
doubly on guard with modern literature. The chances are overwhelming
that the writer will offer for approval viewpoints that oppose Christianity. This is a way of saying that Christian readers will inevitably
find themselves a minority when they read and discuss modern literature, as anyone who has sat in a secular literature classroom or book
discussion can attest. This is not surprising: our broader culture is, after
all, secular, pagan, existential, and many another thing espoused in
modern literature.

A good operating procedure is for Christian readers simply to pay
attention to their responses to a piece of modern literature. These responses are self-revealing. If they are informed by Christian ideas and attitudes, they will confirm that the reader is Christian in outlook and
allegiance. In the case of *The Stranger*, everything comes to focus on the
narrator who bares his inner thoughts to us throughout the novel.
Meursault's behavior and attitudes are so foreign to what a Christian
believes that I have always found it hard to believe that the book itself
espouses the attitudes that the narrator embodies. Left to my own
designs, I would interpret the story as a satire—an implied exposure of
the deficiencies of the character who stands at the center of the story.
But we have the author's very clear statement that he himself admired
Meursault and regarded him as a Christ figure (though Camus may
have partly changed his mind in later years).

Camus himself, despite his lifelong dialogue with Christianity,
rejected the Christian faith. He embodied this rejection in the experience
of his fictional hero. Two characters in the story attempt to convert
Meursault after his imprisonment, and neither is portrayed sympatheti-
cally. The examining magistrate waves a crucifix before Meursault in a
display of genuine religious fervor, but Meursault is bored and embar-
rassed. When the prison chaplain makes a similar appeal, "something

seemed to break" inside Meursault as he began shouting and assaulting the chaplain. As so often in modern literature, the author here makes his anti-Christian bias apparent.

Although I have suggested that Christian readers should pay attention to their responses as pointing to a valid Christian assessment of the truth claims of a work, I need to urge a caution. As we scrutinize our responses, we must also be critical of them. A frustration that I have in teaching *The Stranger* is that because students find much of themselves in Meursault's attitudes, they conclude that this makes Meursault an exemplary character. But we should read literature partly to discover what Augustine called "the dark corners of the heart"—aspects of ourself that are wrong and usually hidden from our consciousness.[12]

Several principles emerge from what I have said. One is that we are under no obligation to agree with an author's viewpoint, no matter how great a work of literature is. Another is that modern literature is a litmus test of the reader's view of life. Christian readers, like other readers, should have the courage to be themselves as they respond to modern literature.

A third principle is that we can benefit from reading literature that espouses viewpoints that we find uncongenial. Not only do the alien world views of modern literature represent attitudes by which most people in our society live, they can also serve as a catalyst to our own thinking. With good reason we reject Meursault's emotional deficiency, but the author's praise of him for refusing to lie about his feelings raises a very important question: how *should* we live with the discrepancy between our feelings and the conventional rules that society expects us to follow? Meursault finds the people around him a frequent nuisance and the institutions of his society corrupt. Do we not all share this problem? If Meursault's response is deficient, what is the right response?

*Summary.* Modern literature continues to elicit contradictory responses from Christian readers. At the extremes are indiscriminate endorsement of modern literature and indiscriminate rejection of it. A proper Christian response is a middle way between the extremes. A statement by T.S. Eliot provides dependable guidance: "So long as we [Christian readers] are conscious of the gulf fixed between ourselves and the greater part of contemporary literature, we are more or less protected from being harmed by it, and are in a position to extract from it what good it has to offer us."[13] We will not go far wrong if we read modern literature in an awareness of the three things that Eliot names about modern literature—the gulf that divides it from Christianity, its potential harm, and its potential good.

## Notes to Chapter 9

[1] I have used the Stuart Gilbert translation of *The Stranger* (New York: Vintage, 1946).

[2] Lewis attributes this quality to Shakespeare's sonnets in an introductory essay on Spenser in *Major British Writers*, ed. G. B. Harrison (New York: Harcourt, 1959), 1:102.

[3] Camus, as quoted in James W. Woelfel, *Albert Camus on the Sacred and the Secular* (Lanham, N.Y.: University Press of America, 1987), p. 125.

[4] Rene Girard, "Camus's Stranger Retried," *PMLA* 79 (1964): 521.

[5] Albert Camus, *Lyrical and Critical Essays*, ed. Philip Thody, trans. Ellen C. Kennedy (New York: Vintage, 1970), p. 335.

[6] Edmund Fuller, *Man in Modern Fiction* (New York: Vintage, 1949), p. 12.

[7] C.S. Lewis, "Christianity and Culture," as reprinted in *The Christian Imagination: Essays on Literature and the Arts*, ed. Leland Ryken (Grand Rapids: Baker, 1981):, p. 33.

[8] Woelfel, p. 19.

[9] Martin Esslin, *The Theater of the Absurd* (Garden City: Doublday, 1961), p. xix.

[10] Jean-Paul Sartre, "An Explication of *The Stranger*," in *Camus: A Collection of Critical Essays*, ed. Germaine Bree (Englewood Cliffs, NJ: Prentice-Hall, 1962), p. 114.

[11] Ibid., pp. 119-120.

[12] I have quoted Augustine from Simon Lesser, *Fiction and the Unconscious* (Chicago: University of Chicago Press, 1957, 1975), p. 253.

[13] T.S. Eliot, "Religion and Literature," as reprinted in *The Christian Imagination*, ed. Ryken, p. 153.

## Conclusion

## Where Do We Go from Here?

✳

*The fullest friendships [with books] are likely to be with the works that the world has called classics. . . . I meet in their authors friends who demonstrate their friendship not only in the range and depth and intensity of pleasure they offer, not only in the promise they fulfill of proving useful to me, but finally in the irresistible invitation they extend to live during these moments a richer and fuller life than I could manage on my own.*

*I might say to any one of these in reply: . . . your company is in some ways superior even to the best company I can hope to discover among the real people I live with. . . . You lead me first to practice ways of living that are more profound, more sensitive, more intense, and in a curious way more fully generous than I am likely to meet anywhere else in the world. You correct my faults, rebuke my insensitivities. You mold me into patterns of longing and fulfillment that make my ordinary dreams seem petty and absurd. You finally show what life can be, not just to a coterie, . . . but to anyone who is willing to work to earn the title of equal and true friend.*[1]

✳

Having looked at selected classics, it is good to ponder some concluding questions that emerge naturally from what I have said. What role should the classics fill in a Christian's life? How does our reading of the classics relate to the rest of our reading experience? Are the classics elitist? What are the limitations of the classics? What can they *not* do for us?

*Why Christians Need the Classics.* Readers need the classics first of all because these works are foundational. Writers themselves acknowledge this by both their testimony and their practice as writers. They praise the classics, allude to them, and follow them as models. The history of literature is an ongoing dialogue between individual works and the classics that have preceded them. The resulting body of literature is a huge interlocking family.

This tradition, which I do not hesitate to call the great tradition, rests on two foundations—the classical (Greco-Roman) and the biblical (Hebraic-Christian). To try to make sense of literature without a knowledge of the masterworks is to labor under a handicap—like trying to play basketball with one arm tied behind one's back. It can be done, but not well.

Why do writers and students of literature gravitate so naturally to the classics? Partly because these works are prototypical. They are a definitive example of various aspects of literature. Writers are interested in the classics for the same reason painters are interested in still life—in order to discover the fundamental principles of their craft. I could have chosen lesser works in raising the literary issues I have discussed in this book, but the resulting discussion would not have possessed quite the same authority. If we want to know about the value of myth, we can never have the final word until we have considered Homer. No discussion of literary tragedy or the literary influence of the Bible is complete if it omits the greatest practitioners of these things, Shakespeare and Milton, respectively.

In addition to being foundational and prototypical, the classics are simply the best. Matthew Arnold, the Victorian champion of the classics, stated the case very succinctly: "The best poetry is what we want; the best poetry will be found to have a power of forming, sustaining, and delighting us, as nothing else can."[2]

The classics give us what the French writer Flaubert called "contact with greatness." To illustrate what he meant, he shared how violently his heart leaped at the sight of one wall of the Acropolis. The classics serve as an inspiration to the human spirit. They do for a reader what a professional sports event does for an amateur athlete.

The classics provide a balance to the clatter of contemporary events. In the view of one writer, "The ideal thing would be to hearken to current events as we do to the din outside the window that informs us about traffic jams and sudden changes in the weather, while we listen to the voice of the classics sounding clear and articulate inside the room."[3] Alternately, adds this writer, "A classic is something that persists as a background noise even when the most incompatible momentary concerns are in control of the situation." In either case, the classics stand in a vital relation to real life.

*Standards of Excellence.* Because they are the best, the classics can refine and mold our literary taste and serve as a touchstone by which to evaluate other literature, including contemporary literature. When we teach children neat handwriting, we show them examples of good handwriting rather than bad handwriting. The same principle applies to our judgment of literature.

The manager of a Christian bookstore once asked me if I thought her store should stock such classics as Homer's *Odyssey* and Dickens' *Great Expectations*. After writing this book, my answer is "yes." In a day when religious fiction is notable for its mediocrity, we need standards by which to distinguish between what is inferior and superior. Furthermore, the classics, whether or not they are written by Christians, are rich in the truth and beauty that Christian readers need.

One thing that the classics demonstrate at once is that literature needs a balance between its entertaining function and its status as a form of knowledge or truth. Homer's *Odyssey*, in addition to being an epic, contains descriptions of epic performances. From these we learn that literature was, from the beginning, a form of entertainment. Here is Odysseus' account of his delight in being entertained at an epic performance during his visit to Phaiacia:

> *I declare it is just the perfection of gracious life: good cheer and good temper everywhere, rows of guests enjoying themselves heartily and listening to the music, plenty to eat on the table, wine ready in the great bowl. . . . I think that is the best thing men can have.*

But in addition to filling the human need for pleasure, literature was also from the beginning regarded as instructive. Plato tells us that some Greeks believed that a person should regulate the whole of life by following Homer. The writers of the works that I discuss in this book would not have shared the common fallacy that understanding is antithetical to beauty and enjoyment.

The dual criterion of beauty and truth, or entertainment and edification, remains a valid test for the latest short story or poem that we read from a current periodical. A great deal of twentieth-century literature lacks this breadth. Some of it shows the author's interest in technique for its own sake and is apparently *about* nothing. Contrariwise, much of it is propagandistic and adds little to our enjoyment of literary technique as something having value in itself.

The classics encourage us to value both form and vision in literature. They begin in delight and end in wisdom. To use Matthew Arnold's formula, they touch upon life powerfully at many points. A work does not have to be long in order to measure up to this blend of truth and beauty. It is something that can characterize a lyric poem as readily as a novel.

The classics show a similar comprehensiveness in the range of experiences that they embody. When they take human tragedy or misery as their subject, they find ways to enclose the terror in some type of reassuring framework that ensures us that this is not the whole picture. When these works make affirmations, they earn the right to make those affirmations by looking into the abyss of human suffering.

Aldous Huxley speaks of the ability of great literature to give us "the Whole Truth." In such literature, the experiences that the author records "correspond fairly closely with our own actual or potential experiences—and correspond with our experiences not on a single limited sector, but all along the line of our physical and spiritual being." These experiences, moreover, are presented "with a penetrative artistic force that makes them seem peculiarly acceptable and convincing."[4]

A further quality of the classics that commends them as touchstones of literary excellence is their ability to clarify life. They do not preach at us. They rarely convey new information to us. Instead they clarify some aspect of life and bring that insight to our awareness in a way that makes us take note of what we usually overlook. The classics thus allow us to assess a contemporary piece of literature by training us to expect some clarification of life from what we read.

The classics are also inexhaustible. They meet us at whatever level we are prepared to experience them. Because our experiences of life keep changing, we continually see more and different things in them every time we read them. In this sense we can never exhaust them. If we judge books and poems by whether they keep us coming back to them because they always have something new to tell us, some contemporary literature measures up and some strikes us as rather thin and one-dimensional. Someone has said that "every rereading of a classic is as much a voyage of discovery as the first reading. . . . A classic is a book that has never finished saying what it has to say. . . . The classics are books that we find . . . new, fresh, and unexpected."[5]

It is of course the case that in order to clarify life a work of literature must itself be clear to our understanding. The classics adhere to the time-honored artistic qualities of unity, coherence, and emphasis. In doing so, they are clear to us. They do not confuse us. In reading modern literature, much of which is governed by the cult of obscurity, we must not be cowed into thinking that the obscurity of the literature is somehow our fault. The classics show us that great literature clarifies rather than confuses.

Two of the greatest benefits of reading the classics will come as byproducts. First, we can expect our reading of the classics to make us discontent with shallow forms of literature, including examples from television drama and movies. As our taste is trained by contact with excellence, lesser works will inevitably seem inferior. Secondly, contact with the classics will alert us to the literary excellence of the Bible. The Bible, too, is a literary classic. It possesses the literary beauty, power, and wisdom that the best literature possesses. It is more than a literary classic, but not less.

*Are the Classics Elitist?* I can imagine someone asking, "Who says the classics are the best? *For whom* do they represent the best?" My answer is simple: they are considered the best by people whose literary education enables them to appreciate their excellence and who are free from the partisan spirit that leads some people to reject the classics because they were not written by Christians or women or some other specific group.

There is nothing elitist about valuing the classics. The classics that I have discussed in this book are accessible to anyone with a college education. Most of the works I have discussed are accessible to literate high schoolers. The classics are generally no more difficult to assimilate than the Bible. The claim that studying the classics is elitist did not emerge until the literary and educational establishment gave in to the claims of a mentally lazy society.

If the classics are elitist, they are elitist in the same way that the pursuit of excellence always is. Judged by such a criterion, Jesus' Sermon on the Mount is elitist. It calls people to live a life nothing short of perfection: "You, therefore, must be perfect, as your heavenly Father is perfect" (Matthew 5:48). Jesus himself acknowledged that such a high moral standard would appeal to the few rather than the many (Matthew 7:13-14). In literary pursuits, as in other areas of life, Christians are called to excellence because the God they serve is supremely excellent.

Because most people first encounter the classics in literature courses, they wrongly think that the classics are not works with which one would want to curl up for an hour of relaxation. The very title "classic" sets up a distance that is unwarranted. The works that I discuss in this book are for ordinary people who want the maximum of delight and wisdom that literature can afford.

*The Limitations of the Classics.* The very excellence of the classics suggests one of their limitations: only a minority of people today read them and count them as favorite friends. Far from discouraging us from reading them, this should encourage a close sense of fellowship among those who do read them. We need a revival of literary clubs (no matter how informally organized) and book discussion groups in which readers share their enthusiasm for the classics and enrich each other's relish for the truth and beauty that they offer.

It is no disparagement of the classics to say that they cannot constitute a person's entire diet of reading. No one wants to attend a banquet every night. Even people who love the classics do not read only them, just as people who love major league baseball nevertheless take time to watch little league games or play softball at a picnic. Professors of literature read much besides the classics they teach. They may deliberately include lesser works in the courses they teach in order to achieve specific goals. But even in these cases the classics retain their usefulness as a touchstone of excellence and a repository of the fundamental principles of literature.

One of the things that the classics do not do is portray the specific social issues of our place and time. For this we need contemporary literature. The classics are perpetually up to date, but they portray human issues in universal terms. As a result, they require translation into our own situation. By focusing on the universal human condition, the classics omit some things that are important to our own era, such as the minority experience and women's experience written from a feminine viewpoint. Not that the experiences of oppression and women are omitted from the classics that I have discussed in this book, but they are portrayed by people who did not belong to the groups I have named.

*Practical Suggestions.* Several practical pieces of advice follow naturally from what I have said throughout this book. One is the recommendation to keep reading the classics. They never disappoint. I hope that this book might encourage my readers to choose to spend an evening reading a classic whereas before they would not have considered it an option. The classics offer a depth of insight into human experience and a quality of aesthetic beauty that other works do not.

That is why, incidentally, the attempt to drive too deep a wedge between the classics and works that are relevant to current social concerns is misguided. Studied in depth, Shakespeare or Tolstoy will always yield a more profound insight into the human condition than more propagandistic writing that may appear to provide more relevant social commentary. This is not to say, of course, that the classics always say what we want said on an issue. But even when we disagree with them, they serve as a catalyst to our thinking in a way that more ostensibly current literature often fails to do.

A second piece of advice that I would offer is that every reader is entitled to his or her own list of classics. If we define a classic as the best of its type, the list of such classics is far longer than the small list I have discussed in this book. We all have our favorites in a wide range of categories. For us, these are classics.

While I was writing this book, I received a phone call from an office on my campus where a debate was under way about what constituted a classic. The consensus was that Tolkien's fiction could not rank as classic because it does not find its way into major anthologies of literature. My response is that Tolkien's fiction is classic because it is the best of its type of modern fantasy literature.

I recall an era when as a student I decided to compile and type my own anthology of favorite poems and prose passages. The project grew beyond my power to sustain it as my acquaintance with literature grew, but I have carried over the same attitude to the question of literary classics. In addition to the standard entries that people of good literary taste agree belong on the list of classics, a person's list of classics should contain a personal touch—works that for a given reader meet the test of being an essential work for which no other comes close to satisfying the appetite it arouses.

A related recommendation is that everyone would benefit from claiming an author as his or her own specialty. There are several reasons for this. One is the sheer exhilaration that comes from having thoroughly mastered a field. The second is that we have never completely mastered an author until we have read widely in biographical and critical studies of him or her. Our own insights into an author's work are by themselves meager compared with the insights that the broader world of readers has discovered and recorded. In the process of reading what others have said about "our" author, we are also reminded that literature is a social institution—a shared possession of kindred spirits. One of the most natural responses after finishing a book is to compare our impressions with those of others.

An additional reason for becoming an expert on an author is that the more we read by an author, the more of life we see. Great writers have a comprehensiveness that emerges from their total canon. They have a remarkable way of covering the bases. By comparison, to read only the best works of the greatest writers is piecemeal and fragmented. One of the rewards of reading a writer's whole canon is the feeling that this conveys of a world complete—a sense that we have been put in touch with all of the essential features of life. Part of the completeness is that we see the writer's relative failures as well as successes, and the writer's development from youthful strivings to mature achievement.

*Summary.* The classics matter because literature itself matters. They offer the rewards of all great literature—pleasure, recreation, heightened awareness of human experience, involvement with life, expanded viewpoint, and the occasion to focus our own thinking about the great issues of life.

## Notes to the Conclusion

[1]Wayne Booth, *The Company We Keep: An Ethics of Fiction* (Berkeley: University of California, 1988), p. 223.

[2]Matthew Arnold, "The Study of Poetry," in *Criticism: The Major Statements*, ed. Charles Kaplan (New York: St. Martin's, 1975), p. 405.

[3]Italo Calvino, "Why Read the Classics?" *New York Review of Books* 9 October 1986: 20.

[4]Aldous Huxley, "Tragedy and the Whole Truth," in *Tragedy: Vision and Form*, ed. Robert W. Corrigan (San Francisco: Chandler, 1965), p. 77.

[5]Calvino, 19.

# Index